American Literature Readings in the 21st Century

Series Editor
Linda Wagner-Martin
University of North Carolina
Chapel Hill, NC, USA

American Literature Readings in the 21st Century publishes works by contemporary critics that help shape critical opinion regarding literature of the nineteenth and twentieth centuries in the United States.

More information about this series at
http://www.palgrave.com/gp/series/14765

Laura Rattray

Edith Wharton and Genre

Beyond Fiction

palgrave
macmillan

Laura Rattray
University of Glasgow
Glasgow, UK

ISBN 978-0-230-36166-9   ISBN 978-1-349-59557-0 (eBook)
https://doi.org/10.1057/978-1-349-59557-0

© The Editor(s) (if applicable) and The Author(s) 2020
The author(s) has/have asserted their right(s) to be identified as the author(s) of this work in accordance with the Copyright, Designs and Patents Act 1988.
This work is subject to copyright. All rights are solely and exclusively licensed by the Publisher, whether the whole or part of the material is concerned, specifically the rights of translation, reprinting, reuse of illustrations, recitation, broadcasting, reproduction on microfilms or in any other physical way, and transmission or information storage and retrieval, electronic adaptation, computer software, or by similar or dissimilar methodology now known or hereafter developed.
The use of general descriptive names, registered names, trademarks, service marks, etc. in this publication does not imply, even in the absence of a specific statement, that such names are exempt from the relevant protective laws and regulations and therefore free for general use.
The publisher, the authors and the editors are safe to assume that the advice and information in this book are believed to be true and accurate at the date of publication. Neither the publisher nor the authors or the editors give a warranty, expressed or implied, with respect to the material contained herein or for any errors or omissions that may have been made. The publisher remains neutral with regard to jurisdictional claims in published maps and institutional affiliations.

Cover illustration: © Granger Historical Picture Archive / Alamy Stock Photo, Image ID: FF6WR0

This Palgrave Macmillan imprint is published by the registered company Springer Nature Limited.
The registered company address is: The Campus, 4 Crinan Street, London, N1 9XW, United Kingdom

Edith Wharton and Genre

Laura Rattray's meticulously researched and beautifully written study fully establishes not only Wharton's amazing versatility as an author, but her virtuosity in genres as diverse as poetry, travel-writing, play-writing, design, life-writing, and literary theory. In lively prose, *Edith Wharton and Genre* also offers a more socially conscious and feminist Wharton, a woman who was often, as Rattray argues, a "trailblazer." So, too, is Rattray, who has changed the way we will think of Edith Wharton.
—Julie Olin-Ammentorp, Professor of English, *Le Moyne College*, is the author of *Edith Wharton, Willa Cather, and the Place of Culture* and of *Edith Wharton's Writings from the Great War*. She is a past president of the *Edith Wharton Society*

Edith Wharton and Genre offers a radical and radicalizing perspective on Wharton and American literary history. By making the author's poetry, drama, autobiography, and—most impressively—literary theory the center of her inquiry, Laura Rattray reveals the creative and intellectual deliberateness of Wharton's generic choices and their significance to the long nineteenth century.
—Susan Tomlinson, Associate Professor of English, *University of Massachusetts Boston* and editor, *Legacy: A Journal of American Women Writers*

In Rattray's hands, Edith Wharton is re-presented as a writer mastering a wide range of genres beyond the celebrated fiction. Wharton's achievements in poetry, drama, architecture and design, criticism, memoir, and travel writing emerge as sites for her most confident, radical experiments. This game-changing book will lay to rest the image of the grand dame, showing Wharton to defy categorization and to be as "large" and full of "multitudes" as the Whitman she so admired.
—Emily J. Orlando, Professor of English at *Fairfield University (USA)* and author of *Edith Wharton and the Visual Arts*

Rattray's volume shows that Wharton consistently rejected shortcuts across the multiple genres in which she wrote. The same might be said of Rattray's scholarship. In an authoritative, critical voice based on careful research, Rattray transforms the successful lady novelist created, in part, out of gender and social biases into the experimental woman artist who embraces risks in both subject matter and presentation.
—Rita Bode, Professor of English Literature, *Trent University, Canada*

Laura Rattray places between the covers of a single book an original study of all Wharton's work apart from her fiction. Her constantly interesting arguments make intriguing new connections between disparate material and she brilliantly demonstrates how the different genres in which Wharton wrote nourish and sustain each other. Wharton emerges as a far greater literary figure than most of her (often dismissive) critics have been willing to recognize.
—Virginia Ricard, *Bordeaux Montaigne University*

In this lively and superbly written survey of Edith Wharton's writings in genres other than prose fiction, Rattray demonstrates the broad repertoire of a writer who was more than a novelist of manners. A welcome addition to Wharton scholarship, Rattray's study gives us yet more reason to be in awe of Wharton's breadth of knowledge and her indefatigable energy.
—Maureen E. Montgomery, Adjunct Associate Professor, *University of Canterbury, New Zealand* and author of *Displaying Women: Spectacles of Leisure in Edith Wharton's New York*

Acknowledgements

I am deeply grateful to the people who were there for me over the six years I worked on this book. Heartfelt thanks to the Leverhulme Trust for a research fellowship that made it possible for me to undertake this project. Huge thanks to Wharton scholars Ailsa Boyd, Mary Chinery, Irene Goldman-Price, Susan Goodman, Jennifer Haytock, Cecilia Macheski, Julie Olin-Ammentorp, Virginia Ricard, and Linda Wagner-Martin for their incisive feedback, enthusiasm, generosity, and expertise. I am immensely grateful to series editor Linda Wagner-Martin for her encouragement, insight, and support for this project from its inception. My thanks to the Edith Wharton Society for the privilege of giving the keynote presentation on Wharton and Genre at the Wharton Society International Conference in Washington, DC, in June 2016 at a pivotal stage of the project. Excerpts from unpublished writings by Edith Wharton are reprinted by permission of the estate of Edith Wharton and the Watkins/Loomis Agency. My thanks to Julia Masnik at the Watkins/Loomis Agency for facilitating permissions. Earlier versions of parts of Chaps. 3 and 7 appeared in my two-volume edition of *The Unpublished Writings of Edith Wharton* and are reproduced with permission of the Licensor Informa UK Ltd through PLS clear. Thanks to my colleague Faye Hammill at the University of Glasgow for her insightful, constructive feedback. My thanks to Lina Aboujieb and Rebecca Hinsley at Palgrave Macmillan. Thanks to Nynke Dorhout, Librarian at Edith Wharton's home, the Mount; to Kate O'Donnell, Assistant Archivist at Somerville College, University of Oxford; to Erika Dowell, Associate Director and

Curator of Modern Books and Manuscripts at the Lilly Library, Indiana University; and to University of Glasgow College of Arts Librarians Richard Bapty and Morag Greig. My thanks to Ann Heilmann at Cardiff University, to Anna Grundy at the Leverhulme Trust, Philippa Osmond-Williams and Bryony Randall at the University of Glasgow, Emma Harding, and Margaret P. Murray, former President of the Wharton Society. Thanks to my students for their incisive discussions and energising enthusiasm for Wharton. As always, deepest thanks to my lovely family for being there, believing in me, and for putting up with the inordinate amount of time I spend in the company of Edith Wharton.

Contents

1 Introduction 1

2 Edith Wharton as Poet 19

3 Playwriting 55

4 Travel Writings 87

5 Architecture and Design 121

6 Critical Writings and Literary Theory 147

7 Life Writings 179

8 Afterword 209

Select Bibliography 217

Index 231

CHAPTER 1

Introduction

I have always known what I wanted & done it![1]

Edith Wharton was one of the most versatile writers of her time. Her career comprised so much more than the novels, novellas, and short stories for which she is deservedly acclaimed. Indeed Wharton worked—and worked hugely successfully throughout her career—across a variety of other genres, most notably poetry, drama, criticism and literary theory, travel, and autobiography, as well as writing on architecture and design. This diverse narrative has been obscured over the years, however, primarily by the fascination with Wharton as a novelist, and at times by the imposition of a series of restrictive, and often contradictory, scripts: the society novelist, the anti-modernist, the author who captured society in transition, the writer of New York, the chronicler of the elite, the grande dame, the first woman to win the Pulitzer Prize for fiction, the writer who lost touch. On her death in August 1937, the literary world paid tribute to a *novelist*—its scale of acclaim ranging from 'noted', 'great', to 'one of the greatest'.[2] Many of Wharton's obituaries recorded very precisely the volume, but not the range of her output, observing that she had written thirty-eight books, with another collection of stories proof read and in the final publication stages at the time of her death, along with the unfinished, final novel, *The Buccaneers*. Of that total, however (in fact forty-three books published in her lifetime), a third fall outside the categories of novels, novellas, or short stories. Include the numerous other texts that were

© The Author(s) 2020
L. Rattray, *Edith Wharton and Genre*,
https://doi.org/10.1057/978-1-349-59557-0_1

uncollected or unpublished—not least a series of plays, scores of individual poems, and various unfinished memoirs, essays, and travel writings—and it equates to an even more substantial and significant body of work. The stories of these other Edith Whartons, born through her extraordinary dexterity across a wide range of genres, and their impact on our understanding of her career, have not been fully told, and they are the focus of this study.

Wharton's work was often radical, subversive, and transgressive—the full extent of which becomes clear only when viewing her oeuvre across its span of less familiar genres. The author who wrote about child prostitution, drug addiction, child suicide, blasphemy, vivisection, domestic abuse, illegitimacy, euthanasia, and incest would still come to be associated by the public with an antique image of 'violets and old lace'.[3] Wharton's diversity of output was part of her radicalism. She could so easily have stuck to the success achieved in any one of a variety of genres—but instead refused to allow her talent and creative vision to be curtailed. Her prowess across a range of genres spoke to this author's confidence and sense of authority on the one hand, and to her vision of artistic cohesion and connectedness on the other. (As will be seen repeatedly in this study, here was a writer who loathed any kind of short-cut.) It is often in the genres for which she is least well-known that Wharton is shown at her boldest, most adventurous, and most radical—which in part explains why a full recognition of those characteristics of her work has been obscured. The author who penned the powerful critical volume *The Writing of Fiction* (1925) had indeed more than the writing of fiction to her name.

Wharton rebelled early. In many ways, the very act of writing as a young girl in the privileged, leisured society into which she was born was itself an act of rebellion. And that rebellion was advertised early. Of her first published poem, 'Only a Child' (1879), which appeared in the *New York World* when she was seventeen, Wharton recalled sending a note to the editor in which she carefully explained that she 'knew the rules of English versification' and 'had put in the extra syllables on purpose!'[4] At seventeen, Edith Jones knew the form—and was prepared to transgress it. Before that obscuring gauze of 'violets and old lace' was lowered, Wharton's work caused fierce controversy. In November 1901, for example, *Harper's Monthly Magazine* published her now little-read dramatic monologue, 'Margaret of Cortona', in which Margaret on her death bed makes a blasphemous confession to the priest that she would not have entered the convent had her lover lived: 'I, who have known both loves, divine and human, / Think you I would not leave this Christ for that?' 'He was my Christ.'[5] The Catholic Church's Margaret was fully repentant and duly canonised; Wharton's dissatisfied Margaret was still teeming with physical desire and passion thwarted in a second-rate substitute life of the church. The poem caused outrage, with the Catholic press denouncing 'a subtle love of evil in the literary world', Wharton's 'shameful misrepresentation' and her flagrant offence against 'good taste, historical accuracy, Catholic tradition, and Divine teaching': 'Miss Wharton has erred.'[6] The furore was such that by January 1902 the editor felt obliged to issue a fulsome apology for the 'injury to the religious sensibilities' of readers, claiming historical ignorance on the part of both poet and editor, who 'rather than have knowingly done the wrong, would have given up writing and editing altogether'.[7] The idea that the cultured Wharton, who often spent months of every year in Italy, would be ignorant of an Italian saint about whom she was writing was almost as unconvincing as the notion she would lay down her pen. Wharton, like her Margaret, was evidently unrepentant, not only republishing the poem in her volume, *Artemis to Actaeon* (1909), but doing so without any amendments to appease 'religious sensibilities' and atone for the 'offence'.

Only months before 'Margaret of Cortona' was first published, *The Shadow of a Doubt*—a play Wharton scholars were unaware existed until 2016—appeared set for the Broadway stage, having been taken on by Charles Frohman, the leading producer of his age. The play's startling theme was euthanasia, with its revelation that the character of Kate Derwent, formerly a professional nurse, had helped her husband's first wife to die, after she had begged for an end to her pain. By making Kate a figure of quiet integrity and honour who elects to give up her newly acquired life of luxury because her husband doubts that she acted out of compassion, Wharton refuses her audience an easy, unquestioning condemnatory stance, inviting instead recognition of euthanasia as a complex moral issue. To write a play pivoting on a theme of euthanasia for the commercial stage was brave and controversial—and the theme may offer one explanation for Frohman's production being abruptly shelved. Wharton would later include euthanasia as one of several plotlines in her novel, *The Fruit of the Tree* (1907), but its impact was partially blunted by a multiplicity of themes. It was Wharton as *playwright* who made the bolder artistic decision, one which professionally may have cost her a Broadway debut.

In her notebook, 'Quaderno dello Studente', begun in 1924, Wharton claimed as her motto a phrase from 'The Vision' by seventeenth-century poet, Thomas Traherne: 'Order the beauty even of Beauty is.'[8] Her novels, poems, and plays often illuminate the allure, but also the dangers, especially for women, of disorder, of crossing the threshold, of going 'beyond'. Kate Derwent's choice takes her from London's affluent Park Lane to a drab lodging-house in the East End, as she struggles to find employment without a reference to attest to her character or professional skills. In the poem, 'May Marian', written when Wharton was only fourteen, a young woman's naïve choice to follow a man to London proves fatal. In the unfinished early novel *Disintegration*, the divorced Mrs Clephane is 'banned to a desert place outside the geography of the visiting-list',[9] while 'beyondness' ultimately brings *The House of Mirth*'s Lily Bart to the shabby and dingy existence she most feared, on the 'rubbish heap' from which only chloral provides an effective release.[10] 'In the established order of things as she knew them', reflects the narrator of Charity Royall in the closing stages of *Summer* (1917), 'she saw no place for her individual adventure....'[11]

In her non-fiction, however, Wharton *is* able to find space for and reward the individual adventure, to suggest guiding rules, but encourage flexibility within them. In *The Writing of Fiction*, the author deploys 'Order the beauty even of Beauty is' as the volume's epigraph, yet directly warns against excessive prescription: 'General rules in art are useful chiefly as a lamp in a mine, or a hand-rail down a black stairway; they are necessary for the sake of the guidance they give, but it is a mistake, once they are formulated, to be too much in awe of them.'[12] *The Writing of Fiction* will be seen to push critical writing beyond prescriptive boundaries and advocate a flexibility essential for Wharton's artistic vision in which 'genius' and 'inspiration' are the *sine qua non*, but insufficient on their own to make art. As a critical writer, Wharton produces a user-friendly handbook that acknowledges and validates the space, the mystery, the licence to be individual, while holding out to fiction writers 'a future rich in untried possibilities' (*WF* 8).

In turn, Wharton's 1903 critical essay, 'The Vice of Reading', delights in 'intellectual vagrancy', 'the improvised chase', a book as 'the keynote of unpremeditated harmonies, as the gateway into some *paysage choisi* of the spirit'.[13] Reader response and engagement are crucial considerations, bringing combined responsibilities and rewards. In an unpublished autobiographical fragment, 'Adventures with Books', Wharton would build this sense of communication into her definition of a library, a definition that opened up ownership beyond the elite, prioritising prosperity of the imagination over that of the cheque book. 'I have known people with a handful of books who had a library', she writes, '& others who possessed rows on rows of <the classics>, beautifully bound, works, & priceless first editions & had none.' She continued, 'In other words, <what I understand by> a library is the <give-and-take> relation between an individual & his books. Everything but this live area of communication between the book & its reader is dead lumber.'[14] In her travel writing, she advocates stepping off the beaten path and forging one's own. Wharton is often criticised as elitist, yet her writing in the genres for which she is less well-known will repeatedly be seen to offer a very pragmatic sharing of knowledge, empowering her reader, while always remaining resistant to dumbing down, indeed demonstrating an early faith in her audience that editors will be shown at times to lack. The work examined in this study often unapologetically offers up a life-affirming paean to culture, validating knowledge, a rich, full, civilised life, and denying short-cuts.

It is often forgotten that at times Wharton's own rich, full, civilised life was reduced to scandal-sheet fodder. As highlighted in Chap. 7 in the discussion of life writings, her life choices, social position, talent, behaviour (as a woman), and her success all came in for very public scrutiny. At the age of twenty, she was publicly shamed over the ending of her first engagement. *Town Topics* reported in October 1882 that 'the only reason for the breaking of the engagement hitherto existing between Harry Stevens and Miss Edith Jones is an alleged preponderance of intellectuality on the part of the intended bride.' 'Miss Jones', the report flagged, 'is an ambitious authoress, and it is said that, in the eyes of Mr. Stevens, ambition is a grievous fault.'[15] Wharton was criticised for affectation, for not being 'a beauty', for aloofness, ambition, for being a pale copy of Henry James, for her relationship with Walter Berry, for the premature death of her former fiancé, for her choice of husband, for writing *The House of Mirth*, both for living in Lenox and for leaving Lenox, for the fact her husband was 'left behind' when she travelled, for allegedly breaking an agreement to sell the Mount (after the men of the party had a 'gentlemen's agreement' no less), and later for living in France.[16] Before the 'grande dame' mantle settled, her behaviour was read for decades on a shifting scale of the inappropriate, improper, rebellious, and transgressive.

A study of Wharton's less familiar genres as a body of work also reveals that the writer encountered much greater and more pernicious levels of sexism in both the production and reception of her work than is generally acknowledged. She faced sexism of both the overt and indirect, insidious varieties—a fact that at times has been rendered less visible because of her success in spite of it and in counteracting it, but also in large part because it is the now under-read genres considered in this study towards which sexist responses were most energetically directed. In her writing on architecture and design, for example, Wharton was expected (but refused) to produce the 'chatty' work her editors wanted on Italian villas, to play the supporting role to a male collaborator (she resisted) and to adapt her ideas in a way her collaborator was not. Her vision for *Italian Villas and Their Gardens* (1904) was ultimately compromised by her editors' refusal to include her architectural plans in the book, a decision interpreted by the author as their way of punishing her for rebelling against their wishes.[17] Undoubtedly, Wharton could herself be sexist and did not always support other women—she was certainly no vocal advocate of women's suffrage even as she lived through the vital period of campaigning and constitutional change in much of Europe and the United States. But she was much more often a victim than a perpetrator of sexism, and persistently saw her work viewed and judged through a sexist lens.

The Henry James comparative scenario appeared early, while throughout her career in fiction Wharton was accused of being incapable of writing men: one reviewer of *Old New York* (1924) memorably decreed that a 'few deft touches from a masculine hand would set … [her male protagonist Hayley Delane] right'.[18] Displays of sexism, however, reach a new degree of intensity in responses to a number of the genres with which Wharton is less often identified. Consider G. R. Carpenter's extraordinary 1905 *Bookman* review of her travel book, *Italian Backgrounds*: 'Mrs. Wharton unwittingly has allowed herself to be hypnotised by Italian art. She has denationalised, defeminised herself. Her writing is not that of an American of today, not even of a woman, but merely of the art-antiquarian.'[19] Meanwhile, Wharton's published poetry was often assessed as derivative, lacking masculine rigour and passion, and the author seen as a poor (wo)man's Browning. The *New York Times* wrote Wharton almost entirely out of her own poetry in unmistakably gendered terms, when it suggested that dramatic monologues of *Artemis to Actaeon* (1909) 'owe more to Browning than to their foster mother'.[20] In 1925, when Wharton published her volume of criticism *The Writing of Fiction* (examined in Chap. 6), she was an author in her sixties, still at the height of her powers, earning more money than at any point in her career, winner of the Pulitzer, and internationally renowned. It is almost inconceivable that a male writer in such a position would have been denied respect and due consideration for his voice and views. Wharton, by contrast, found herself under attack as a woman trespassing on a male literary realm. In a breathtaking sexist and ageist reduction, her volume was judged as 'slight' and 'scrappy', not even presenting a 'closely-woven argument', only a 'bundle of notes'.[21] The young Percy Lubbock's *The Craft of Fiction* (1921) was held up as the standard bearer, which the female critic could not match. Wharton's contribution was quite literally belittled as a 'little volume', 'little study', 'little book'.[22]

The critical responses to *The Writing of Fiction* offer a powerful reminder that Wharton was never one of the boys' club. The internationally acclaimed, prize-winning author remained in many ways always a literary outsider. While she is memorialised as a writer who chose the company of men, it is often forgotten that she was also surrounded by brilliant women, from Anna Bahlmann to Vernon Lee, Mary Cadwalader Jones, Mary Berenson, Claude Silve (Philomène de Lévis-Mirepoix), Sara Norton, Beatrix Farrand and others, either in person or via avid correspondence—some of the women famous in their own right, but others whose brilliance was obscured. When *The Times* (London) obituary noted Wharton 'was fortunate in her friends', producing a list that included only one woman (Vernon Lee),[23] it prompted a now forgotten letter from an anonymous, female 'old friend' who wished 'to bear testimony to [Wharton's] generous, sympathetic understanding and kindness to herself and many others of the same sex and calibre', informing *The Times*' readers that 'the blank she leaves in her women friends' hearts will never be filled.'[24] The letter publicly undercut the myth that Wharton had no women friends at the exact moment it was forming, but the myth built nevertheless, reaching its apotheosis half a century later in the *New York Times* headline, 'The Woman Who Hated Women'.[25]

Though it is an epithet Wharton herself would have roundly rejected, her oeuvre emerges from a study that considers her span of genres as more overtly feminist than we have appreciated. Perhaps surprisingly, it is often the genres outside the novel, novella, and the short story—in texts both published and unpublished—that display most clearly an unfettered, unapologetic feminism (which in turn likely feeds the heightened responses of sexism in relation to the published work noted above). There are dramatic monologues that reverse the poetic status quo: men are silenced, women speak and claim the account of their lives. In the notebook poem, 'Lucrezia Buonvisi remembers', a vilified woman tells and owns her story:

Wharton does not demonise her and does not judge. In 'Ante-Mortem', still unpublished, a woman makes a death-bed confession of unfaithfulness to her husband. The woman dominates; her husband is voiceless, the reader witnessing only his 'wordless tears'. The marriage in a more familiar poem, 'The Last Giustiani', which I will suggest has been too easily read as a hymn to romance and mutual longing, sees Wharton re-envisage a purportedly romantic idyll with a disturbing subtext of a young woman caught in a male narrative of objectification, silencing, and control.

In her writings on travel, on architecture and design, as well as in her literary criticism, Wharton is assured, authoritative, and professional, and declines to apologise for her knowledge and expertise. In her travel writing, she does not present herself as a 'woman traveller', but is a trailblazer: at times a woman in a man's world, at others a traveller in a country without a guide book, promoting individualism and adventure, again endeavouring to empower her readers to pursue their own paths. In contrast to the travel writing, Wharton sets up and embraces a form of critical writing that will be seen at times as decidedly *gendered*. While the author has been accused of being tentative, uncertain in her critical voice, she is, I suggest, dazzlingly assured—berating perceived shortcomings of male critics and critical double standards. In *The Writing of Fiction*, Wharton legitimises individual space, offering up a less elitist vision of the artist, a vision that never suggests 'men only'. In *The Decoration of Houses* (1897), Wharton and Ogden Codman insist on viewing interior design as a branch of architecture, thereby giving equal priority to the field so often considered the inferior design arena, for women. While Wharton's social mindset could at times be closed, locked into the prejudices of her age, her imagination and creative vision were always open to an extraordinary world of possibilities, her capacity for wonder undiminished.

Examination of Wharton's work across the span of genres in this study often reveals a writer who identifies less conflictedly than is often supposed, as *American*, both before and during her long residence in France. Her travel writing, for example, both promotes an intensely American narrative of individualism and independence of spirit, evoking the pioneer ethos, and compellingly (re)aligns her own identity with the country of her birth. Much of *French Ways and Their Meaning* (1919) illuminates a route to being a better American. None of her writing advocates an artificial recreation of Europe or European ways in the United States—'a marble sarcophagus and a dozen twisted columns will not make an Italian garden' as she pithily observes in *Italian Villas and Their Gardens*[26]—but espouses fidelity to the spirit rather than the letter, appreciating and benefitting from cultural exchange. In *A Backward Glance* (1934), after decades living in Europe, Wharton will be seen to build and embed herself into an American narrative, with descriptions of portraits in the Capitol's Rotunda positioning her family as *literally* part of the nation's history, presenting herself not only as an American, but an American for the age.

A study of Wharton's writing beyond the novel, novella, and short story also underlines Wharton's experimentalism and the extent to which it has been critically obscured. That experimentalism often surfaces in the genres in which one might least expect it. *Italian Backgrounds* (1904) is the closest Wharton will ever come to producing a modernist manifesto; in her critical writing, the author redefines the concept of the American novel; in her autobiography she redefines contemporary 'Americanness' itself, with *A Backward Glance* reimagining the genre of life writing. Wharton made bold, on occasion costly choices. She also had the courage to be unfashionable, to propose that looking back was not necessarily a nostalgic, regressive artistic act, but could be progressive, radical, and essential in equal measure.

Edith Wharton and Genre: Beyond Fiction offers the first study of Wharton's full engagement with original writing in genres outside those with which she has been most closely identified and for which she is best remembered, namely the novel, novella, and short story. A significant part of this obscured narrative lies within neglected dimensions of the author's published record, while another is uncovered only in the rich Wharton archives in both Europe and the United States, which have been mined for this work. The focus is on original writings, so the study does not comprehensively examine Wharton's translations or adaptations (and simply does not have the space to do so). Nevertheless, arguably the most prominent of these—the author's stage adaptation with Clyde Fitch of her own *The House of Mirth*, of Abbé Prévost's novel *Manon Lescaut*, and her translation of Hermann Sudermann's play *Es Lebe das Leben (The Joy of Living)*— are considered in Chap. 3 in the contexts of her work for the stage. What war scholars have categorised loosely as Wharton's 'war writing', I class with the more precisely defined genre of travel writing, examining *Fighting France: From Dunkerque to Belfort* (1915) as a text which enhances understanding of both the development and cohesion of the author's record as a travel writer. Similarly, short poems and articles published in newspapers during the war are discussed with their audience and placement very much in mind, but within the genres to which their content and form assign them—poetry, life writing, and travel writing. In a number of genres Wharton will be seen to push their boundaries; in others actively to relish those boundaries and the diverse possibilities within them. The chapters of the study span a very considerable volume and variety of work, both published and unpublished, including unfinished work, writing from juvenilia to late diaries, notebook poems, variant drafts, and plays.

The study first considers two of the most critically neglected of the genres in which Wharton worked—poetry and playwriting—and endeavours to establish the primacy of both to a full appreciation and understanding of the writer's oeuvre and artistic development. Following on from this introduction (Chap. 1), Chap. 2 examines Wharton's poetry, starting with her early work, including childhood experiments with poetics in letters to her governess Anna Bahlmann, individual poems appearing first or solely in periodicals, and her overlooked volume, *Verses*, published privately by her parents when Edith Jones was sixteen and key to a formative stage of artistic growth. The chapter then explores a notebook housed at the Lilly Library at Indiana University packed with poems written in the late 1880s and early 1890s, almost all of which were unpublished in her lifetime, and her collection *Artemis to Actaeon and Other Verse* (1909). This volume was published when Wharton was an international star, yet reviewers responded to her poetry as though she were a novice writer. Discussion includes the volume *Twelve Poems* (1926), which appeared when the author was at the height of her commercial success, alongside poetry published during the war, diary poems written at emotional highs and lows, and draft variants. The chapter explores the genre's address to Wharton's sense of herself as an artist, the influences and traditions from which she learned and which she outgrew, her ease across a broad spectrum of forms and themes, her sometimes bold feminist reworking of traditions, the openness and flexibility of her approach which often evades easy categorisation, and the preview of motifs developed in her fiction. Wharton's poetry was at times inspired by her extraordinary bank of historical cultural knowledge and at times by gritty newspaper reports of the day, leading to explorations of social injustice and deprivation. The results range from the dull and pedestrian to some of the boldest, most exciting and transgressive work of Wharton's career. Recognition of Wharton as a significant poet of the late nineteenth and early twentieth centuries and of the impact of the genre on a fuller understanding of her as a writer and thinker are both long overdue.

In Chap. 3, with the emergence of recent new evidence, I develop the argument I first made in volume one of my critical edition, *The Unpublished Writings of Edith Wharton* (2009), that at the turn of the century Wharton was as much—if not more—interested in seeking success as a playwright than as a novelist. Original plays discussed include *The Man of Genius, The Arch., an untitled play, The Necklace, Kate Spain*, and *The Shadow of a Doubt*. This chapter examines Wharton's appropriation and subversion of dramatic stereotypes, her openness to experimentation, her harnessing of controversial plotlines, on occasions her embrace of populist melodrama, on others her deployment of minimalism and quiet economy in what would otherwise have been a sensationalist drama. Wharton's confidence in the genre spans deft comedies of manners to grittier realities of life below stairs. A number of plays offer plot and character prototypes of later, better-known Wharton novels, while we also see the imprint of her playwriting techniques on the novels that in many ways came to define her career. Wharton was interested in playwriting from the beginning to end of her professional life, but while she was still writing plays after 1906, she no longer actively pursued them to production. One of the likely explanations for this, I suggest, lies in the frustrations Wharton experienced with the collaborative nature of theatre work. Collaboration had led to aborted productions, creative disagreements and misunderstandings, a compromised artistic vision, and the glare of unsavoury publicity, with full-scale rows reported by the press. In a scenario that will partly echo in Wharton's work on architecture and design, collaboration was seen to bring risks, an abnegation of control, a threat to the integrity of her creative vision—and, as the most pragmatic of bottom lines, the prospect of a shared, reduced financial return. Playwriting as a form, however, remained a life-long fascination and an influential, though critically long-neglected genre in Wharton's career.

An inveterate traveller became an inveterate travel writer. Chapter 4 examines Wharton's work in the genre of travel writing, including *The Cruise of the Vanadis*—Wharton's little-read account of her three-month Aegean voyage in 1888 which remained unpublished in her lifetime, *Italian Backgrounds* (1905), *A Motor-Flight Through France* (1908), *Fighting France: From Dunkerque to Belfort* (1915), *French Ways and Their Meaning* (1919), *In Morocco* (1920), and depictions of her travels in Spain. Important scholarship by Jennifer Haytock and others has addressed the often unorthodox modernism of Wharton's fiction in recent years. I suggest it is at times in her travel texts that the modernist dynamics of her writing are most clearly on display, with work that both advertises modernity and journeys into the past. This chapter challenges biographical assumptions, which I claim have contributed to diminished readings of the author's work in this genre as apprentice texts or as journeys of Wharton's personal 'self-discovery'. The chapter considers her refusal to present herself as 'woman traveller' and her place among travel writing contemporaries, including her sister-in-law, Mary Cadwalader Jones. While Wharton's role as explicator of Europe to an American readership is secure, I also discuss her later evocation of dream-like states with *In Morocco*, where Wharton is faced with a culture she cannot fully understand or convey. Travel writing will be seen to present Wharton (in Europe) at her most American: the pioneer, often prioritising individualism and adventure, and while work in the genre inevitably speaks to a level of elitism—her travels made possible by disposable income—the writer empowers her reader, encouraging individual journeys, real or imagined, into a realm of rich possibilities. Wharton produced a very substantial body of varied travel writing, with the boldness of her achievements in this genre still partially obscured.

Wharton's first professional book publication was her 1897 design collaboration with Ogden Codman Jr, *The Decoration of Houses*, while six years later she received a commission that resulted in *Italian Villas and Their Gardens* (1904), Wharton's research on almost eighty villas accompanied by twenty-six drawings by the renowned American artist, Maxfield Parrish. Chapter 5 examines Wharton's writings on architecture and design, focused primarily on her two volumes, but also encompassing early letters to the *Newport Daily News* protesting the loss of Newport's old houses and advocating the decoration of schoolrooms, as well as much later works on gardening design, most unpublished in her lifetime, notably 'Gardening in France', an unfinished account of her restoration of the gardens at Pavillon Colombe. Wharton and Codman looked to Europe for inspiration, but to America for application and impact, insisting on viewing house decoration as a branch of architecture. Wharton's work in this field is not entirely original, but its scholarship and authority, underpinned by immaculate research, elevated American public discourse on interior design and architecture to another level. As in her travel writing, the author offers an undaunted advocacy of culture, of a meaningful, connected life, and empowers the reader in a determination to share expertise and knowledge—offering both scholarly text and practical, can-do guide. Again we see that at the end of the nineteenth century, and beginning of the twentieth century, much of Wharton's professional work was rooted in collaboration—which brought both frustrations and rewards. Architecture and design will be shown as one area in which Wharton increasingly stepped away from theory in favour of practice, her early work at The Mount followed by the design of two internationally renowned gardens in France.

'True originality', suggests Wharton in *The Writing of Fiction*, 'consists not in a new manner but in a new vision' (*WF* 18). Chapter 6, 'Critical Writings and Literary Theory', considers work including the mock reviews Edith Jones devised to accompany her 'novelette' *Fast and Loose*, a series of illuminating, early twentieth-century book reviews, the essays 'The Criticism of Fiction' (1914), 'The Great American Novel' (1927), 'Tendencies in Modern Fiction' (1934), 'Permanent Values in Fiction' (1934), and *The Writing of Fiction*. Discussions encompass the critical reception, contemporary critical writing, and Wharton's place within it. The chapter centres on an examination of Wharton's most developed and significant thesis on the theory and art of writing, her volume *The Writing of Fiction*, now generally neglected, summarily dismissed or misremembered as an anti-modernist howl. Wharton's critical writings, sustained and substantive, are often unfashionable, difficult to categorise, and subversive. At times in her critical writings Wharton will be seen to be setting out an alternative, explicitly feminist critical agenda, while more broadly her work in this field, notably *The Writing of Fiction*, often opens up possibilities, argues against narrow thinking, against standardisation, and sets a different range of priorities. And the immediate audience is often the practising writer not the armchair reader, distinctive from other critical texts—the author speaking up against the pressures facing writers to produce (quickly) more of the same. Wharton opened up possibilities only to find herself excluded: her gender, at times career stage, age, class and image have persistently worked against her receiving due recognition for the innovations of *The Writing of Fiction*.

Work considered in Chap. 7, 'Life Writings', includes 'Life and I'—Wharton's incomplete memoir devoted to her formative years that would remain unpublished until many decades after her death, *A Backward Glance* (1934), 'A Further Glance' (published posthumously in *Harper's Magazine* as 'A Little Girl's New York' in March 1938), and the manuscript fragments 'Adventures with Books'. Discussion extends to the private pages of 'The Life Apart (L'âme close)', with entries from October 1907 to June 1908 covering the period during which Wharton's friendship with Morton Fullerton turned into an affair, and the entries stretching over a decade from May 1924 to December 1934 in her notebook, 'Quaderno dello Studente', which Wharton advertised to future biographers. I consider the serialisation of *A Backward Glance*, which ran from October 1933 in the *Ladies' Home Journal*, very substantially abridged, and the targeted public constructions of Wharton's life in the weekly periodical that became *Town Topics: The Journal of Society*. *Town Topics* presented itself as an essential source of information on culture, art, and society, but was read primarily for its society gossip and scandal. The chapter reflects on the place of *A Backward Glance* in the 1930s' autobiography boom, and Wharton's contribution to both a personal and national record, including ways in which she explicitly links her story to the story of America itself, with the author increasingly concerned about a legacy image. Wharton's published autobiographical writing taps into a popular market, but also resists that market by pushing the boundaries of the genre, challenging readers' perceptions of what really comprises the signpost events of life, the Lady Godiva moments of autobiography. A work presented as discreet and evasive is considered in this study as Wharton's bold and unexpected rewriting of the conventional hierarchies of importance in both autobiography and life—all in the presence of the volume's formal studio portrait of the artist in choker pearls, a fur drape around her dress, hands concealed by a fur muff, suggesting a woman belonging to another age.

Indeed Wharton's longevity has also traditionally been read as problematic, as the cause of perceived routine, even fag-end late work and an unnecessarily bloated oeuvre. Edmund Wilson opens his essay 'Justice to Edith Wharton' with the sweeping statement: 'Before Edith Wharton died, the more commonplace work of her later years had had the effect of dulling the reputation of her earlier and more serious work', implicitly defining 'later years' as spanning almost twenty years of her career.[27] Yet the writer's longevity, and the ongoing, diverse productivity that accompanied it, also proves part of what makes her 'un-boxable', despite the imposition of critics' labels, labels that Wharton recognised and to each of which she gave a shelf-life of 'about ten years' ('Edith Wharton in Profile'). This is an author whose publishing record spans almost sixty years, her writing record longer, the writer whose poetry was encouraged by Longfellow at one end of her career and dismissed by T.S. Eliot at the other. After all, who exactly *are* Wharton's contemporaries? The longevity of her career makes them difficult to pinpoint, in a shifting cast. There were of course always lazy reviews. Writing in the *Spectator* in May 1933, Graham Greene was still making his review of Wharton's volume of stories, *Human Nature*, as much about Henry James as Edith Wharton—almost twenty years after James' death.[28] In his January 1923 essay, 'American Authors of Today', Percy H. Boynton presented 'Mrs. Wharton' in terms that suggested a conduit in a literary séance: 'With the death of William Dean Howells in 1920, Mrs. Wharton was left as the connecting medium in American fiction between his generation and ours. She is not a writer to stir enthusiasms, but she wins her full share of respectful admiration, as a distinguished representative of the old school is certain to do.'[29] In a short piece for the *Washington Post*, published one month after Wharton's death, William Lyon Phelps recalled a lunch with the author in the summer of 1928, during which he had 'asked her if she were working on a new book, and she answered *with a melancholy smile*, "I am always writing"' (my italics)—a vignette that intimated a bittersweet compulsion of an unfulfilled life.[30] Readings of Wharton's longevity and ongoing varied productivity as creating a 'burden' of quantity over quality, of a writer who had outlived her time, have only formed another stubborn block to a full recognition of the depth and versatility of genre that were intrinsic to that sixty-year publishing record. As this study will repeatedly illuminate, for all the accusations to the contrary, for all the restrictive tags and labels, Edith Wharton possessed—exactly as she wrote of Geoffrey Scott in her June 1914 review of his *The Architecture of Humanism*—'a mind unwilling to rest in accepted formulas'. . .[31]

Notes

1. Letter from Edith Wharton to Mary Cadwalader Jones, 23 January 1919, Edith Wharton Collection, Yale Collection of American Literature, Beinecke Rare Book and Manuscript Library, Yale University. Box 28, folder 845.
2. 'Edith Wharton Dies of Stroke At 75 in Her French Chateau', *The Washington Post (1923–1954)*, 13 August 1937, ProQuest Historical Newspapers: The Washington Post, 26; 'Edith Wharton', *New York Times*, 13 August 1937, ProQuest Historical Newspapers: The New York Times with Index, 16; 'Edith Wharton Dies in France', *Philadelphia Bulletin*, undated clipping, Beinecke; Edmond Jaloux, 'Edith Wharton Un Très Grand Romancier', 17 August 1937, clipping, Beinecke; 'La Première Romancière Des États-Unis Edith Wharton Est Morte', *Le Petit Parisien*, 14 August 1937, clipping, Beinecke. *The Times* (London) was rare in list-

ing a broad range of Wharton's work, but headlined her as 'A Great American Novelist' upgraded in the first line of its obituary to 'one of the greatest novelists America had produced', 'Edith Wharton', *The Times*, 14 August 1937, 12, The Times Digital Archive.
3. Loren Carroll, 'Edith Wharton in Profile', Paris edition of the *New York Herald Tribune*, 16 November 1936. Clipping, Edith Wharton Collection, Yale Collection of American Literature, Beinecke Rare Book and Manuscript Library, Yale University. Subsequent references are included in the text.
4. 'Life and I', in Laura Rattray (ed.), *The Unpublished Writings of Edith Wharton*, Vol. 2 (London: Pickering and Chatto, 2009), 183–204; 200. Subsequent references to this work are included in the text ('LI').
5. 'Margaret of Cortona', *Harper's Monthly Magazine* (November 1901), 884–87; 887, 886: https://www.unz.com/print/Harpers-1901nov-00884/.
6. '"Harper's Magazine" and St. Margaret of Cortona', *The Sacred Heart Review* 26:22 (30 November 1901), 9: https://newspapers.bc.edu/?a=d&d=BOSTONSH19011130-01.2.26. Subsequent references to this work are included in the text.
7. 'Editor's Study', *Harper's Monthly Magazine* (January 1902), 339–42; 342: https://www.unz.com/print/Harpers-1902jan-00339/.
8. Edith Wharton, 'Quaderno dello Studente', in Laura Rattray (ed.), *The Unpublished Writings of Edith Wharton*, Vol. 2 (London: Pickering and Chatto, 2009), 205–15; 209. Subsequent references to this work are included in the text ('QS').
9. Edith Wharton, *Disintegration*, in Rattray (ed.), *The Unpublished Writings of Edith Wharton*, Vol. 2 (London: Pickering and Chatto, 2009), 65–118; 93. Subsequent references to this work are included in the text.
10. Edith Wharton, *The House of Mirth* (New York: Charles Scribner's Sons, 1905), 498. Subsequent references to this work are included in the text (*HM*).
11. Edith Wharton, *Summer* (New York: D. Appleton and Company, 1917), 235.
12. Edith Wharton, *The Writing of Fiction* (London: Charles Scribner's Sons, 1925), 42. Subsequent references to this work are included in the text (*WF*).
13. Edith Wharton, 'The Vice of Reading', *The North American Review*, 177: 563 (October 1903), 513–21; 516: https://www.jstor.org/stable/25119460.
14. Edith Wharton, 'Adventures with Books', Wharton Collection, Beinecke. Box 19, folder 581.

15. Cited in Shari Benstock, *No Gifts from Chance: A Biography of Edith Wharton* (London: Hamish Hamilton, 1994), 46. Subsequent references to this work are included in the text.
16. See Chap. 7, 'Life Writings'. *Town Topics: The Journal of Society*, 17: 25, 23 June 1887, 2; 47:5, 30 January 1902, 14–15 ('The disparity between the original and the copy is typically great in this as in other cases: Mr. James's story is the notable bit of work in the magazine, while the Wharton verses ['Uses'] are as futile as possible'); 69:23, 5 June 1913, 9; 70:12, 18 September 1913, 8; 17:25, 23 June 1887, 2; 20:3, 19 July 1888, 2; 67:22, 30 May 1912, 8; 66:9, 31 August 1911, 9; 62:27, 30 December 1909, 6–7; 62:14, 30 September 1909, 8; 66:10, 7 September 1911, 7. *Everyday Life & Women in America c.1800–1920:* www.everydaylife.amdigital.co.uk. For a discussion of contemporary American responses to Wharton's decision to live abroad, see Kristin Olson Lauer, 'Can France Survive this Defender? Contemporary American Reaction to Edith Wharton's Expatriation', in Katherine Joslin and Alan Price (eds.), *Wretched Exotic: Essays on Edith Wharton in Europe* (New York: Peter Lang, 1996), 77–95.
17. Edith Wharton, *A Backward Glance* (New York: D. Appleton-Century Company, 1934), 138–39. Subsequent references to this work are included in the text (*BG*).
18. Stanley Alden, 'Edith Wharton, as Writer of Comedy', Springfield *Republican*, 31 August 1924, 7-A, cited in James W. Tuttleton, Kristin O. Lauer and Margaret P. Murray, 'Introduction', in Tuttleton, Lauer, Murray (eds.), *Edith Wharton: The Contemporary Reviews* (Cambridge University Press, 2009), ix–xxii; xvii, 375.
19. G. R. Carpenter, 'Mrs. Wharton's *Italian Backgrounds*', *Bookman*, 21 (August 1905), 609–10, reprinted in *Edith Wharton: The Contemporary Reviews*, 100–1.
20. 'Books of Poems by Two Writers', *New York Times*, 8 May 1909, ProQuest Historical Newspapers: The New York Times with Index, BR300.
21. J. B. Priestley, 'The Novelist's Art', *Spectator*, 135 (5 December 1925), 1047, reprinted in *Edith Wharton: The Contemporary Reviews*, 386–88.
22. Brander Matthews, 'A Story-Teller on the Art of Story-Telling', *Literary Digest International Book Review*, 3 (October 1925), 731–32; 'This Week's Books', *Spectator*, 135 (7 November 1925), 836; Lloyd Morris, 'Mrs. Wharton Discusses the Art of Fiction', *New York Times Book Review*, 15 November 1925, reprinted in *Edith Wharton: The Contemporary Reviews*, 379–93.
23. 'Edith Wharton', *The Times*, 14 August 1937, 12. The Times Digital Archive: http://tinyurl.galegroup.com/tinyurl/9ksdb0.
24. An old friend, 'Edith Wharton', *The Times*, 17 August 1937, 15. The Times Digital Archive: http://tinyurl.galegroup.com/tinyurl/A76tq9.

25. Janet Malcolm, 'The Woman Who Hated Women', *New York Times*, 16 November 1986: https://www.nytimes.com/1986/11/16/books/the-woman-who-hated-women.html.
26. Edith Wharton, with pictures by Maxfield Parrish, *Italian Villas and Their Gardens* (New York: The Century Co., 1904), 12. Subsequent references to this work are included in the text (*IVG*).
27. Edmund Wilson, 'Justice to Edith Wharton' [1941], in Irving Howe (ed.), *Edith Wharton: A Collection of Critical Essays* (Englewood Cliffs, N.J.: Prentice-Hall, 1962), 19–31; 19. Subsequent references to this work are included in the text.
28. Greene states: 'Mrs. Wharton writes in the tradition of Henry James; from that superb portraitist she has borrowed a trick or two of style, the use of alliteration for example, the habit of introducing her minor characters in an ironic vignette and her general scene—the more "visited" of Continental cities'; 'Deception, which was Henry James' prevailing theme, is Mrs. Wharton's also in these stories.' Graham Greene, 'Fiction', *Spectator*, 150 (5 May 1933), 654, reprinted in *Edith Wharton: The Contemporary Reviews* 508–9.
29. Percy H. Boynton, 'American Authors of Today: V. Edith Wharton', *The English Journal*, 12:1 (January 1923), 24–32; 25.
30. William Lyon Phelps 'Edith Wharton: Author Of 44 Books', *The Washington Post (1923–1954)*, 21 September 1937, ProQuest Historical Newspapers: The Washington Post, 9.
31. Review, 'The Architecture of Humanism', *Times Literary Supplement*, 25 June 1914, reprinted in Frederick Wegener (ed.), *Edith Wharton: The Uncollected Critical Writings* (Princeton University Press, 1999), 130–34; 130.

CHAPTER 2

Edith Wharton as Poet

In sonnet form, Miss Wharton should some day achieve something…[1]

Poetry opened doors for Edith Wharton. In 1894, it was her work as a poet (more than the letter of introduction from Paul Bourget) that provided her with an entrée into the highly selective Florentine household of Vernon Lee and her seriously ill brother Eugene Lee-Hamilton. Lee tellingly invited Wharton to call if she 'chanced to be the Edith Wharton who had written a certain sonnet … in "Scribner's Magazine"' (*BG* 130).[2] The meeting initiated a mutually supportive friendship. Wharton was already a longstanding admirer of Lee's work, crediting *Studies of the Eighteenth Century in Italy* (1880) and *Euphorion: Being Studies of the Antique and the Mediaeval in the Renaissance* (1884) with ushering her as a young woman 'into that wonder world of Italy which [she] had loved since [her] childhood without having the key to it'.[3] She held Lee-Hamilton's poetic talents in similarly high, even exalted regard, proclaiming shortly after his premature death in 1907 that his volume *Sonnets of the Wingless Hours* (1894) contained 'some twenty sonnets of exceptional beauty, and four or five which rank not far after the greatest in the language'.[4] Wharton regretted that his sonnets were 'far less known than they should be to readers of verse in America' ('The Sonnets of Eugene Lee-Hamilton' 251), a position reiterated almost thirty years later in *A Backward Glance* with the reflection that she had 'never understood why the poignant verse written during his illness…is not more widely known' (*BG* 131).

Wharton's reputation as a poet remains only slightly higher than Lee-Hamilton's. With a few telling exceptions—most notably 'Terminus', determinedly interpreted by biographers as an account of a night of passion with Morton Fullerton in a Charing Cross Hotel—her poetry remains little read or discussed. Yet Wharton was a prolific and dedicated poet, working seriously in the genre throughout her career. Poetry, for Wharton, represented the highest form of literary discourse. She described it emotionally in *A Backward Glance* as 'my chiefest passion and my greatest joy' (170), and reverentially in a letter to William Crary Brownell in October 1908 as 'so august a thing that I always feel as if I should be struck by lightning when I sidle up to the shrine'.[5] Her first publication was a volume of poetry, the anonymous, privately printed *Verses* (1878), followed much later by *Artemis to Actaeon and Other Verse* (Scribner's, 1909), and *Twelve Poems*, published by the Medici Society in London at the Riccardi Press in 1926. Her final publication was the posthumous *Eternal Passion in English Poetry* (Appleton-Century, 1939), favourite love poems across the centuries selected by Wharton and Robert Norton with the collaboration of her literary executor Gaillard Lapsley, and with a preface by the author. In addition there exist numerous individual poems, published in periodicals including *Scribner's Magazine, The Atlantic Monthly, Harper's Magazine, Century Magazine* and the *New York World*, and scores of unpublished poems, manuscript drafts, and variants, spread across various archives. Even when she expressed doubt that she 'ever reached the "poetry line"', Wharton's 'warbling' as she termed the production of poetry, played an important role from beginning to the end of her career.[6]

Wharton's poetry composition began early. The recovery of the author's letters to her governess Anna Bahlmann was seized upon by readers primarily for its biographical realignment of Wharton's childhood and young adulthood. The discovery also illuminated, however, an extraordinary early focus on poetry and poetics—a focus largely overlooked in the critical reception of the letters, reflective of both the value of the biographical treasures unearthed and the abiding fascination with Wharton's *life*, but also of an ongoing failure fully to absorb her oeuvre in genres outside the remit of fiction. Biographical dazzle aside, the Bahlmann letters prove of equal importance in terms of Wharton's development as a writer, specifically for their underscoring of a literary apprenticeship in poetry—the young Edith Jones writing poems, agonising over word choice, metre, debating the work of other poets.

'Please, if it not be troubling you too much, tell me which lines you do not like, in your next letter' urged the fourteen-year old writer to Bahlmann in August 1876.[7] Edith Jones was looking early for people who engaged with her work, who offered constructive critique. Parents offered easy praise; Wharton wanted more—and found it in Bahlmann's guidance (though she would outgrow her governess' advice). 'I have been more than rewarded by your frank criticism, which is so much more of compliment to me than the polite, unmeaning, "Oh, it's lovely," which I so often get when I beg for an honest opinion', wrote the young author, again in August 1876 (*My Dear Governess* 30–31). Early letters concern Wharton's translation of poetry, notably two 'Mignon' poems from Goethe's *Wilhelm Meisters Lehrjahre*, which the teenage writer is referencing above, then swiftly move on to original compositions. A number of the poems do not appear to have survived, including a piece, again Goethe related, about Friederike, which Wharton mentions in her correspondence of August 1876 as having written that spring (*My Dear Governess* 31), and the intriguingly titled 'Phantoms', referenced in a letter of 17 October 1878, the same letter in which we hear for the first time of 'June and December', one of the poems included in the volume *Verses*. (Wharton professes herself 'very glad' that 'June and December' pleased Bahlmann 'especially' and that she liked the last stanza [*My Dear Governess* 42].) There are gaps in the correspondence, the timings of which can be infelicitous, notably just short of two full years between letters of 23 September 1876 and 2 September 1878 during which Wharton writes her novella *Fast and Loose* and works on a number of the poems that will be collected in *Verses* (1878).[8] Yet the correspondence charts a vivid map of the young poet's creative processes and means of production. This is a writer very focused on the pragmatic mechanics of construction ('The last stanza is flat—cramped—horrid—excepting, again, in the last line—which couldn't help itself' [*My Dear Governess* 36]), who knows her own mind ('I do not like the "no" you suggest as an alteration' [*My Dear Governess* 35]), who is earnest, committed, and occasionally 'breathtakingly audacious', as Irene Goldman-Price terms it, memorably pronouncing Shakespeare's *Julius Caesar* as 'too much like my own earliest attempts at tragedy to move me in the least' (*My Dear Governess* 30, 38).

As a consequence both of interruptions in the correspondence and of the shifting dynamics of the Jones-Bahlmann relationship, no contemporaneous authorial commentary on *Verses* or its reception survives. The volume will resurface briefly in Wharton's memoirs, by which time she appears roundly to dismiss her 'oeuvre de jeunesse' ('LI' 199).[9] Wharton looks back on her own early poetry with self-deprecation, and with a veiled, barbed charge at her mother, fostered in the years since their relationship soured. In 'Life and I', the author credits her mother for arranging the private printing of *Verses*, only to phrase it in such a way that damns her for poor judgement, understanding, and taste: 'My mother took an odd inarticulate interest in these youthful productions, & kept a blank book in which she copied many of them. She ~~even~~ <also> perpetrated the folly of having a "selection" privately printed when I was sixteen; & from a recent perusal of these two volumes I am reluctantly obliged to conclude that, ~~my "se~~ with one exception, nothing in my oeuvre de jeunesse showed the slightest spark of originality or talent' ('LI' 199).[10] That one exception, Wharton reflected, was the short poem 'Opportunity', written when she was 'about sixteen'. Published in fact as 'Opportunities', this assured, if undeveloped verse offers a precursor of a prominent leitmotif of Wharton's *oeuvre*—lost chances, here opportunities going unrecognised in 'the narrow present' as they 'walk beside us with unsounding feet'.[11]

The author inscribed her copy of *Verses*, published anonymously by the Newport firm C.E. Hammett, Jr., in late November or December 1878[12] with the lines: 'Who wrote these verses and this volume owns / Her unpoetic name is Edith Jones', while the frontispiece carries a Bettine Brentano quotation as a plea for a kindly disposed reading, 'Be friendly, pray, to these fancies of mine' (cited by Lee 43). The little criticism that exists on *Verses*, the volume comprising twenty-four original poems and five translations from German, largely echoes Wharton's own late life assessment. Lee notes that Wharton would look back on these verses as 'completely unoriginal' and suggests that 'Daises' (dated 1878) 'confirms this judgement' (43); Shari Benstock proposes that in *Verses* the young writer 'used the device of parodying or copying standard subjects and poetic forms as a way of analyzing poetic method'; Blake Nevius notes of 'the thin pamphlet' that 'without exception the poems are derivative', while Millicent Bell states that as late as the 1880s when Wharton first met Henry James she 'could scarcely call herself a writer, having done little besides some verses of amateur quality', singling out 'Some Woman to Some Man' from *Verses* as 'a pale, poor little poem'.[13] In 'Life and I' Wharton portrayed her earliest writing as a 'new refuge from ...outward miseries' (198). Jennie Kassanoff has used this to suggest that for a young Edith Newbold Jones who 'frequently felt menaced by some unnameable lurking source of turmoil and emotional devastation', 'poetry answered a very private need for order in a world that seemed threatening and confusing', though the dark hues of Wharton's childhood reminiscences, explored in the chapter 'Life Writings', are markedly at odds with the archival materials that have surfaced in the years since.[14]

The poems selected for *Verses* date from 1875, when Edith Jones was thirteen (the opening two sonnets dated 10 November and 11 November 1875 respectively) to the year of publication, when she was still sixteen. They largely offer conventional, but often accomplished meditations on the natural world, the beauties of the seasons, ageing, unreciprocated longing, musings on the fleeting nature of first love. A dramatic monologue '"The Last Token"' sees a young Christian woman in the Roman arena about to be killed by lions, while her helpless lover looks on. Its Browningesque quality—also apparent in *Verses*' 'Some Woman to Some Man', reminiscent of his 'Any Wife to Any Husband' (1855)—provides an early indication that poetry will present the genre in which we discern some of the strongest European inflections and influences on Wharton's work. (Her posthumous selection, *Eternal Passion in English Poetry*, would include thirteen Robert Browning poems.) While Louis Auchincloss seems unpersuasive in his speculation that the lover in '"The Last Token"' 'might be a forecast of Lawrence Selden in *The House of Mirth*, the cultivated dilettante who can do little more for his ill-fated sweetheart than toss her a rose from his own high immunity' (*Poems* iv), we will see in the poetry many of Wharton's mature themes in bud: hieroglyphic worlds, unexpressed longings, lost time and opportunities, thwarted passion. At the same time, the consolidated focus on nature will not be repeated until *Summer* almost forty years later, by which point Charity Royall's blossoming sexuality is explicitly linked to the glories of the natural world (though May 1876's 'Spring Song' with '[t]he first warm buds that break their covers', the 'flush of branches with fair blossoms', the '[f]resh rapture of the early Spring!' gives an indication of the direction of travel [*Poems* 3]). The opening lines of 'Some Woman to Some Man'—'We might have loved each other after all, / Have lived and learned together! Yet I doubt it' (*Poems* 13)—preview, at sixteen, a major motif of Wharton's mature work.

In *Verses*' 'May Marian' a fourteen-year old poet takes a conventional ballad form, but neatly offsets it with a chillingly unflinching eye, showing the fatal cost of women's naïveté and sentimentality. Marian has her 'silly heart' stolen by a gentleman riding through town one summer day. She follows him to London only to find he is already engaged. The role open to Marian is not wife, but 'serving maiden' to his 'betrothed bride'. 'Weeping sore' Marian turns away and travels home alone, only to find the door 'shut against her': 'All night long alone she wandered, / Wandered weeping through our town' (*Poems* 8–10). At sunrise she is found dead in the street. The poem ends with a jaunty 'MORAL': 'Ladies, listen to my ballad: / Maidens are too lightly won; / Home is best for country lasses, / Men are false in London town' (*Poems* 10), but women paying the price for their social errors was evidently a theme Wharton nailed young. Meanwhile, the evocative 'Heaven', dated January 1877, rejects an idea of the divine as 'Star-sentinelled from our humanity, / Beyond the humble reach of every day', positing instead that 'there is no line / That marks our human off from our divine'. Offering a perhaps surprisingly inclusive, though not necessarily democratic vision that 'For all one household, all one family / In different chambers labouring are we', 'Heaven' presages Wharton's threshold motif, the beyond, and the aligning of domestic architecture to the design of human nature and the soul, later demonstrated vividly in her short story 'The Fulness of Life': 'though across the threshold, in the gloom, / We cannot see into that other room, / It may be that the dear ones watching there / Can hear our cry of passionate despair, / And wait unseen to lead us through the door...' (*Poems* 5–6). Youthful and flawed certainly, *Verses* nevertheless serves notice of Wharton's emerging themes, interest in form, and considerable talent.

It was the publication of the poem 'Only a Child' the following year, however, that Wharton later marked as a 'great event' in her early life—publication by a professional editor rather than supportive parents ('LI' 200). The poem appeared in the *New York World* on 30 May 1879, under the pseudonym of 'Eadgyth', an early English spelling of 'Edith', but also the name of the Saxon Queen (c. 910–946), who was the granddaughter of Alfred the Great and wife of Otto I, Holy Roman Emperor—the choice marking a decided, confident shift from the earlier lack of pretension or ego in the 'unpoetic' epithet noted in the frontispiece of *Verses*. 'Only a Child' was inspired by a newspaper account the author had read 'of a little boy who had been put in the "lock-up" for some childish offense, & had hanged himself in the night'—Wharton noting that the subject 'appealed' to 'the morbid strain' in her nature ('LI' 200). Breaking regular metre—her reassurance to the editor that she knew the 'rules' of versification ('LI' 200) only highlighted the young writer's willingness to defy them—Wharton plies sentimental tropes to evoke pity for a boy, incarcerated, terrified to the point of taking his own life: 'Poor little hands! And little heart / That ached so long alone'; 'Think of him …Four walls of brick and mortar / To shut the child's soul in' (*Poems* 109). The writer who will be misremembered as the almost exclusive purveyor of high-class worlds offers here a very early focus on the voiceless and dispossessed, and directs an unforgiving spotlight on moral hypocrisy ('In a Christian town it happened, / In a home for children built' [*Poems* 110]).

Talent notwithstanding, social connections undoubtedly played a significant role in Wharton's launch as a poet. Less well-to-do young women would not have seen editors' doors open with ease. For Edith Newbold Jones, the chain of privilege worked its favours. In a letter of 16 October 1879 to Anna Bahlmann, Wharton named four of her five poems that would appear in *The Atlantic Monthly* in 1880—and alluded to the patronage that brought about their publication (*My Dear Governess* 45–47). Wharton's brother Harry showed the poems to Newport neighbour and editor of the *North American Review*, Allen Thorndike Rice, who passed them to Henry Wadsworth Longfellow, and Longfellow gave them in turn to Howells, editor of *The Atlantic Monthly*. 'The Parting Day', 'Areopagus', 'A Failure', 'Patience', and 'Wants' appeared between February and May 1880. In Lee's summary, '[l]ike many teenage poems, they were extremely gloomy' (44). Rather they read as mature, muted, resigned reflections, often visions of women's half-lives, half-lived. In 'A Failure', the female speaker reflects 'what I might have been to you / I cannot be to other men', learning 'too late' that she had 'dreamed in vain'.[15] 'Wants', a rare collective address to 'We women', moves down the path of women's emotional compromise: 'When Love goes by / With folded wings [not yet the broken wing that will haunt the ending of *Summer*], we seek a friend.' 'But when both love and friendship fail'—when, not if: this is already Wharton—'We cry for duty, work to do', but 'before our task is done, / With sudden weariness oppressed, / We leave the shining goal unwon, / And only ask for rest.'[16] In 'Patience', meanwhile, the speaker traces the 'lines of sad, sweet beauty' as 'life's golden visions fade'.[17]

In March 1880, again as 'Eadgyth', Wharton wrote the poem 'The Constellation's Last Victory', published in the *New York World*. It relates the story of the war ship Constellation, which was refitted to bring relief supplies to the victims of the Irish famine of 1879–1880. This late famine was widely reported in American newspapers, with its large Irish American population, not least as a result of earlier famines, and a number of papers led fundraising efforts. Once again, the woman who will come to be thought of as the author almost exclusively concerned with the upper social echelons fixes her sights on lives of tangible hardships and suffering: 'She hastes to crown the starving board / 'Mid the dying and the dead.'[18] The poem's subject matter, like that of 'Only a Child', also powerfully underscores that Wharton was clearly au fait with contemporary events, following and finding literary inspiration in newspaper reports of the day. The young writer pens 'The Constellation's Last Victory' as a poem of dual, redemptive second chances: both for the suffering who are to receive 'salvation' and for the deadly old battleship reinvented as a 'messenger of peace'.

In 'Life and I' Wharton claimed she could not remember 'what the [*Atlantic Monthly*] poems were about, or when they appeared', asserting that at this point her 'literary activity was checked by a much more important event' (201): coming out into society at seventeen (a year early). In 1880 concerns over the health of Wharton's father would lead the family back to France in search of a more accommodating climate (he died two years later). The poems of that year would be followed by a publishing hiatus of almost a decade. While Wharton's burgeoning publishing record was checked at this point, her voracious reading was not. As the family prepared for the move to France, Wharton described herself as 'continually on the verge of explosion'—and in the midst of her excitement was the task of deciding which books she could take with her: '…which shall I take? And how hard it will be to leave the rest—Milton, Shelley and Browning must certainly go—and Wordsworth of course' (*My Dear Governess* 51–52). Though Wharton came to treasure most the poetry of Walt Whitman, her lifetime reading in the genre largely drew on a European cultural fund. As a child, her reading included Keats, Shelley, Browning, Tennyson, Goethe. Her surviving library holds a rich collection of poetry, Lee noting that the volumes' markings indicate Wharton paid close attention to Shakespeare's *Sonnets*, Meredith's *Modern Love*, the poems of the Brownings, and those of Christina and Dante Gabriel Rossetti, Donne's 'A Valediction: Forbidding Mourning', Matthew Arnold's 'Resignation', Meredith's 'Lucifer in Starlight', Baudelaire, Dante's *Vita Nuova*, William Morris' 'The Defence of Guenevere' and Hardy, among others—and that many of the poems marked in her library or quoted in her Commonplace Book would surface again in the anthology of love poetry, published posthumously (Lee 673–74). Wharton's poetry books, Lee suggests, are annotated differently from her prose, the poetry 'much marked up: especially passages of deep emotion, romantic descriptions, sad, tender expressions of love, feelings of solitude and longings for death', while in her prose volumes 'she tended to mark ironical epigrams and disillusioned philosophies' (673–74).[19] Wharton's response to poetry was physical as well as emotional. In 'Life and I', citing Wordsworth, she conveyed its power: 'When I read my first poetry I felt that "bliss was it in that dawn to be alive". Here were words transfigured, lifted from earth to heaven!' She describes the movement of metre as 'intoxicating', the 'thump thump' of her heart, her 'plunge' into Tennyson, all the while her 'enjoyment of the rhythmic beauty… undisturbed by <any> intellectual effort' as she understood 'hardly a word' of what she was reading (188).

As noted, much of Wharton's poetry remained unpublished in her lifetime, with manuscript verses, drafts, variants, and fragments spread across multiple archives within the writer's notebooks, Commonplace book, on loose sheets, and at times embedded in journals and letters. The archival prize jewel is a notebook held in the Lilly Library at Indiana University: a notebook of 168 lined pages, containing fifty-eight handwritten original poems—nearly as many as in her published volumes combined.[20] Bar six blanks, Wharton writes on every page, as well as the endpapers, compiling a very substantial volume of material. A number of the poems are scored out with a diagonal cross, including some of the strongest verses, for example 'The Tomb of Ilaria Giunigi', suggesting not a rejection by their author, but an indication perhaps that a typed copy had been made. A few of the poems remain unfinished, along with some fragments of verse, but most are clean or almost clean copies of complete works (including those scored out), which, along with our knowledge of Wharton's composition process and the labour it took to reach a clean copy, strongly suggests that they are final or close to final versions, recorded for posterity. All but one of the poems are undated—a familiar frustration for any Wharton scholar. Beneath the last of three different poems titled 'Song', Wharton records 'Written in Italy, March 1892' (subsequently scored out), while two of the few poems published (the ekphrastic 'The Tomb of Ilaria Guinigi' and one of the 'Life' poems) first appeared in *Scribner's Magazine* in February 1891 and June 1894 respectively. On the opening page of the notebook Wharton lists the titles of eight poems (there is no text of these eight poems in the notebook) with date and place of publication, from 'Last Giustiniani Scribner Oct. 1889' and 'Euryalus Dec 1889 Atlantic' to 'Chartres [Scribner] Sept 1893'. These firm datings primarily, along with the position in the notebook of the rare poems for which we have a publication year (but also allowing for the immediacy of the eulogy 'Browning in the Abbey' [Browning died 12 December 1889], the fact that we know Wharton was determinedly submitting poems to publications during this period, the strong presence of sonnets [primarily Petrarchan], dramatic monologues, miniature verse dramas, and of Italian source material for the poetry), very persuasively indicate that most, probably all, of the poems in the notebook were composed in a period from the very late 1880s to early 1890s.

On the notebook's opening page, Wharton also includes a memorable epigraph, masquerading as epitaph: 'Here lies a mad lover of words, / To whom they sang like a choir of birds.' It prefaces an extraordinary, eclectic collection of themes, styles, and of variable quality, further illuminating understanding of the author's work and direction of that work in a period where information has long been sparse. The mix includes pedestrian poems of the natural world (including 'The Southwind', 'The Northwind', 'An Autumn Day', and 'In the Forest'—a dialogue between an oak tree and a violet), Biblical stories (from the Book of Esther), Greek mythology (Wharton's lifelong fascination with Persephone already in evidence), poems exploring hardship, brutality and poverty, Italian legends, over a dozen sonnets, different poems with the same title (three of 'Song', three of 'Life'), dramatic monologues and dialogues—often with women telling 'their' stories, poems from death's threshold and beyond, of passions realised and passions betrayed, and of women's relationship to shame.

At times Wharton's poetry is most about poetry itself. In the notebook work, the author exhibits supreme confidence, dispensing commanding views on poetic form, or directly addressing the pantheon of male greats. Consider the unblinking assurance of the unpublished 'The Sonnet's Boundaries', which defends the restricted parameters of a form often favoured by Wharton. In a direct address to form, the poet would not have the sonnet widen its boundaries: it is the 'garden of the poets, where they stray / When weary with epic's Alpine way, / Or breathless from the lyric's flight'. The sonnet form evokes and promotes serenity, tranquillity, reflection; there are 'No floods to cross, no peaks are here to climb'. Rather, 'Through lily & rose of alternating rhyme / Thy sinuous windings lead the spirit on'. The speaker ends with a warning in the sestet that the wariest 'wanderer' will be 'undone / If, onward lured by thy recurrent chime / Thy magic boundaries he should overrun.'[21] The sonnet's scale and restrictions are essential to its virtues. The notebook sonnet 'Swinburne', meanwhile, addresses the titular poet who possesses '[a]ll other gifts' to urge on his verse tranquillity, reticence, and restraint: 'Thou that wert' / Born to become the Ocean's vocal heart... / Have not they vigils taught thee that intense / Silence that seals the tempest? Let thine art / Learn the deep calm that sea & air impart / When tranquilly the baffled winds go hence' (Lilly). The woman who had yet to publish a collection beyond the privately printed *Verses* is not bowed here by propriety, or reverence in the presence of gendered genius, but claims her place, her right to evaluate and judge.

Meanwhile, the moving 'Browning in the Abbey' (scored out with a cross, corrected and unfinished) foregoes both sonnet form and the tranquillity Wharton associated with that form for a trumpet fanfare, calling out to Chaucer, the first poet to be interred in Poets' Corner at Westminster Abbey, to make room at his side 'for the dead who comes today / For the brow with laurel burdened'. Browning 'claims the Kinship of the tomb' (Browning was interred in the Abbey on 31 December 1889). The poet calls on the 'greats'—including Coleridge, and on Keats and Shelley 'who sleep far southward from your England's shrine of fame' to 'wake & call him by his long enduring name, / When he joins the choir immortal' (Browning is named only in the title). '[H]e was of you, poets, by his spirit's fiery dusk, / Streaked with lightnings that illumined all... / Till at times our ample English seemed a thin & shrunken husk, / Rent by the exceeding splendour of the thought that bloomed within' (Lilly). The dialogue here is with English poets, all male. One potential exception is the sonnet 'A Vision' (a clean copy, but scored out, again with a single cross), in which there arises from the waves an alluring, 'radiant' female form 'with eyes benign', 'face divine', 'with a smile elusive as the Spring', and her 'bosom's tranquil curve', who comes to the side of the speaker to murmur in the final line '*in a voice like mine*' (my emphasis): 'I am the Sonnet thou hast tried to sing!' (Lilly). The poetic form of 'A Vision' is conventionally inscribed as female, but here the 'voice like mine' also implies a female poet—Wharton again making, and claiming, a space.

A Victorian fascination with death weighs significantly on the notebook poems, the most memorable of this selection focused on death's threshold or beyond, as Wharton evidences an early concern with 'beyondness' and states in-between. In 'The Dead Wife' (the title changed from 'The Ghost Wife', a clean copy, but scored out) the nameless woman wants to look once more on the sitting room of her husband's home, to check the domestic arrangements remain in place. In a compelling, seven-side dramatic monologue 'Ante-Mortem', a woman makes a death-bed confession to her husband. When they had been married two years, she calmly, pragmatically aware, entered into an affair, 'So walked I shameward, gazing at my fate / With tranquil eyes serene': 'Who sins in thought (Christ said it) sins. Why not / Die for an action rather than a thought?' After 'one brief, perfect year', she is abandoned to face the 'outstretched future, a grey solitude', walking 'alone together' until death, with her 'dead sin's ghost'. Death itself will not uncouple them, however, and the poem ends with the wife's exhortation: 'when I die for pity's sake make room / For my sin's ghost beside me in the tomb.' The husband hearing the confession does not speak: the reader is presented only with his 'wordless tears' (Lilly). In the sonnet 'Death', meanwhile, the speaker urges: 'Let me from death draw back a little space, / As from a stranger's face his host might lean, / To read its lines & what is writ between / Before awarding him his household place / Yea, death, let me behold thee face to face / Before thou blottest all that I have seen' (Lilly). In 'The Tomb of Ilaria Giunigi' (a clean, but scored out copy in the notebook, published, with slight modifications, in *Scribner's Magazine* in February 1891[22]), the widower of Ilaria Giunigi commissions an artist to produce the 'perfect image' of his dead wife on her 'sculptured bier'. When her soul '[c]ast the sweet robing of the flesh aside, / Into these lovelier marble limbs it stole' (Lilly). Reminiscent of Poe's poetry of beautiful, dead women, the image of Ilaria is 'perfect'; marble limbs preferred. A number of these poems about death call to mind Emily Dickinson, whose volumes of verse were first published posthumously in 1890 and 1891, around the time that many of the notebook pieces were written, but we simply do not know if Wharton read them. (And if she had at this time it would have been Dickinson highly regulated and conventionalised.) Death, tombs, mourning, the afterlife were all part of a shared nineteenth century cultural fund.

In the eleven-page 'A Dialogue' (a clean copy, but scored out), alienated husband and wife have the conversation that might have spared them years of pain. This Duke and Duchess have been living separate lives for some time. He has taken other lovers, but his estranged wife has come to ask him to spare his latest young target, Philippa, to whom she feels like a guardian: 'if you love her, Sir, / You would not have her branded "the Duke's mistress"'. The Duke, however, wishes to possess Philippa precisely because of her nearness to the Duchess, affirming that he does not love the young woman. The Duchess castigates:

I would I might unhear you—Shame, my lord! [altered from 'oh most base!']
Why, I've been told that a man's tongue will spare
The poorest girl that shares a night with him
In some base brothel [changed from 'mean hovel']; have you not at least Lip-loyalty?

In a frank, unfiltered exchange between the married couple—a dialogue that rarely takes place in Wharton's later hieroglyphic worlds—festering resentments and regrets of a miserable, uncommunicative marriage are aired. The Duchess reveals that as a 'new-made wife' she had seen a woman watching the wedding procession, a figure the courtiers referred to as 'the Duke's past'. 'But is she the past?' one answered—before they laughed. Loving her husband, the word was like a blow that smote the new wife's lips and thereafter she was 'dumb'. Over many years she unlearned the tongue and mastered instead '[s]tout words like duty, pride, & cares of state, / Restraint, denial'. 'I am the thing you made me', she asserts. All this time the Duke has in fact loved his wife, but now it is too late for them—and for Philippa. The Duke does not love her, but he will take her. The poem ends with the Duchess' words 'Poor Philippa' (Lilly). The young woman, not seen in the poem, is to pay the price.

A number of the notebook poems express a poignant longing for a shared life. One of the 'Song' verses repeats the invocation 'Let us be lovers to the end', envisaging life's journey with a soulmate. The ties that bind here are welcome, not the weighty chains that oppress characters of Wharton's later work: 'Dear, let us make of Time a friend / To bind us closer with his cares' (Lilly). The refrain 'Let us be lovers to the end', and finally 'If we are lovers to the end' offers no certainties or guarantees, however. A second 'Song' parades the glories of the natural world ('Blush of the sunrise', 'blaze of the sunset', 'Planets that swim in the sea of the dusk', 'Bird-song like laughter', 'the dawn's rapture of jubilant trilling') only to underscore the brutal physicality of a relationship's end: 'All these I had of thee when I was glad of thee, / Now the fruit's eaten, I hold but the husk' (Lilly). In the notebook's unfinished, fourteen-page verse drama 'The Duchess of Palliano' (fairly clean copy, but scored out), Wharton takes Stendhal's tale of a historical, sixteenth-century Italian account of passion, betrayals, confessions, torture, and execution—and proceeds to remove both sensation and passion. The titular figure, in exile, unhappily married but 'with too proud a soul to sin / Clandestinely', offers the man she loves an alternative proposition:

> But are there no two ways of loving? Look,
> These lips, hands, eyes you thirst for are the Duke's,
> Inevitably his. Will you not rather
> Possess the soul he never sought to reach,
> And smile to think how little has been his?

It is an exchange in which her love Capecce has no interest, however: 'What lover ever asked for less than all?' (Lilly). He wants the body as much as the soul. The Duchess' sentiment recalls the familiar passage of Wharton's short story 'The Fulness of Life', comparing a woman's life to a 'great house full of rooms', where in 'the innermost room, the holy of holies, the soul sits alone and waits for a footstep that never comes.'[23] The timings of composition are similar—the story initially rejected in 1891, but published in *Scribner's Magazine* in 1893—Wharton's early protagonists already expressing a longing for a deep human connection, a longing that ends in a cold reality of resigned disappointment or outright defeat.

'Lucrezia Buonvisi's Lover (Dying at Viareggio)' and 'Lucrezia Buonvisi remembers', on the other hand, present the consequences of passion and betrayal (the latter poem scored out). Again, Wharton draws on Italian inspiration, this time offering variant perspectives on an infamous crime taking place in the city of Lucca in the late sixteenth century. It is the story of an Italian noblewoman complicit in her husband Lelio Buonvisi's murder by her lover, Massimiliano Arnolfini. When the deed is done, Lucrezia Buonvisi does not meet her lover as arranged, but flees to a convent, where she will take a new name and, in time, new lovers. In the first of Wharton's poems, the lover (Arnolfini) reflects, years later. He remembers the thrill of first possessorship ('To think those bridal lips young Lelio kissed / Had fluttered under mine'), the plan of murder ('So great sins, when first they beckon, / Smile & speak childishly to lull our fears'). After the deed is done, however, 'she came not, & the years went by'. Finally, '[w]hen other loves & other murders, piled / Over the grave that old crime... / Effaced it from men's memories', Arnolfini goes to the convent to see Lucrezia only to be told that she has been sequestered because of taking a lover. Arnolfini naively assumes the lover referenced is himself, only to learn there have been many since ('Enough of them to set the town ablush'). He flees. Now glad he is dying, he reflects 'Nothing today seems real / But love, and our first kisses.' The poem ends, 'Lucrezia, my Lucrezia! Still you stand / With the pure brow & virginal faint smile, / Too proud for vindication. God shall judge' (Lilly). Later in the notebook, Lucrezia Buonvisi tells and owns her story. Wharton does not demonise the woman and does not judge. Instead, Lucrezia labels herself a coward for taking flight and now not knowing if her lover is dead or alive. We see the young woman as a possession sold ('they gave me to old Buonvisi'), trapped in an unwanted marriage ('like a fly in amber'), the currency of town scandal ('For shame is sweeter than honey on many a saintly tongue'). Lucrezia offers no apology, no shame; instead this is a woman driven first by passion, then by fear, possessed by 'a madness of terror', fleeing to the convent 'for fear of the rack & the cord', thinking of the dungeons 'where women have grown old for a moment of crime' (Lilly).

As 'Only a Child' years earlier had forewarned, Wharton does not restrict the cast of her poems to those leading empty, frustrated lives of privilege. We also see those—usually women—who have slipped through the cracks to another 'beyond', figures struggling to survive in a society that has abandoned them. In these poems Wharton illuminates a netherworld of hardship, injustice and its consequences, in images that smash prevailing ideologies of the deserving and undeserving poor. Wharton humanises society's outcasts: they could be any of us fallen on hard times. In the poem 'The Rose', a lone mother cannot provide food for her children. As one part of a city entertains itself with balls and privilege, the woman scavenges for a loaf of bread, her bedraggled presence on a wet, bitter night a source of amusement to the footmen attending the wealthy leaving a ball. The precise circumstances that have brought the woman to this point remain undisclosed, but in a poignant flashback she recalls happier times. Memories and an abandoned rose snatched from the streets will not stave off the hunger of her children, however, and the poem ends in the recriminations of her offspring, focused on the distress of her youngest child. 'Cynthia', first published in Louis Auchincloss' edition of Wharton's selected poems in 2005, begins on the streets where a wealthy man finds a child working as a prostitute to provide for her mother. The poem holds out a tantalising scenario of rescue—the woman-child to be adopted and raised as if the man's own—only for it to be brutally undercut. Cynthia is ultimately a pawn in a man's power game, forever tainted by her past in the eyes of her 'rescuer', and she flees the hypocrisies and bigotry of social respectability to return to a life on the streets.[24] Fragments for 'The New & the Old' reference the dismal living and working conditions of children 'born of shame & sin' (Lilly). Several notebook poems shoulder the miseries of the world, most viscerally in the self-identifying 'Weltschmerz', where the speaker longs to flee into the outer night and gather 'the shafts of pain / Of all the world into my bleeding breast':

> Some awful hours there are, when the world's pain
> Transfixes me, & suddenly I hear
> The echo of all the brutal blows that rain
> On animals & children, far & near;
>
> When Hell's antiphony of oaths & lies
> Thickens the air to foulness, & the groan
> Of drowning sailors under leaden skies
> Mingles its horrors with the maniac's moan; (Lilly)

'Weltschmerz' unravels through notably 'dilated eyes' a world of gothic horrors, one transferred in the sonnet 'The Inferno' to the 'kingdom of the dead'. Enter Dante, who is called upon to lead the speaker through the horrors, the 'awful gateway', but here at least there is escape: 'That I, re-issuing from that fatal shade / Serenely sad, once more may see the stars' (Lilly).

From the Autumn of 1889, Wharton's poetry appeared regularly, if infrequently, in America's leading magazines. In October of that year, *Scribner's Magazine* published 'The Last Giustiniani', a dramatic monologue set in eighteenth-century Italy, in which the last surviving member of the family has been compelled to leave his religious calling to take a wife and continue the line (a plot used six years later by Henry James for his play *Guy Domville*). In Wharton's version, the monk's initial fears of worldliness and physical intimacy subside in 'love's new refrain…the whole music of [his] late-found life' (*Poems* 116), the poem opening up the prospect of a rich, full, sexual life. While critics readily disregard Wharton's work in this genre, Lewis goes so far as to judge there is just one stanza (of twelve) of 'The Last Giustiniani' 'that hovers toward poetry' (60). Instead, what we see here is a subtle, unsettling poem, with a subversive undercutting of the surface focus on romantic sensuality. This is the man's story, the male vision. The young bride is given no name other than wife, and she does not speak; she is objectified by body parts and male desire: 'your slim young form', 'lips' soft flame', 'unvisioned beauty', 'left me man to face your womanhood'. The last Giustiniani has been charged with 'add[ing] new honors to the race'—the 'sweetness, *whiteness*, youth' (my italics) of his wife providing the eugenically sanctioned vessel to do so (*Poems* 116–18). By rendering the woman mute, inspected ('stand back'), visually dissected, an uncorrupted vessel to reproduce for an old white patrician caste, the poem exposes a disturbing, camouflaged subtext. This is not a poem of romance, of mutual longing: it is one of male possession, silencing and control. 'The Last Giustiniani' has been labelled the first poem Wharton published professionally (see, e.g., Lee 105)—but we see now the extensive body of poetry that led up to this point, including work for which she was paid. *Scribner's Magazine* would follow up in its December issue with the sonnet 'Happiness', a musing on words' inability to convey the most powerful emotional sensations: 'Let us be silent still, since words convey / But shadowed images, wherein we lose / The fulness of love's light; our lips refuse / The fluent commonplace of yesterday' (*Poems* 114). The same month *The Atlantic Monthly* published Wharton's sonnet 'Euryalus'.

It would be another two decades before the appearance of the volume *Artemis to Actaeon and Other Verse* (1909), but most of the poems in that collection had been written much earlier, and published, primarily in *Scribner's Magazine*. Among the *Scribner's Magazine* publications were 'The Tomb of Ilaria Guinigi' (February 1891), 'Chartres' (September 1893), the volume's title poem (June 1902), 'A Torchbearer' (April 1903). Other appearances included the *North American Review* ('Vesalius in Zante' [November 1902]), *Harper's Magazine* ('Margaret of Cortona' [November 1901]) and, closer to the volume's publication, *Century Magazine* ('Moonrise over Tyringham' [July 1908]) and *The Atlantic Monthly* (the dramatic monologue 'Life' [October 1908]). The sonnets of part II of *Artemis to Actaeon* were mostly first published in the early 1890s. The scattered publication provided one practical challenge. When Scribner's William Crary Brownell proposed a volume in 1902, the author mused: 'One difficulty is that my verse is so "fugitive," that most of it has run quite away' (*Letters* 75). Undeterred, Brownell gathered up the poems and had them sent to Wharton.

By the time Scribner's published *Artemis to Actaeon and Other Verse* in April 1909, forty-seven year old Wharton was the internationally recognised author of works including *The Decoration of Houses* (1897, with Ogden Codman, Jr.), *The Greater Inclination* (1899), *The Touchstone* (1900), *Crucial Instances* (1901), *The Valley of Decision* (1902), *Sanctuary*

(1903), *Italian Villas and Their Gardens* (1904), *The Descent of Man and Other Stories* (1904), *The House of Mirth* (1905), *Italian Backgrounds* (1905), *Madame de Treymes, The Fruit of the Tree* (1907), *The Hermit and the Wild Woman and Other Stories* (1908), and *A Motor-Flight through France* (1908). All bar *Italian Villas and Their Gardens* (Century) were Scribner's titles. The firm capitalised on Wharton's literary pedigree. An advertisement 'SCRIBNER'S SPRING BOOKS' in the 20 March 1909 issue of *The Publishers' Weekly* listed *Artemis to Actaeon* first of its poetry titles ready in April and loftily promised, 'Mrs. Wharton's first volume of collected verse…will prove her right to as high a place among the Poets as she now holds among novelists.'[25] The reviews notably failed to recognise that Wharton had been writing and publishing poems for decades, the *Spectator* observing 'Mrs. Wharton, another novelist, has also turned to verse…', while the *Manchester Guardian* opined 'Miss Edith Wharton's ARTEMIS TO ACTAEON….shows—for the first publication of hers in verse, which we take it to be—singular maturity and facility.'[26] The *North American Review*, meanwhile, offered an oddly contradictory assessment. After observing moments when the writer's 'diction and cadence halt and move in the measure of prose', it reached for superlatives in its closing remarks: 'Mrs. Wharton is of the elect. She is one of those who accomplish whatever they set their hands to and she has innumerable facets of her soul. Having proved that she is among the finest writers of prose America has ever produced, she flashes another facet upon us, and we have a new poet and one we could not spare.'[27] Unhelpfully, Scribner's released *Artemis to Actaeon* in the same month as *Artemision Idylls and Songs* by another of its writers Maurice Hewlett, also his first volume of verse and one taking inspiration from the same Olympian goddess. The *New York Times* found the similarity of title 'odd' and noted the volumes were 'furthermore arranged after the same fashion'.[28] A number of reviews paired the volumes—to the detriment of the female poet. The British publication, the *Spectator* judged '[i]n form she is nearer classical standards, though she has none of the rich imaginative vigour of Mr. Hewlett.'[29] Not for the last time Wharton's work would be held up to that of a male contemporary and found wanting (see, e.g., Chap. 6 and the comparison of Wharton's *The Writing of Fiction* with Percy Lubbock's *The Craft of Fiction*). The appearance of Hewlett's volume had not been missed by the market-vigilant Wharton. Towards the close of a letter, written from Paris on 30 April 1909, the author advised her friend John Hugh Smith that he would probably receive a copy of *Artemis to Actaeon* 'by E.W.' the following week, dryly observing, 'I see that Mr. Hewlett has been before me in addressing himself metrically to the lady, but I don't think his Artemis & mine live in the same street' (*Letters* 178).

Modern discussions of *Artemis to Actaeon* have been framed by the posthumous awareness of Wharton's affair with Morton Fullerton, the dramatic monologue 'Life' and the sonnet sequence 'Mortal Lease' in particular read in the light of that knowledge. Lee asserts that 'certainly the love affair turned her into more of a poet', with *Artemis to Actaeon*, 'which was published in the middle of the affair...her second and most interesting collection of poems' (344); Lewis claims 'The Mortal Lease' is 'a re-enactment, at a sufficient distance of time and space, of the journal she had addressed to Fullerton: a rehearsal, made more orderly in retrospect, of the stages she had passed through in the evolving relationship' (235). Catherine Bancroft suggests 'Life', 'The Mortal Lease', and 'Ogrin the Hermit' (the last was published in *The Atlantic Monthly* in December 1909) 'document her struggle to retrieve herself from the self-betrayal that threatened her artistic voice', with 'Life' shaped as 'a female artistic autobiography' exposing 'in the first throes of exhilaration and bewilderment... a strong impulse to relinquish her artist's voice as the price for her sexuality'.[30] In the 'personal love-literature', Elizabeth Ammons suggests, 'Wharton watches herself in love.'[31] If Wharton feared detection, however, there was evidently no need. Ironically, contemporary reviewers, without that biographical knowledge, almost uniformly remarked on a *lack* of passion. *The Spectator* suggested Wharton's poetry 'very beautiful and perfect in its way, makes its chief appeal to the intellect'; William Payne in the *Dial* judged 'its artifice is too evident, its song (as far as it sings at all) does not well straight up from the heart'; the *Scotsman* noted a 'careful, conscientious artistry', while the *Review of Reviews* found a collection 'without...very much emotional appeal'.[32] The *New York Times* surmised: 'The book has all the grace and loveliness of the intellect, but it is on the whole an academic production. It makes no appeal to the emotions because it has not drawn from them.'[33]

Contemporary reviews notwithstanding, 'Life' and 'The Mortal Lease' stand as the two most erotically charged poems Wharton would ever publish. They are also a timely reminder that the subsequently uncovered 'Terminus' and the prose fragment 'Beatrice Palmato' should not have come as a surprise. Here, passion—both its rapture and its consequences— is Wharton's theme. 'Life', the second poem in *Artemis to Actaeon*, trumpets its intentions in the opening (repeated in the closing) exhortation:

'lift me to thy lips, Life, and once more / Pour the wild music through me—.'[34] Its respectable cover story of a reed, played on by Life, does not mask the eroticism. As Lee terms it, the poem 'throbs with pangs, tremors and kisses, bursting veins and penetrating fingers, suckings, pantings and leaping flanks, in a wild narrative of sexual climax dressed up as neo-pagan allegory' (345). Each moment of ecstasy is accompanied by physical pain. Indeed, pain, disappointment, aching, fear, uncertainty are never far from the surface of most of the unpublished diary poems from 1908–1910, including 'Senlis', inscribed 'For M.F.', and 'The Coming of the God' which ends with the speaker looking into the lover's eyes only to realise '[t]hey see not what I saw.'[35] The unpublished 'Terminus', written in June 1909, and sent to Fullerton, who proceeded to make a copy, does not in fact share the same level of eroticism as 'Life' but it carries a much greater risk: the poetic disguise of the reed transported through woods, mountains, seascapes giving way to human lovers in a bed in a hotel room. In the series of linked dialogues that make up the eight sonnets of 'The Mortal Lease' Wharton offers both thematic and formal tension between giving oneself entirely to a lover ('the currents of our love are poured / Through the slow welter of the primal flood' [*AA* 37]) and the desire not to see everything sublimated by physical passion ('Something more than thou / Shall write the score of what mine eyes have wept' [*AA* 43]). It is a tension beautifully reinforced by the tight parameters, the '[p]ure form' of the sonnet that Wharton had outlined in 'The Sonnet's Boundaries'. Here, four of 'The Mortal Lease' sonnets end in question marks, each bound by the form, but pushing against it, leaving the query hanging.

The range evident in the Lilly notebook is replicated in *Artemis to Actaeon*, the volume spanning with equal confidence blank verse, dramatic monologue, the lyric, the sonnet. Wharton's openness to deviation from metrical rules, seen as early as 'Only a Child', was showcased in her February 1903 review, near dissection, of Herbert W. Paul's study of Matthew Arnold. Here she berates Paul for his straitjacketed approach to the poetry, using that in turn as a springboard to air wider criticisms of the field, namely 'the fact that the average English critic is still afraid of *vers libre*, still in bondage to the superstition of the Latin foot': 'critics are still frightened when poetry ventures out of sight of rhyme, and even rhymed irregular verse is looked upon as a hazardous experiment.'[36] Wharton placed more faith in Arnold's readers, most of whom she suggested 'will probably agree that, although all his later poetry has an individual note, his unrhymed *vers libres* are his most original contribution to English verse'

('Mr Paul on the Poetry of Matthew Arnold', 97). The unrhymed lyric 'Terminus' sees Wharton's theory in practice. And it is often overlooked that Wharton admired and embraced the work of Whitman. Kenneth M. Price reminds us that in 1898 *Leaves of Grass* appeared on her list of favourite books, and that in 1904 she shared her enthusiasm with Henry James, 'who agreed that Whitman was the greatest of American poets—a shared judgment all the more striking for being made at a time when the reputation of *Leaves* remained decidedly mixed.'[37] In June 1906 she praised Bliss Perry's newly published *Walt Whitman*, but not without reservation: 'I only wish you had gone into more detail about his rhythms. It seems to me in *that* side that he was the great and conscious artist, & the great originator...' (cited in Price 48). In 1908, the year before she wrote 'Terminus', Wharton even outlined ideas for a critical essay on Whitman, though the plan would not be realised.[38]

Reviewers did not of course have the opportunity to read 'Terminus'. What they claimed to recognise instead in the dramatic monologues of the first part of *Artemis to Actaeon* were echoes of Browning, and a dash of Tennyson. The *Manchester Guardian* viewed 'Vesalius in Zante' and 'Margaret of Cortona' as 'the two best things in the volume', possessing 'something of the Browning vigour without his fertile intricacies', while the *New York Times* almost removed the author from the creation of her own work, suggesting those two dramatic monologues 'owe more to Browning than to their foster mother'.[39] Undoubtedly Browning was a lifelong poetic inspiration for Wharton, echoes seen as early as *Verses*, notably with 'The Last Token' and 'Some Woman to Some Man'. Yet the dramatic monologue as a form in *Artemis to Actaeon* was almost certainly as much inspired by Wharton's interest in playwriting, at a time when she was prolific in the genre and perfecting dialogue. Most of the monologues that open *Artemis to Actaeon* were written when she was working seriously on a burgeoning playwriting career, with her play *The Shadow of a Doubt* even going into production the same year as 'Margaret of Cortona' was first published (in *Harper's Magazine* in 1901). The dramatic monologue was a form that spoke to Wharton both as poet and as playwright.

Wharton often claims in the dramatic monologue space and authority for a female voice, just as she claimed for her own. 'Margaret of Cortona' also tellingly echoes form and motifs of the Lilly notebook's Lucrezia poems and the deathbed confessional motif of 'Ante-Mortem', where again a woman tells and owns her story, her 'shame'. Here, Margaret of Cortona makes a blasphemous deathbed confession to the priest that she would not have entered the convent had her lover not been killed: 'when my lover gathered me, he lifted / Stem, root and all'; 'I, who have known both loves, divine and human, / Think you I would not leave this Christ for that?' (*AA* 27) The priest in turn can only reach for the convenient tropes of female hysteria, reportedly responding to a clear-sighted confession, with an observation that the woman 'raves' (*AA* 29). As noted in the introduction, the poem's original appearance in *Harper's Magazine* in November 1901 unleashed a furious response from the Catholic press to Wharton's 'shameful misrepresentation'. The *Sacred Heart Review* offered 'strong words to the author of the poem and to the editor and publishers...to show how obnoxious to the Catholic mind is the worse than blunder that has been made.' Observing that 'Tennyson has told of St. Agnes' love for Jesus Christ, and such love is possible for a Mary Magdalene and a Margaret of Cortona', the journalist reflected, 'Why persons knowing their Tennyson, if not their Bible, should so flagrantly offend against good taste, historical accuracy, Catholic tradition, and Divine teaching, as has been the case in this very unfortunate instance, is a mystery, indeed.' In summation, 'There is at present a subtle love of evil in the literary world, blinding many eyes to pure and holy things in a large degree', the *Review* writer protested: 'Miss Wharton has erred' ('"Harper's Magazine" and St. Margaret of Cortona' 9). At the beginning of the twentieth century, Wharton's work was being viewed as controversial and transgressive: in 1901 alone, the 'shameful' blasphemy of 'Margaret of Cortona' and the euthanasia plot of her play *The Shadow of a Doubt*, discussed in Chap. 3. Wharton was making her voice heard.

Wharton's goddess Artemis, in turn, also has her own voice, one often denied in the retelling,[40] and she claims the space usually occupied by the male gaze, as seen in 'The Last Giustiniani'. In 'Vesalius in Zante (1564)', however, gaze and voice return to the male in a terrifying dramatic monologue in which the visual dissection of 'The Last Giustiniani' becomes real. Vesalius, 'one of the first physiologists to dissect the human body' as Wharton's one note of the volume tells us (*AA* 90), recalls cutting open the body of a girl before she was actually dead: 'The girl they brought me, pinioned hand and foot / ...Think what she purchased with that one heart-flutter / That whispered its deep secret to my blade! / For, just because her bosom fluttered still, / It told me more than many rifled graves' (*AA* 15). In the note, Wharton writes of 'the body of a woman' (*AA* 90), but in the poem she is a 'girl' (most likely a girl on the verge of womanhood with the accompanying reference to 'bosom') and with that transformation the dissection becomes even more disturbing in its violation of a child. Most disturbing of all is that the horror is swiftly sidelined in the poem, making way for a story of male ambition, rivalry, and regret. Influences of the 'master' of the dramatic monologue are certainly present, but ultimately, the stamp and expert scalpel are not those of Browning, but uniquely Wharton.

Almost two decades would pass before the publication of the third and final volume of Wharton's original poetry, but individual poems continued to appear in-between. Poems published in the years immediately after *Artemis to Actaeon* included 'Ogrin the Hermit' (*The Atlantic Monthly* December 1909), 'The Comrade' (*The Atlantic Monthly* December 1910), 'Summer Afternoon (Bodiam Castle, Sussex)' (*Scribner's Magazine* March 1911), and 'Pomegranate Seed' (*Scribner's Magazine* March 1912). During the years of the First World War and immediately after, Wharton wrote a number of poems inspired by and in response to the conflict. As scholars have noted, the author's time and energies were very heavily invested in her extraordinary relief work, yet while the premise that Wharton's literary production almost halted in the process has been overturned, the replacement theory that her literary production took a different form during the war years is flawed. Certainly Wharton produced articles for American newspapers and magazines, a number of them describing her trips to war zones in France and Belgium, later collected in *Fighting France: From Dunkerque to Belfort* (1915), but poetry also formed a significant portion of her work during the war and its aftermath, and poetry had been a staple for Wharton from the beginning. Poetry offered a cathartic release, at times a public rallying to the cause, and, in its concise, contained form, a pragmatic solution to Wharton's often limited available time. One of the poems 'The Tryst' Wharton would include in *The Book of the Homeless* (*Le Livre des Sans Foyer*), her fundraising anthology of 1916 of essays, poems, drawings, and other pieces from a series of distinguished contributors. Her poem 'Belgium' appeared in the compendium, *King Albert's Book. A Tribute To The Belgian King And People From Representative Men and Women Throughout the World*, in December 1914. (Wharton in fact was one of the few female contributors, along with suffragette leader Emmeline Pankhurst). Most of Wharton's war-related poems, though, were first published in newspapers and magazines. One week after the British ocean liner the Lusitania was torpedoed in May 1915, with the loss of 1198 lives, including 128 US citizens, the *New York Herald* ran Wharton's translation 'The Hymn of the Lusitania' on its front page. The *New York Times* published 'The Great Blue Tent' in August 1915, while the following month the poem 'Battle Sleep' appeared in *Century Magazine* (reprinted in *Twelve Poems* a decade later). In November 1918 *Scribner's Magazine* published the poem '"On Active Service"'; 'You and You' appeared in the *Pittsburgh Chronicle Telegraph*, with the longer version of the poem printed in *Scribner's Magazine*, both early 1919.[41] In March 1919, the *Saturday Evening Post* published 'With the Tide' (reprinted in *Twelve Poems*).

Alan Price, author of the immaculately researched *The End of the Age of Innocence: Edith Wharton and the First World War*, notes Wharton's observation that 'she had to sound the "tremolo note"' during the war in her frequent appeals for money for her charities. Such a note, writes Price, 'initially stuck in Wharton's throat'; its 'obvious appeals to sentimentality and bathos struck her as inauthentic—it was making a private situation public....Yet if stooping to a sentimental appeal would save the lives of the children and aged refugees for whom she had assumed responsibility, then Wharton could sustain a vibrato that would shake dollars from the pockets of a neutral American public.'[42] And the tremolo note that served its purpose well here was not entirely new for Wharton: it marked a return to the harnessing of sentiment, the emotional tugging at readers' heartstrings that we see to varying degrees in a number of her early poems, most notably 'Only a Child', with a terrified boy 'starving on bread and water / For—some little childish sin!' (*Poems* 109). During the war, that tremolo often resonated loudly in Wharton's public prose, but also in some of her poetry, particularly in the early years of the conflict—'The Great Blue Tent', for example, is largely a drum-beating appeal to a noble cause, working its *New York Times* readership, a calling card to both idealism and patriotism: 'O flags of freedom, said the Flag, / Brothers of wind and sky; / I too was once a tattered rag, / And I wake and shake at your cry' (*Poems* 135). Artistic distinction was not the primary objective here. The poem was designed to move hearts and minds, notably among the readership of a nation that remained neutral. In 'The Tryst', a displaced woman relives the murder of her husband and child: 'They shot my husband against a wall, / And my child (she said), too little to crawl, / Held up its hands to catch the ball / When the gun-muzzle turned its way' (*Poems* 93). Wharton, in her fifties when the war broke out, would see and hear of many atrocities, both in her relief work and her visits to the front line. She does not spare the reader of 'The Tryst': 'The streets are foul with the slime of the dead, / And all the rivers run poison-red / With the bodies drifting by' (*Poems* 93). The timing, context, and first placing of the poem in *The Book of the Homeless*, the volume sold for the benefit of the American Hostels for Refugees (with the Foyer Franco-Belge) and the Children of Flanders Rescue Committee, perhaps inevitably encourage identification of the nameless woman as a Belgian refugee and the killers of her husband and child as German soldiers.[43] Tellingly, though, the poem does not in fact identify the woman as Belgian, or the killers as German soldiers or even specify the dead child's gender; instead the focus is on the loss, the trail of devastation and the testimony of a female survivor. She is 'the woman'. In February 1916, Wharton labelled 'The Tryst' as 'doggerel', but the fact that she chose to reprint it as one of four war-related pieces in the highly selective *Twelve Poems* a decade later suggests she came to re-evaluate its worth.[44]

Wharton's poetry during the war and its immediate aftermath perhaps inevitably included a sequence of elegies. The author mourned the deaths of friends, family, and household staff, including in the space of just a few months in 1915 Jean du Breuil de Saint Germain, her friend and translator Robert d'Humières, and her former footman Henri. Julie Olin-Ammentorp establishes that the author's grief at du Breuil's death 'elicited her first war-related elegy', the unpublished 'Beaumetz, February 23rd 1915' (46). Later, the deaths of Ronald Simmons and long-standing friend Theodore Roosevelt would prompt '"On Active Service"' ('He is dead that was alive. / How shall friendship understand?' [*Poems* 138]) and 'With the Tide' respectively. The late elegy 'You and You' of early 1919 simultaneously succeeds in striking both a democratic, yet exclusionary, partisan note. The sacrifices of young foot soldiers are seen to have won the war, but the poem is addressed '*To the American private in the great war* [*Poems* 139, my emphasis]', again speaking to its US readership. In its full *Scribner's Magazine* manifestation, many of the opening lines patriotically namecheck North American home towns and states ('You from the piping prairie town', 'You from the bleak New England rocks', 'You from the Rockies, you from the Coast, / You from the burning frontier-post' [*Poems* 139]), ensuring the soldiers are US produced and stamped. In the extracted version of the poem, meanwhile, it is only the parenthetical subtitle (in this version 'To the American Private Soldier in the Great War'[45]) that marks nationality: the city, ranch, farm, church, college, mill et al are not country specific. In its *Scribner's Magazine* tour of duty, 'You and You' becomes a heightened, patriotic roll call and death knell. In the self-titled 'Elegy', a poem Olin-Ammentorp suggests was written in 1918 but first published in *Twelve Poems* in 1926 (112), Wharton's focus is again on the death toll of the young: 'Ah, how I pity the young dead, whose eyes / Strain through the sod to see these perfect skies, / Who feel the new wheat springing in their stead, / And the lark singing for them overhead!' (*Poems* 94). As Olin-Ammentorp observes, here however 'Wharton does not suggest the dead "are on some farther quest" [the phrase that closes the elegy, 'With the Tide'] ... nor that their rest is complete. Instead she suggests that the dead maintain a certain residual consciousness, just enough consciousness to be aware of what they have lost' (114). There is no easy recourse to religious consolation. Instead we see an unsettling, gothic-infused return to Wharton's threshold motif where the 'dead' are sufficiently present to be sentient of everything from which they are forever excluded.

Almost half a century stood in between the publication of Wharton's first volume of original poetry and her last. During the 1920s, the author was at the height of her commercial success, her work earning her in the first four years of the decade the modern equivalent of nearly three million dollars (*Letters* 418). This was the backdrop against which she arranged with the Medici Society in London for the publication of *Twelve Poems* in 1926, with a print run of 130 copies. In the midst of Wharton's fierce commercial acumen, the volume was both a labour of love and a marker of prestige. A royalty report dated 21 December 1926 indicates that 59 copies had been sold, while Wharton herself bought 30 further copies (cited in Garrison 314). Other poetry volumes published that year included those by Hart Crane (*White Buildings*), Dorothy Parker (*Enough Rope*), Langston Hughes (*The Weary Blues*), Siegfried Sassoon (*Satirical Poems*), e. e. cummings (*is 5*), and Amy Lowell (the posthumously published *East Wind*), many of them indicators of the extent to which the literary landscape had transformed in those years in between. The *Times Literary Supplement* offered a lazy, lukewarm review of *Twelve Poems*: most of the 'review' simply reprinted the poetry, including 'Elegy' in its entirety, only to compare it unfavourably to Wilfrid Gibson's 'Lament' (also quoted). Once again, the female poet was found wanting. 'In these poems familiar things remain familiar', remarked the reviewer, deeming an 'absence of surprise, this failure to move us from our accustomed standpoint' characteristic of the volume as a whole.[46]

The opening pieces of *Twelve Poems*, meditations on the beauties of nature, advertise their French origins, and were almost certainly written in the country that Wharton had made her permanent home ('Nightingales in Provence', 'Mistral in the Maquis',[47] 'Les Salettes'). The word 'Beauty' resonates through a number of the opening poems—beauty of the natural world, and of life, even when it is accompanied by disappointment and a heightened awareness of waning powers. In the poignant 'Les Salettes', the 'lost years' hasten to the poet's feet to declare 'All is not pain': 'such glories still renew / To transient eyes the morning's hue'; 'Life's last drop of evening wine / Shall like a draught of morning shine'; 'life is Beauty, fringed with tears' (*Poems* 89–90). 'Les Salettes' unmistakably mirrors the tone of 'Quaderno dello Studente', Wharton's late notebook with entries from May 1924 (discussed in Chap. 7) in which an ageing author exposes personal vulnerabilities while continuing to grasp life: '…to wake in the morning is an adventure…!' (8 Dec. 1934, 'QS' 215), 'Love & Beauty have poured such glowing cups for me that when the last drop i̶s̶ <of the last is> drained I shall go away grateful—if not satisfied' (12 May 1933, 'QS' 215). Meanwhile, the free-flowing dramatic monologue 'The First Year' is impressive and deeply unnerving. One year after death a woman leaves the darkness of her grave, her 'dungeon', to return to earth and her old home only to find the soul of another woman sitting in her chair. Her presence violates all memories of her intimate life:

> Was she always there?
> Were her lips between all our kisses?
> Did her hands know the folds of his hair?
> Did she hear what I said when I loved him?
> Was the room never empty? Not once?
> When I leaned in that chair, which one of us two did he see?
> Did he feel us both on his bosom? (*Poems* 106)

'The First Year' explodes the domestic idyll and the veneer of middle-class respectability. One woman is any woman. It makes no difference whether the returned soul is present or not, and indeed the poem opens up the prospect of a flesh and blood replacement woman within the year. Domestic life, partnership, intimacy—all are lies.

Though Wharton would not publish another volume of original poetry, she was far from finished with the genre. In addition, plans for an anthology of English love poetry (the project would be abandoned by Wharton, but the volume was published posthumously by Appleton-Century in 1939 as *Eternal Passion in English Poetry*) were hatched, according to Frederick Wegener, as early as the mid-1920s in poetry evenings at Ste.

Claire, with Robert Norton recalling that at least two thirds of the suggestions came from Wharton.[48] The brief preface to the volume was determined and unapologetic. There was no 'pandering' to schools, fashions, no careful allocations of popular poems offset against neglected works. Wharton, along with Norton, simply picked the poetry she loved: 'These are poems read aloud again and again by the winter fireside, and again and again found enchanting and satisfying to reader and listeners' ('Preface' 253). The selection included works by Elizabeth Barrett Browning, Robert Browning, Robert Burns, John Donne, William Ernest Henley, Charles Kingsley, Christopher Marlowe, Alice Meynell, Dante Gabriel Rossetti, Walter Scott, Shakespeare, Swinburne, Tennyson, and William Butler Yeats. In September 1939, *Publishers' Weekly* ran the 'Fall Announcement for D. Appleton-Century Company', promising a 'unique' anthology of love poems, one that 'reveals Mrs. Wharton's fine critical faculty and selective ability'.[49] However, the decision of Wharton's literary executor, Gaillard Lapsley, to arrange for a posthumous publication of the volume did nothing to enhance the writer's reputation. Tom Boggs in his *Poetry* 'Review: Five Anthologies' was a swift executioner: '103 love lyrics, that everybody knows, with an appropriately colorless introduction by Edith Wharton—the cost of the book $2.50, making the introduction $0.83 a page'.[50]

The most poignant poem of Wharton's last decade was written on the day of Walter Berry's death on 12 October 1927. Poleaxed by grief ('The Love of all my life died today, & I with him', she wrote in her notebook 'Quaderno dello Studente' [213]), Wharton picked up her pen and drafted an untitled poem that would be published in *Scribner's Magazine* in January 1928 as 'Garden Valedictory'. A number of drafts of this poem exist, including one recorded in 'Quaderno' on the day of Walter Berry's death following the moving diary entry above. 'I will not say that you are dead, but only / Scattered like seed upon the autumn breeze, / Renewing life where all seemed locked & lonely' opens the twelve-line poem that runs as a single sentence, conveying movement and with it a sense that a spirit has not been controlled and contained ('QS' 213). On one of the worst days of Wharton's life, poetry was the genre that evidently came to the writer's aid, providing an emotional and creative release.

And yet, despite her long history, despite multiple volumes of poetry and dozens of periodical publications, Wharton never earned a reputation as a poet. Only in July 1931 did it look as though things might change when an article by Robert Sencourt, 'The Poetry of Edith Wharton', appeared in the *Bookman*—'Mr. Sencourt' listed as the author of *The Life of George Meredith*, and of the recently published *Life of the Empress Eugénie*. (Decades later, he would go on to write a memoir of T.S. Eliot, posthumously published in 1971.) In a snobbish, elitist piece, Sencourt blamed a 'declension in the standards of taste' for 'divert[ing] attention from Mrs. Wharton's best work', one that explained 'why her remarkable poetry is everywhere, and particularly in America, practically unknown'.[51] Sencourt suggested that 'the joy of admiring excellence no longer marks anything but the standards of a few' (478); he praised the 'chaste music' (484) of Wharton's poems, their 'careful pattern' (480), their 'classic splendor of phrase' (483), and the writer herself for remaining 'so elastically upright in the tumble of intellectual disorder mark[ing] an unusual individual strength' (479). Sencourt calls *Artemis to Aactaeon* 'the most august volume of poetry ... that has come from the pen of an American, and the sanest vindication of America's unity with Europe' (482): 'one asks why it is that Mrs. Wharton should be known rather as novelist than poet?' (484). Wharton's poetry, concluded Sencourt, was 'beyond all argument the best that has been written by an American woman, and most American men' (486). In his bibliographical essay four decades later, James Tuttleton noted Sencourt's article with a straightforward assessment that it 'overpraises her verse'.[52] In part Sencourt's approach foreshadowed Edmund Wilson's problematic essay 'Justice to Edith Wharton' a decade later. 'Justice to Edith Wharton' was an essay focused not on poetry, but on her fiction, Wilson duly concerned to salvage the writer's posthumous reputation, but resorting to easy stereotypes in the process, playing one phase of her oeuvre against the other—writing off Wharton's later work (while admitting he had not read it), calling her 'important' during the period 1905–1917, but only with a crippling qualification that it was a period 'when there were few American writers worth reading' ('Justice', 19). In his closing paragraph, Sencourt knocked down the work of Sara Teasdale ('cannot compete'), Emily Dickinson ('poignant cries'), Emerson, and Lowell (of both: 'uninspired verse') to claim a place for Wharton's poetry 'in the same rank as the best of Longfellow or Whitman' (486). Sencourt's essay is perhaps most memorable today for the overlooked response it elicited from T.S. Eliot the winter before it appeared in *The Bookman*. If Wharton's poetry inspired one extreme from Sencourt, it was quite another from Eliot. On 30 December 1930, he wrote to Sencourt from *The Criterion*, with a stinging dispatch:

> I am sending you back your essay on Mrs Wharton's poetry.... I am afraid, judging solely by the extracts you give, I cannot concur with your admiration of Mrs Wharton's verse. It may be due to defective understanding or to some weakness of the flesh, but this poetry leaves me feeling as cold as if I had been reading the Sonnets of Mr Santayana or stroking a dead fish.[53]

In a final analysis, the extremes of Sencourt and Eliot prove equally misplaced. Wharton's output in the genre, however, remains important and requires attention—both in its own right, but also for our understanding of Edith Wharton as a writer more broadly. Some writers work exclusively, or near exclusively, with poetic form. Wharton—novelist, short story writer, dramatist, poet, travel writer, design writer, critic et al—did not. In terms of quality, her poetry is the most mixed of any genre in which she created. Wharton received multiple literary accolades—but minimal critical or financial reward for her poetry. Nevertheless, she worked seriously and prolifically in this genre throughout her career. Wharton is still afforded no place in the canon of American poetry, one underlying reason for which is likely the fact that her body of work in this genre evades easy categorisation, a neat 'fit', partly by virtue of her longevity, the poetry from child to woman spanning seven decades, and a mutating literary landscape. She produced an extraordinary variety of poetry across a wide spectrum of form and theme. This is a writer who could work a sonnet to perfection, but also push against its parameters, take a dramatic monologue and revise it as a feminist script, dissect a romantic idyll and its conventions to reveal the horror at its heart, embrace the unrhymed lyric. The poems showcase her remarkable cultural fund of learning and knowledge, with inspirations from the Bible to Greek mythology, sixteenth century Italian legend, and pagan allegories that on occasion serve as means of camouflage and subterfuge. They also underscore deep concerns about social injustice, dispossession, and moral hypocrisy, while at times previewing motifs developed in her fiction, illuminating early interests in beyondness, states in between, in passion and shame, in hieroglyphics and silencing, in women's lives, half lived. Her poetry can be dull and predictable, but also subversive, blasphemous, feminist, transgressive—and deeply unsettling. The neglect of the poetry on one level is also almost certainly a consequence of Wharton's own productivity. There is so much work for consideration—and poetry, much of it less readily available than her fiction, has come at, or near, the bottom of the list. In the more than eight decades from work on the immediate posthumous reclamation of her reputation to the discoveries and realignments of twenty-first century Wharton scholarship, analysis of her poetry has largely been left behind. Yet to achieve a full understanding and appreciation of her work, Wharton's readers and scholars must also cross the 'poetry line'.

Notes

1. 'New Books: Recent Verse', *Manchester Guardian*, 16 August 1909, ProQuest Historical Newspapers: The Guardian and The Observer, 5.
2. Cited by Hilda M. Fife, 'Letters from Edith Wharton to Vernon Lee', *Colby Library Quarterly* (February 1953), 139–44; 139.
3. Letter from Wharton to 'Miss Paget', 31 December [1902], Vernon Lee Papers, Special Collections, Somerville College, University of Oxford, courtesy of the Principal and Fellows of Somerville College, Oxford. My thanks to Kate O'Donnell, assistant archivist.
4. Wharton, 'The Sonnets of Eugene Lee-Hamilton', *The Bookman: A Literary Journal* XXVI (November 1907), 251–53; 251. Subsequent references to this work are included in the text. https://babel.hathitrust.org/cgi/pt?id=njp.32101077277000&view=1up&seq=267.
5. Letter cited in Frederick Wegener, '"Enthusiasm Guided by Acumen": Edith Wharton as a Critical Writer', in Wegener (ed.), *Edith Wharton: The Uncollected Critical Writings* (Princeton University Press, 1999), 3–52; 17. Subsequent references to this work are included in the text.
6. Letter to Brownell, 6 November 1902, cited in R. W. B Lewis and Nancy Lewis (eds.), *The Letters of Edith Wharton* (New York: Collier, 1989), 75; letter to Brownell, cited in R. W. B. Lewis, *Edith Wharton: A Biography* (London: Constable, 1975), 234. Subsequent references to these works are included in the text.
7. Irene Goldman-Price (ed.), *My Dear Governess: The Letters of Edith Wharton to Anna Bahlmann* (New Haven: Yale University Press, 2012), 31. Subsequent references to this work are included in the text.
8. The extant notebook with the handwritten text of *Fast and Loose* in the Special Collections of the University of Virginia provides a rare recorded date of composition: 'Begun in the Autumn of 1876 at Pencraig, Newport; finished January 7th 1877 at New York.' See Laura Rattray (ed.), *The Unpublished Writings of Edith Wharton*, Vol. 2 (London: Pickering and Chatto, 2009), 2.
9. In 'Life and I', Wharton resolutely insists her childhood and youth were 'an intellectual desert' (198). 'If I had only had a tutor', she writes, 'some one with whom I could talk of what I read, & who would have roused my ambition to study' (198).

10. Referencing Elsinia Tyler's 'memoir', a number of biographers note that on her deathbed Wharton remembers her father arranging to publish *Verses*. See Benstock, 36, 479, n.66, and Hermione Lee, *Edith Wharton* (New York: Alfred A. Knopf, 2007), 43. Subsequent references to Lee's work are included in the text.
11. 'Opportunities', from *Verses*, reprinted in Louis Auchincloss (ed.), *Edith Wharton: Selected Poems* (New York: Library of America, 2005), 11. Subsequent references to Auchincloss' edition of Wharton's poetry are included in the text (*Poems*).
12. Stephen Garrison, *Edith Wharton: A Descriptive Bibliography* (Pittsburgh: University of Pittsburgh Press, 1990), 3. Subsequent references to this work are included in the text.
13. Shari Benstock, 'A Brief Biography' in Carol J. Singley (ed.), *A Historical Guide to Edith Wharton* (New York: Oxford University Press, 2003), 19–48; 24; Millicent Bell, *Edith Wharton and Henry James: The Story of their Friendship* (London: Peter Owen, 1966), 217. Even with the inverted commas, the title of Blake Nevius' note advertises condescension with its use of Wharton's nickname: '"Pussie" Jones's Verses: A Bibliographical Note on Edith Wharton', *American Literature*, 23: 4 (January 1952), 494–97. Subsequent references to Bell's work are included in the text.
14. Jennie A. Kassanoff, 'Edith Wharton (1862–1937)', in Eric L. Haralson (ed.), *Encyclopedia of American Poetry: The Nineteenth Century* (Chicago; London: Fitzroy Dearborn Publishers, 1998): https://literature-proquest.com.
15. Edith Jones, 'A Failure', *The Atlantic Monthly*, April 1880: https://www.theatlantic.com/magazine/archive/1880/04/a-failure/376166/.
16. Edith Jones, 'Wants', *The Atlantic Monthly*, May 1880: https://www.theatlantic.com/past/docs/issues/1880may/wants.htm.
17. Edith Jones, 'Patience', *The Atlantic Monthly*, April 1880: https://www.theatlantic.com/past/docs/issues/1880apr/patience.htm.
18. Eadgyth, 'The Constellation's Last Victory', newspaper clipping, Edith Wharton Collection, Yale Collection of American Literature, Beinecke Rare Book and Manuscript Library. Box 64, folder 1790. Sincere thanks to Irene Goldman-Price for first making me aware of this poem.
19. See also Lee, 'Foreword', in George Ramsden (comp.), *Edith Wharton's Library* (Settrington: Stone Trough, 1999), xi. Subsequent references to this work are included in the text.
20. Only four of the unpublished notebook poems belatedly appeared in Auchincloss' 2005 Library of America volume of selected Wharton poetry: 'Song ["Mirth of life's blooming time"]'; 'Gifts'; 'October in Newport', and 'Cynthia'. Wharton scholars will be greatly indebted to Irene Goldman-Price who at the time of writing is preparing for Scribner

a new edition of Wharton's poetry, including a selection of previously unpublished poems.
21. Wharton mss., box 8. Courtesy The Lilly Library, Indiana University, Bloomington, Indiana. Bar two corrections ('his outspread realm' changed from 'outstretched realm', and 'Yet here' changed from 'But here') it is a clean copy of 'The Sonnet's Boundaries'. Subsequent references to the Lilly poems are included in the text and cited parenthetically as 'Lilly'.
22. The notebook version reads 'thy widowed husband's eyes', 'its sculptured bier', and 'Upon the breast'. These are amended to 'thy husband's widowed eyes', 'the sculptured bier', and 'Beneath the breast' in the versions published in both *Scribner's Magazine* and *Artemis to Actaeon*.
23. Wharton, 'The Fulness of Life', in Maureen Howard (ed.), *Edith Wharton: Collected Stories 1891–1910* (New York: Library of America, 2001), 12–22; 14.
24. For a fuller discussion of the manuscript poems 'Cynthia' and 'The Rose' and Wharton's treatment of poverty, see Laura Rattray, 'Edith Wharton's Unprivileged Lives', in Jennifer Haytock and Laura Rattray (eds.), *The New Edith Wharton Studies* (New York: Cambridge University Press, 2019), 113–28.
25. 'SCRIBNER'S SPRING BOOKS' advertisement, *The Publishers' Weekly*, 75:12 (20 March 1909), 1131.
26. 'Recent Verse', *Spectator*, 103 (3 July 1909), 20, reprinted in *Edith Wharton: The Contemporary Reviews*, 169. 'New Books: Recent Verse', *Manchester Guardian*, 16 August 1909, ProQuest Historical Newspapers: The Guardian and The Observer, 5.
27. 'New Books Reviewed', *North American Review*, 190 (November 1909), 702–3, reprinted in *Edith Wharton: The Contemporary Reviews*, 170–1.
28. 'Books of Poems by Two Writers', *New York Times*, 8 May 1909, ProQuest Historical Newspapers: The New York Times with Index, BR300.
29. 'Recent Verse', *Spectator*, 103 (3 July 1909), 20, 169.
30. Catherine Bancroft, 'Lost Lands: Metaphors of Sexual Awakening in Edith Wharton's Poetry, 1908–1909', in Alfred Bendixen and Annette Zilversmit (eds.), *Edith Wharton: New Critical Essays* (New York: Garland, 1992), 231–43; 232–33.
31. Elizabeth Ammons, *Edith Wharton's Argument with America* (Athens GA: University of Georgia Press, 1980), 58. Ammons writes that Wharton 'poured her creative energies into poetry, with the result that she produced some very bad verse, the worst being "Ogrin the Hermit," but also at least one very good poem, "Terminus"' (58). Subsequent references to Ammons' study are included in the text.
32. 'Recent Verse', *Spectator*; William Morton Payne, 'Recent Poetry', *Dial* 47 (16 August 1909), 101, and 'The New Books', *Review of Reviews* 40 (July 1909), 123, reprinted in *Edith Wharton: The Contemporary Reviews*,

169–70; 'POETRY', *The Scotsman*, 17 May 1909, ProQuest Historical Newspapers: The Scotsman, 2.
33. 'Books of Poems by Two Writers', *New York Times*, 8 May 1909.
34. Wharton, 'Life', *Artemis to Actaeon and Other Verse* (New York: Charles Scribner's Sons, 1909), 7–13. Subsequent references to this edition are included in the text (*AA*).
35. Wharton, 'The Coming of the God', in *Poems*, 158–59; 159. Auchincloss notes that a copy in Morton Fullerton's handwriting, at Simmons College, is titled 'Colophon to *The Mortal Lease*' (*Poems* 177).
36. Wharton, 'Mr. Paul on the Poetry of Matthew Arnold', *Lamp*, February 1903, reprinted in Wegener (ed.) *Edith Wharton: The Uncollected Critical Writings*, 94–98; 95, 96. Subsequent references to this work are included in the text.
37. Kenneth M. Price, *To Walt Whitman, America* (Chapel Hill and London: University of North Carolina Press, 2004), 37. Subsequent references to this work are included in the text.
38. See Susan Goodman, 'Edith Wharton's "Sketch of an Essay on Walt Whitman"', *Walt Whitman Quarterly Review* 10:1 (Summer 1992), 3–9.
39. 'New Books', *Manchester Guardian*, 16 August 1909; 'Books of Poems by Two Writers', *New York Times*, 8 May 1909.
40. See Kassanoff, 'Edith Wharton (1862–1937)'. Kassanoff writes, 'In Ovid's original narrative, Artemis, the virgin goddess of the hunt, punishes Actaeon, the mortal hunter, for spying on her while she bathes in a spring. Mortified by this transgression, Artemis transforms Actaeon into a stag and, in a sweepingly ironic move, dooms him forever to flee his fellow hunters. As Nancy J. Vickers has pointed out, the classical Petrarchan version of this myth denies Artemis a voice and subverts Actaeon's punishment: by lyrically praising his lady's beauty, Petrarch's speaker inverts the goddess' silencing intent. "A modern Actaeon affirming himself as poet cannot permit Ovid's angry goddess to speak her displeasure and deny his voice; his speech requires her silence"... (*Writing and Sexual Difference*, edited by Elizabeth Abel [1982]).'
41. The *Pittsburgh Chronicle Telegraph* version of the poem is reprinted in Julie Olin-Ammentorp, *Edith Wharton's Writings from the Great War* (University Press of Florida, 2004), 241–42, while Auchincloss (ed.), *Edith Wharton: Selected Poems* reprints the version that appeared in *Scribner's Magazine* (139–42). Subsequent references to Olin-Ammentorp's study are included in the text.
42. Alan Price, *The End of the Age of Innocence: Edith Wharton and the First World War* (London: Robert Hale, 1996), xiv–xv. The phrase, 'the tremolo note', explains Price, comes from a letter to Elsinia Tyler on 12 April 1916.

43. Olin-Ammentorp identifies the woman as 'a Belgian refugee whose home and family have been destroyed by the Germans' in her article 'Edith Wharton's War Elegies', *Edith Wharton Review* (Spring 2004), 6–12; 7, and as a 'Belgian woman' describing 'the Germans' execution of her husband and son' in *Edith Wharton's Writings from the Great War*, 223.
44. Letter from Wharton to Cadwalader Jones, 11 February 1916, cited in Benstock, 319.
45. Wharton, 'You and You', in Olin-Ammentorp, 241.
46. 'Twelve Poems', *Times Literary Supplement*, 17 March 1927, 183, reprinted in *Edith Wharton: The Contemporary Reviews*, 411–12.
47. Garrison notes that Wharton's poem 'In Provence', published in *Yale Review* in January 1920 is comprised of two poems reprinted separately elsewhere: 'Mistral in the Maquis' here in *Twelve Poems* and 'The Young Dead', reprinted in *Current Opinion* 68 (April 1920). See Garrison, 459.
48. Wharton, 'Preface' to *Eternal Passion in English Poetry*, reprinted in Wegener (ed.), *Edith Wharton: The Uncollected Critical Writings*, 253–55. Subsequent references to this work are included in the text. The origins of the Ste. Claire poetry evenings and Norton's recollections are cited by Wegener, endnote 1, 254.
49. 'Fall Announcement for D. Appleton-Century Company', *Publishers' Weekly*, 136: 12 (16 September, 1939), 929.
50. Tom Boggs, 'Review: Five Anthologies', in *Poetry*, 57: 3 (December 1940), 221–23.
51. Robert Sencourt, 'The Poetry of Edith Wharton', *Bookman*, 80 (July 1931), 478–86; 478. Subsequent references to this work are included in the text.
52. James Tuttleton, 'Edith Wharton: An Essay in Bibliography', *Resources for American Literary Study*, 3:2 (1973), 163–202; 186.
53. Letter from T. S. Eliot to R. E. Gordon George (Robert Sencourt), 30 December 1930, in Valerie Eliot and John Haffenden (eds.), *The Letters of T. S. Eliot Volume 5: 1930–1931* (New Haven: Yale University Press, 2015), 447.

CHAPTER 3

Playwriting

It is a feather in the cap of Mr. Charles Frohman that he has been the first manager to appreciate the dramatic worth of Mrs. Wharton.[1]

Theatrical settings and motifs are pervasive in Wharton's fiction. Pivotal scenes in her novels take place at the theatre, most memorably perhaps with the opening of *The Age of Innocence* (1920), which sees a more elaborate, scripted scenario playing out among the audience than onstage. The theatre offers an ideal venue for Wharton's women to display themselves and be displayed. *The House of Mirth*'s Lily Bart is trained to perform expertly on the New York social stage, casting herself as the desired object, the ultimate prize of the male gaze. Indeed, Wharton's fiction parades a cast of versatile actresses, skilfully changing roles as the occasion demands. Undine Spragg in *The Custom of the Country* (1913) lives for the limelight: 'she might have been some fabled creature whose home was in a beam of light.'[2] She has a dress and a role for every scene. At the early Dagonet dinner, 'she found that to seem very much in love, and a little confused and subdued by the newness and intensity of the sentiment, was, to the Dagonet mind, the becoming attitude for a young lady in her situation. *The part was not hard to play*…[my emphasis]' (91). Wharton wittily situates Undine's cultural vacuity within the paradigms of theatre-going:

> On the theatre they were equally at odds, for while Undine had seen "Oolaloo" fourteen times, and was "wild" about Ned Norris in "The Soda-Water Fountain," she had not heard of the famous Berlin comedians who

were performing Shakespeare at the German Theatre, and knew only by name the clever American actress who was trying to give "repertory" plays with a good stock company. The conversation was revived for a moment by her recalling that she had seen Sarah Burnhard in a play she called "Leg-long," and another which she pronounced "Fade"; but even this did not carry them far, as she had forgotten what both plays were about and had found the actress a good deal older than she expected. (*CC* 37–38)

Undine's face is 'like a theatre with all the lustres blazing' (173), associated throughout with mirrors and artificial light. A classical performance at the Théâtre-Français in Paris leaves her 'too weary and puzzled', while husband-of-the-day Ralph Marvell later escapes to attend the theatre by himself and is emotionally transfixed, '[c]aught up in the fiery chariot of art', feeling 'the tug of its coursers in his muscles', the 'rush of their flight' throbbing within him (*CC* 172).

Visits to the theatre are part of the foreplay to George Darrow and Sophy Viner's affair in *The Reef* (1912). Darrow's concern that their box should not be visible to young Owen Leath, a 'smeared' copy of a theatrical journal, the airless atmosphere, his swift boredom at the Théâtre-Français, and wandering attention all signal unpromising omens for the relationship.[3] Ellen Olenska in *The Age of Innocence* always feels as though she were '…on the stage, before a dreadfully polite audience that never applauds',[4] the opening scene powerfully serving notice that this unconventional woman will live under surveillance for as long as she remains in New York. In *The House of Mirth* Sim Rosedale likens Lily's increasingly desperate situation and its solution to the world of popular drama, as he visualises an alternative climactic act: 'You see I know where you stand—I know how completely she's in your power. That sounds like stage-talk, don't it?—but there's a lot of truth in some of those old gags; and I don't suppose you bought those letters simply because you're collecting autographs' (*HM* 415). Wharton's first surviving juvenile novella, *Fast and Loose*, illuminates a scenic narrative arc underpinned by stage conventions, with narrative description at times replaced with stage-directions, while Chap. 7 closes with an explicit address to the stage: 'How the curtain lifted, what scenes it disclosed, & how unexpectedly it fell, our next chapter will ~~disclose~~ reveal.'[5] The theatre offers a variety of scenarios in Wharton's fiction: a cultural shorthand, both setting and script, a frame, a means of character and social delineation, a costumed law court in which judgements are passed down, an experience that can either be emotionally transformative or sink to the realms of tired cliché.

The author's deployment of theatrical motifs in her fiction reflected her deep interest in playwriting, with Wharton invested in the theatre and in playwriting from the beginning to the end of her career. She reviewed, translated, adapted, and wrote a series of original plays, from high-society comedies of manners to bold, socially conscious dramas treating euthanasia, poverty, and the exploitation of workers who made possible the leisured, privileged lives for which her career is still best remembered. And Wharton was more closely connected to the theatre world than was long supposed. She moved in theatre circles on both sides of the Atlantic and worked with leading producers, agents, and theatre exponents of the age, among them theatre impresario Charles Frohman, theatrical and literary agent Elisabeth Marbury who represented a list of star clients, and Clyde Fitch one of the most popular and prolific playwrights of the late nineteenth and early twentieth centuries before his premature death in 1909. Wharton was taken seriously as a playwright, with preeminent figures of the theatre world investing in her talent. Her interest in and writing for the theatre was widely reported in newspaper theatre columns of the day. In fact at the turn of the century, Wharton's work was focused more on achieving success as a playwright than as a novelist. During the years 1899 to 1902, her writing for the stage included the translation of Hermann Sudermann's *Es Lebe das Leben* (*The Joy of Living*); a dramatisation of Abbé Prévost's novel *Manon Lescaut*; and her original plays *The Tightrope*, *The Man of Genius*, and *The Shadow of a Doubt*. Meanwhile, two early stories, 'The Twilight of the God' from Wharton's first collection of short stories, *The Greater Inclination* (1899) and '"Copy": A Dialogue', first published in *Scribner's Magazine* in June 1900 and collected in *Crucial Instances* (1902), were both written as dialogues in play format, offering further evidence of the author's fascination with theatre and dramatic form (and Frohman would secure permissions for both pieces). By the time of a December 1902 review of a Frohman-produced matinee of 'The Twilight of the God', *The New York Times* announced, 'MRS. WHARTON, PLAYWRIGHT'.[6]

Wharton scholarship has been slow to recognise the author's playwriting either in its own right or in terms of its significance to her wider career. Any reference is often still limited to a brief acknowledgment of her work with Fitch on the adaptation of *The House of Mirth* in 1906, by which time Wharton was an experienced, seasoned playwright. Among her papers, a box of incomplete playscripts at the Beinecke archive appeared to be almost entirely overlooked by scholars for many decades, even though it held substantial materials for five original plays: *The Man of Genius*, an untitled play, *The Arch.*, *The Necklace*, and a complete first act for *Kate Spain* on which Wharton worked in 1935. (In 2009, the surviving, incomplete texts of these plays were published for the first time in volume one of my critical edition, *The Unpublished Writings of Edith Wharton* [London: Pickering and Chatto].) Also in the Beinecke are fragments of several other original plays (all fewer than eight pages), among them 'The Children's Hour' set in a Catholic church in an unidentified poor district of New York and 'Crichton of Cluny' set in a palace in Mantua, Italy, which appears designed to present a version of the story of Scottish prodigy James Crichton (the sixteenth-century historical figure behind 'the Admirable Crichton'), in addition to the holograph manuscript and corrected typescript of the brief verse drama 'Pomegranate Seed', published in *Scribner's Magazine* in March 1912. In 2016 Wharton scholars became aware for the first time of the existence of another original play, *The Shadow of a Doubt*, the play first published and discussed by Mary Chinery and myself in *The Edith Wharton Review* the following year. *The Shadow of a Doubt* gave us for the first time an extant full-length complete original play by Wharton—a compelling play in its own right exploring the theme of euthanasia, but also a text that changes our understanding of some of Wharton's work as a novelist and its genesis, notably *The House of Mirth* and *The Fruit of the Tree* (1907).

Playwriting appealed to Wharton on a number of levels, including a desire for commercial success, and the form spoke to two of her greatest gifts as a writer: dialogue and character creation. Unrivalled one-liners pepper her playscripts: 'My dear, after twenty, all life is pretending, and it's easier to pretend in a good house, with everybody's cards on the hall table, than alone in a garret under a false name!' scolds Lady Uske in *The Shadow of a Doubt*.[7] Wharton toys with character stereotypes in her plays—a form of shorthand and popular stage convention—but then at times she will be seen brilliantly to undermine those with the nuance and complexity for which the protagonists of her novels became renowned. As a playwright, she was totally unafraid to embrace melodrama—*The Arch.* and *The Necklace* will amply demonstrate that, but her plays can also be subtle, quiet, understated, and strikingly modern. The plays at times remind us that Wharton can indeed 'do' happy endings, that she is an expert at comedy when it suits, the knowing wit foreshadowing the tone of the narrative voice of a number of later novels. The unfinished nature of some of the manuscripts is revealing about Wharton's writing practices and working processes—this writer one of the great recyclers of American literature, reusing plot lines, and bits and pieces of dialogue. Wharton's playwriting themes are varied, at times bold and controversial—and if her work in this genre was more widely known, her oeuvre might be less vulnerable to easy charges of elitism and snobbery. The plays on occasion reveal her openness to experimentation, offer a potential dress rehearsal for plotlines that will be expanded in later novels, and early expositions of motifs that would fascinate throughout her career. Plays and playwriting were embedded in Wharton's thinking and career plan from the beginning, in part the foundation that made the writer we know today.

In 'A Further Glance', a memoir begun after the publication of *A Backward Glance*, later developed, and published posthumously (March 1938) in *Harper's Magazine* as 'A Little Girl's New York', Wharton openly acknowledged the influence of the theatre on her life. When she 'look[ed] back across the blurred expanse of a long life' she saw theatre and church going 'standing up like summits catching the light when all else is in shadow'.[8] Alongside church, '[t]he other great emotion of my life was connected with the theatre' she wrote ('FG' 26), a sentence later relegated to '[t]he other great emotion of my *childhood*' (my emphasis) in *Harper's Magazine*.[9] Though unable fully to immerse herself in a play, the theatre was 'something new, a window opening on the foam of faeryland' ('FG' 27), the young theatre-goer rapturously 'listening to voices' ('FG' 28), watching acting that the writer in her seventies believed was mostly 'much better' than any she had seen since ('FG' 27). In *A Backward Glance*, recollections of *The Decoration of Houses* and *The Greater Inclination* are framed by references to playwriting: difficulty with writing *The Decoration of Houses* was 'deeply discouraging to a young woman who had in her desk a large collection of blank verse dramas and manuscript fiction' (107), while 'Out of the Pelion and Ossa of slowly accumulating manuscripts, plays, novels and dramas, had blossomed a little volume of stories' (113). Still, *A Backward Glance* insists the writer 'had never taken [her] dramatic impulses very seriously' (160)—Wharton, the Pulitzer Prize winning novelist, publicly downplaying in her official memoir her work in a genre for which, by 1934, she no longer received recognition.

For all the avowed denial of her playwriting 'career' in *A Backward Glance*, rare surviving correspondence from Walter Berry to Wharton reinforces her enthusiasm for, and deep interest in, the theatre. Notably his letters covering the years 1900 to 1902 are peppered with references to plays—Wharton's own works-in-progress, works by other playwrights, reading, viewing, and reviewing plays. 'Wouldn't it be fun knocking about the theatres together!' exclaims Berry in January 1900.[10] When it came to responding to Wharton's own plays-in-progress and her playwriting aspirations, Berry was enthusiastic, encouraging, and eminently practical. The letters offer most of the few remaining clues to the play on which Wharton was working in 1900, *The Tight-Rope*—the script of which does not appear to have survived. Conceived as a comedy of manners, with characters including Mr Perth and Mrs Smash, Berry suggested it should be called 'A Comedy of Distemperament' and thought Wharton should work up some good 'society gags'. The manuscript was complete ('It's written, any how', concluded Berry), and while the play did not have 'the big situation', Berry still thought it would 'go', especially with the staging and business of the Musicale and ball, and he went so far as contemplating the casting of the role of Mrs Smash.[11] In a letter of February 1900, Berry enthusiastically asked his friend when 'Tightrope' was to be 'stretched'.[12] From the only surviving letter of 1900 from Wharton to Anna Bahlmann, we learn that *The Tight-Rope* was being read and taken seriously in professional London theatre circles, notably by prestigious actor, theatre manager, and producer George Alexander. His productions included Oscar Wilde premieres at his St. James's Theatre in London of *Lady Windermere's Fan* in 1892 and *The Importance of Being Earnest* in 1895, plays in which Alexander also acted (as Lord Windermere and John Worthing respectively). Wharton wrote to Bahlmann from London on 15 May 1900 that she was to see Alexander later that week and that he had informed Marbury, not knowing they knew each other, that 'he thought "The Tightrope" the best play (written by an American) that he had ever read' (*My Dear Governess* 187). No false modesty for Edith Wharton. Her work for the stage was evidently being taken seriously in professional theatre circles at the start of the new century, with real prospects for commercial production.

The Tight-Rope, however, would ultimately not be stretched on the professional stage. The loss of this script from a crucial stage in Wharton's career is keenly to be regretted, though Lewis' suggestion that 'it may have been a dramatic version of what became *The House of Mirth*' (109) appears unsubstantiated and at odds with Berry's description of the play above. Potential alternatives were *The Man of Genius*, *The Shadow of a Doubt*, and Wharton's complete, five-act dramatisation of Abbé Prévost's novel, *Manon Lescaut*. In the same 15 May letter to Bahlmann noted above, the writer explained that there was a chance that Frohman's version of *Manon Lescaut* 'may have fallen through' and that Marbury was 'going to see what she can do' about hers (*My Dear Governess* 187). In *A Backward Glance*, Wharton recalls being asked 'to make a play out of "Manon Lescaut" for that delightful actress, Marie Tempest' only for her subsequently to 'renounce "costume plays" for modern comedy' (*BG* 166). The writer claimed it was 'a resolve [she] could not but applaud; and that was the end of that' (*BG* 166). In fact, the project was picked up as a vehicle for another actress, Julia Marlowe, but by 22 February 1901 she too had decided against the production—Berry writing to Wharton that the theatrical path was indeed 'rugged!'[13] The adaptation of *Manon Lescaut* was to be another 'almost', Wharton's ambitions as a writer for the commercial stage again thwarted.[14]

Wharton, however, was determined, with scripts of two original plays also in circulation in early 1901. In its theatre column of 3 February 1901, the *Boston Herald* announced that 'Edith Wharton, who wrote "The Twilight of the Gods" [sic] has turned out plays called "The Shadow of a Doubt" and "A Man of Genius"[sic]', news repeated in the *Detroit Free Press* a week later.[15] *The Man of Genius*, an original social comedy set in England, concerns the trials and tribulations of Claud Hartwood, a renowned writer struggling to complete his latest novel, and caught up in a web of comic misunderstandings. (Over a decade later, 'Man of Genius' would be employed as a subtitle to Wharton's unfinished novel, *Literature*, whose chief protagonist, Dick Thaxter, first writes a play, which is produced professionally—only to flop.) *The Man of Genius* envelops an engaging discussion of the role of the artist and of the creative life, a recurring motif of Wharton's work, but the play exudes a light, bright touch, with what would become trademark one-liners on fulsome display. Lewis suggests *The Man of Genius* 'never reached production' because it was simply too good for the American stage: the play 'was alive with subtlety and wit, and deep insight into the creative life: elements that in 1901 the New York stage, which at its most adventurous had yet to get beyond *The Count of Monte Cristo*, was not prepared to accept' (109–10). It is a charming proposition, if somewhat undermined by the diversity of New York theatre-going in this period. Cynthia Griffin Wolff notes that Wharton was 'an avid theater-goer' in 'the busy, varied world of Edwardian drama'.[16] Between 1890 and 1905, Wolff continues, 'the New York theater world was lively and varied. There was a relatively flexible sense of international theater: major productions in London and Paris were regularly reviewed in the New York papers; touring companies travelled back and forth across the Atlantic' (413). There was certainly 'theatrical clap-trap and triviality', as Wharton herself phrased it,[17] but there were also many diverse, strong productions and performances—to the latter of which the writer's May 1902 review of Minnie Maddern Fiske's portrayal of Hardy's Tess enthusiastically testified, as she admired the actress' 'remarkable sobriety of method, …her marvellous skill in producing effects with the smallest expenditure of voice and gesture' ('The Theatres' 79).

Conceived as a four-act comedy, only an incomplete playscript of *The Man of Genius* appears to have survived: a corrected typescript comprising forty-four pages of Act I (complete), twenty pages of Act II (incomplete), nine typed pages of a scenario, beginning where Act II breaks off, and six pages of handwritten notes. The corrected, handwritten notes consist primarily of a dialogue between the characters Cynthia Tressadeane and Mark Lovat, in which the latter attempts to warn his former ward against her behaviour, witty lines, and gems of dialogue (among them 'I adore seeing literary people but I hate having to talk to them'[18]), which would eventually find their way, at times slightly modified, into the typescript. Again, the opportunity to indulge an extraordinary talent for dialogue was clearly one of the attractions of playwriting as a genre for Wharton, and it is one of the most striking and skilful components of all her plays. However rough or unfinished some of them remain, the dialogue is always beautifully polished, Wharton entirely confident of her terrain.

Lewis astutely recognises the play's 'deep insight into the creative life' (109) as the writer, Claud Hartwood, endeavours to meet literary and financial expectations, his current novel faltering as he struggles even to find space to work—his small study in demand for bridge lessons, dress making, and children's classes. With his work buffeted by incessant interruptions and his papers constantly disturbed, he is eventually driven out to the garden on a wet, miserable day in overcoat and goloshes to attempt to write. In an impassioned outburst, the author vents his frustrations:

> It must be bad enough to feel there's nothing left here— (tapping his forehead.)
>
>   that you've said you're [sic] say, that the tank's empty— but to know it's full to overflowing— to feel the torrent rushing in and to have no outlet— none!— to be perpetually choked off by one petty obstacle after another— (He walks up and down, nervously.) Did it never strike you, Belle, that works of art are like children? That they need care and love and congenial surroundings to grow strong and beautiful in? (He lays his hand on his ms.) This ought to have been my best book— and it's nothing but a poor misshapen mutilated failure! (*Man of Genius* 25)

Only his devoted new secretary, Miss Quairn, can see his latest novel is not 'what it ought to be' (*Man of Genius* 33)—a recognition that brings the writer considerable relief.

Hartwood's secretary, however, is also not what *she* should be, and the discussions of creative processes are framed throughout with the comedic business of misunderstandings and mistaken identities. The secretary, Miss Quairn, is in fact Cynthia Tressadeane, a 'beautiful heiress', the former ward of the Hartwoods' close family friend. Anxious to help the writer in his work, Miss Quairn/Cynthia has resorted to subterfuge and disguise. Intentions are misunderstood, however, and by Act II, Hartwood is separated from his wife, living in the tranquil luxury of the heiress's home. Material that in other circumstances could so easily have borne the hallmarks of tragedy (cue Wharton's female intruder) is mined here for its comic potential. The pairings of husband and wife, former guardian and heiress threaten to go awry, but all is to be resolved in—what would become unfamiliar territory for Wharton readers—a projected happy ending. Hartwood is a man who is, of all things, in love with his wife.

The Man of Genius showcases many of Wharton's literary gifts. Like many of the plays, it also discloses some of the inherent frustrations of the genre with regard to other talents. Without the luxury of the prominent narrative voice of her later society novels with which to oversee control, stage directions in the plays become at times lengthier and more elaborate, or actors are stretched by difficult demands: Miss Quairn, on entrance, must instantaneously convey that she is both 'haughty and impulsive'; she is 'about twenty-one but looking older' (*Man of Genius* 10). Nevertheless, the play exudes an appealing lightness and sureness of touch, evidencing a writer in tune with the commercial demands of the theatre, and a scenario of tremendous possibilities for production. With her oeuvre's catalogue of unhappy endings, it is easy to forget that this is a writer who also has firstrate comedic skills, and an Oscar Wildean tonality permeates the dialogue here and in the early stages of *The Shadow of a Doubt*. The pace and lightness of touch in *The Man of Genius* are not too far removed from the spirited exuberance of some of her juvenilia, while also recalling the knowing, pretension-dismantling wit of her short story 'Xingu', first published a decade later in *Scribner's Magazine*.

Of all Wharton's plays, *The Shadow of a Doubt* came closest to realised success: the production taken on by Frohman, with Elsie de Wolfe to play the leading role. Its progress was reported in a variety of newspapers and theatre columns. On 10 March 1901, *The Atlanta Constitution* announced,

'"The Shadow of a Doubt," a play in three acts by Edith Wharton, will have a trial performance at the Empire Theatre in New York in about a fortnight. If it is successful, Elsie de Wolfe, who takes the leading role, is likely to star in it.'[19] The same month *The Critic* reported that 'Miss Elsie de Wolfe will play the leading role in "The Shadow of a Doubt," and she will be supported by an exceptional cast. It is hardly necessary to say that the occasion will be a notable one' ('Lounger' 197). And Berry explicitly references *The Shadow of a Doubt*, or rather 'The Shadow' as he calls it, in a February 1901 letter to Wharton, in which he wishes he could see 'the first rehearsal' of the play. In the same letter, he reports gossiping with Irene Vanbrugh, the lead actress in *The Gay Lord Quex*, suggesting that she would be perfect in the role of 'the wife' in 'The Shadow'.[20]

The opening scene of *The Shadow of a Doubt*, set in a drawing room in London's affluent Park Lane, gives no forewarning of the edginess of its plot, which will pivot on a theme of euthanasia. At the play's opening Kate Tredennis is happily married to John Derwent, the couple just returned from an extended honeymoon tour of Europe accompanied by John's daughter Sylvia whom Kate adores. Kate was a professional nurse to John's first wife, Agnes, who died after a tragic accident. Lord Osterleigh, Agnes' father, is unhappy about the marriage and about Kate's lowly background, as he explains to his friend Lady Uske. The couple's happiness is shattered when the blackmailing Dr Carruthers reveals to John that his new wife administered a fatal dose of chloroform to his first. The couple continue to live together, but lead separate lives. Lord Osterleigh seizes the opportunity to separate his former son-in-law and second wife by securing for him a Foreign Office posting to China without his family. Kate is numbed at witnessing her husband's discomfort at the idea of leaving his child alone with her: Lord Osterleigh is to have sole custody. Act III opens in a drab lodging-house in the East End, Kate's new home as she struggles to find work as a nurse without character references. Lord Osterleigh tracks her down and threatens her with the police if she does not consent to a divorce from John. Pushed to extremes, Kate produces a letter written by Agnes in her final hours that proves both the veracity of her story (that she provided the fatal dose only when Agnes had begged her to end the unbearable pain) and suggests an extra-marital affair between Agnes and John's best friend, destroying Lord Osterleigh's image of her as the perfect daughter and wife. Derwent appears and entreats Kate to return to him only to be told 'It's too late…The moments when you believed in me would only make the others harder to bear...If I haven't convinced you yet nothing will ever convince you' (*Shadow* 253). This is to be a play in which everyone loses.

Again, however, the production was cancelled. *The Atlanta Constitution* announcement above appears to have been obsolete, for two days earlier a column in *The New York Times* reported that 'The proposed special matinee to be given by Charles Frohman to present Mrs. Edith Wharton's three-act play, "The Shadow of a Doubt" with Miss Elsie de Wolfe in the leading part, has been abandoned by Mr. Frohman for the present. This will enable Mrs. Wharton to strengthen some of the roles. The play will be produced next season.'[21] This may have been code for artistic differences, clashing schedules, or Frohman may have become wary of the play's controversial topic of euthanasia and its prospects for success on the commercial stage. Or, the reason for the 'postponement' may have been that Frohman and de Wolfe's ideas of 'strong' roles did not match Wharton's. Just one year later Wharton used her review of the Manhattan Theatre's production of *Tess of the D'Urbervilles*, with the muted performance of Fiske she admired, to take issue with 'accepted code of signals' the 'hieroglyphs of speech and gesture' of 'the Anglo-Saxon stage', which usually meant 'a person who in real life would be likely to sit quietly and speak in restrained tones, is required to pace the stage like a panther and bellow out his sentiments or pronounce them in a slow, chanting drawl.' Objections to 'this tissue of unrealities', continues Wharton, are met with a reply of 'unanimous contempt' from managers and critics 'that the stage perspective must be preserved, and that natural acting will not "carry"' ('The Theatres' 78). By contrast, Wharton can be seen employing the same 'sobriety of method' ('The Theatres' 79) she would admire in her review, with her creation of the understated but resolute character of Kate in *The Shadow of a Doubt*.

Indeed, the quiet, dignified, honourable figure of Kate would not have passed the test of the perceived Anglo-Saxon theatre code. In showmanship she is entirely overshadowed by the dazzling repartee of Lady Uske (who nevertheless contains her own sadness in a miserable marriage and a 'what might have been' scenario with Lord Osterleigh). Lady Uske walks off with the best lines, but it is still Kate's play. Kate's quiet feminism, moral integrity, and independence of spirit contribute to making her one of Wharton's remarkable early female characterisations. Even, or rather especially, in her marriage Kate is always the outsider looking in. 'I'm so ridiculously unused to being happy. It's like a ready-made gown that doesn't fit me', she observes ominously in Act One (*Shadow* 153). Kate's honesty and integrity remain intact—but at an extraordinary cost, leading her to that sparse lodging-house, as a professional woman whose training means little without references to secure employment.

Through Kate's journey, *The Shadow of a Doubt* offers up a bold indictment of male entitlement, social privilege, and class divides. Lord Osterleigh's objections to Kate (other than her not being Agnes) are that she does not meet his standards 'for a future Cabinet Minister's wife': 'If I could have seen him [John] choose a woman of his first wife's rank and traditions. Why, this girl was a hospital nurse—a poor protegee [sic] of Agnes's, who took her in out of charity. She has had no experience of the world, no education, no advantages' (*Shadow* 133). Notably John also did not come from the same social privilege as his first wife. He was originally 'a young fellow who had nothing to recommand [sic] him but his brains' (*Shadow* 132). The man's social shortcomings would be forgiven and assimilated, however, while those of the woman who takes the place of Lord Osterleigh's daughter never will. As Wharton will go on to illuminate starkly in her fiction, one standard of judgement exists for a man, a very different standard for a woman. In an impassioned outburst that frightens her friend in the closing act, Kate underscores her marginalisation and the abhorrent nature of a society that feeds on its own:

> -- What do I care for your world?
> I wasn't born into it, I have no claim on it, and I owe it nothing but misery! ---
> (Rising and walking excitedly about the room)
> What is it, after all -- this world that you're all so afraid of? An idol that you've carved out of your own prejudices and that you all fall down and worship! A monster that feeds on the blood and brains of the wretched beings who created it! Ah, no --- it's better so, after all. I never could have satisfied your world. I never could have filled my place in it as Agnes did ---. (*Shadow* 232)

In her discussion of turn of the century theatre, Wolff indicates that 'the drama of the day was remarkably heroine-focused' (416). With so few surviving clues it is impossible to ascertain whether such a focus might be applied to *The Tight-Rope*—although a character by the name of 'Mrs. Smash' certainly suggests a character role of tremendous comic potential, if also a type. In *The Man of Genius*, meanwhile, Claud is the titular man, taking centre stage, while the brilliance of his wife Belle is stated rather than represented, his young sister-in-law is a flighty ingénue figure, while Cynthia/Miss Tressadeane largely serves the purposes of plot rather than individual characterisation. It is in *The Shadow of a Doubt*, as the only extant complete original play we have at present, where we see most clearly of the plays Wharton's extraordinary gift for character creation, an asset she would later express as the life force of fiction (discussed in Chap. 6). And that gift was for both male and female protagonists. The author who would be charged early with producing unsatisfactory, unconvincing male characterisations disproves the theory in *The Shadow of a Doubt*, as Wharton cleverly toys with dramatic stereotypes of the stage, only to subvert them. The seemingly villainous Lord Osterleigh is also revealed as a desperately grieving father, while the blackmailing Dr. Carruthers is at his wits' end, desperate for money so that his family will not starve. The doctor is even described by one character as 'a tall black theatrical-looking fellow, with a kind of seedy good-looks—' (*Shadow* 198), and he will address the stereotype directly in his dealings with Kate: 'I'm not a stage villain trying to frighten the heroine in order to give the hero a chance to rescue her. I'm simply a poor devil who's down on his luck' (*Shadow* 158). John is ultimately an unsatisfactory character, but not characterisation: even as he tries to win back his wife he does not believe her. For all the heightened dramatic business, nuanced ambiguities seep through these characterisations from a writer who would never be afraid to present flawed, not always sympathetic characters in the mould of Lily Bart four years later in her hugely successful novel, *The House of Mirth*. *The Shadow of a Doubt* also anticipates a number of thematic and structural concerns of her second novel, not least in the final act with its spiral down the social scale from the upper echelons of affluence and perceived respectability to that lodging-house in the East End. Modern readers familiar with *The House of Mirth* will swiftly see echoes in *The Shadow of a Doubt*'s plotlines of blackmail, a fatal dose of chloroform (rather than the equally effective chloral), the burning of letters to conceal an affair, and in the final scene the incineration of a letter which protects both the man Kate loves and the memory of her friend.

At the heart of *The Shadow of a Doubt* being prepped for the commercial stage in 1901, however, was a remarkable plotline of euthanasia. The topic was a fiercely contested one in America in the first years of the new century. In October 1905 a resolution before the American Humane Association would seek approval of 'the practice of physicians who in cases of helpless suffering make painless the last hours of life by an aesthetic'.[22]

It has long been known that Wharton contributed to this heightened discussion with her novel *The Fruit of the Tree* in 1907, but *The Shadow of a Doubt* reveals that she was engaged earlier, and more deeply, in the era's euthanasia debate than previously recognised. The theme was both brave and unmissable in *The Shadow of a Doubt*, while it would be partially masked by several competing plotlines in *The Fruit of the Tree*—the novel that many critics have found too packed, too busy. (There are 'too many "subjects" in the book', suggests Lewis [181].) *The Shadow of a Doubt* challenges and complicates our understanding of the genesis and a number of popular readings of *The Fruit of the Tree*—throwing into doubt, for example, biographical readings, assertions as fact that accidents of friends around 1904/1905 were the specific source and inspiration for the novel.[23] As noted above, the unhidden, controversial nature of such a theme at the turn-of-the century may even have been one of the reasons why the production was shelved.

Early in 1902 the writer attended a production of *Magda*, the English title of Herman Sudermann's play *Heimat*, starring Mrs Patrick Campbell. That same year Wharton accepted a commission from the actress to translate Sudermann's play, *Es Lebe das Leben*—'a tragedy based on the German "point of honour" in duelling' (*BG* 167). The episode is briefly and inaccurately represented in *A Backward Glance*, with Wharton recalling that it took place 'A good many years after "Manon"', that it was a commercial failure, and that it was her 'last theatrical venture, which, like the others was thrust on me and not solicited' (167). The play opened in New York at Frohman's Garden Theatre in October 1902, before touring and playing London the following year. Scribner's would publish the translation, for which Wharton wrote a brief, defensive preface. On its publication *The New York Times* reported that 'it was rumored among those who were intimate in inner circles that there had been friendly differences between Mrs. Wharton and Mrs. Campbell over certain phrases of the translation.'[24] Protesting the 'absurd' (*BG* 167) choice of 'The Joy of Living' for its English title ('"Long Live Life", in its most bitterly ironic sense…virtually untranslatable' [*BG* 167]), the author drew attention to the 'special difficulties' inherent in '[t]he translation of dramatic dialogue' in her note to the publication.[25] The astute business woman also recalled—with crystal clarity in this case—that, decades later, the publication continued to figure 'on a modest scale' in her royalty returns (*BG* 168).

The final item in a box of Wharton's plays at the Beinecke Rare Book and Manuscript Library of Yale University is the incomplete manuscript of a play without title, scenario or the crucial first page with its identifying cast of characters (henceforth *Untitled*). Without date or apparent reference to its genesis, there remains only circumstantial evidence to suggest it is likely to have been composed during this early period: we know, for example, that Wharton worked on at least five plays between 1899 and 1902; the handwriting tension (which altered through her lifetime) is similar to the six pages of pencil notes for *The Man of Genius*, as is the untitled play's opening tone of upper class social comedy and intrigue—and its English setting. The name of *Untitled*'s reluctant central protagonist, maid Alice Wing, is certainly a name in use early in Wharton's repertoire. It was also employed for the pivotal, outcast figure of her abandoned novel, *Disintegration*. While the author worked on *Disintegration* in 1902, the narrative was conceived before she wrote her first published novel, *The Valley of Decision* (1902). Variable in quality, rough, and unpolished, *Untitled*, nevertheless, takes an unexpected turn to transform into one of Wharton's boldest and most socially conscious dramas.

At the play's opening, Mrs Lyas believes she has a problem. As she explains to her friend, Mrs Frayne, her husband is standing for Parliament, and the backing of Lord Julian is essential if he is to carry the seat. The Lyas family have Lady Julian to stay, only for her to repay the hospitality by continuing her affair with another man ('every night'!) under Mrs Lyas' roof. Mrs Lyas is now concerned that if public word reaches Lord Julian that such things go on in their home, it will irreparably damage her husband's political prospects. Lord Julian knows of the affair, but appearances are all. Now Lady Julian is pregnant—and her husband is not the father. It is, in Mrs Lyas' words, 'a beastly fix'.[26]

What appears familiar Wharton literary territory of high-society manipulation and manoeuvring, however, is dramatically transformed when the focus shifts to reveal that Lady Julian is not the only expectant mother—there is also Mrs Frayne's unmarried, pregnant maid. A situation that can be 'managed' in the higher echelons (a child might make Lady Julian more stable, Mrs Frayne suggests) is a disaster on the bottom rungs of the social ladder. The language of the privileged classes casts its censorious hue: 'horror', 'contaminated', 'perfectly horrible', 'corrupting', 'disgusting'. Pregnancy for Alice Wing threatens disgrace, permanent unemployment (she is to be denied a reference from her employer), penury not only for herself and her unborn child, but also the mother and sister her work supports. 'There's always a lame sister' scoffs an unsympathetic employer (*Untitled* 83). There may be a convenient employment of ellipsis—with little open mention of pregnancy, sex, abortion, illegitimacy—but these topics, nevertheless, are explicit presences on the page. Stripping bare the classic double standards that feature throughout Wharton's oeuvre, a woman's behaviour—social and sexual—is judged more severely than a man's, a maid's more harshly than her mistress. Mr Frayne initially attempts to retain his butler Branwell (the child's father) if the maid agrees 'not to persecute him any longer' (*Untitled* 83). 'There can be no happiness in a marriage where there's no confidence,' lectures employer to employee. 'You ought to know sir,' comes the 'respectful' reply (*Untitled* 87). In the Fraynes' own miserable union, the wife, her employees indicate, is engaged in her own illicit affair, but class affords a rare protection. Hypocrisy and social inequality rule the day.

While the men of Wharton's novels often fail to act or act too late (cue: Lawrence Selden), Branwell, though certainly flawed (and one notes with discomfort his swiftness to question Alice's fidelity), says 'the word', makes the bold, outspoken defence. This 'damnable insolence' will cost him both his job and future prospects:

> Have you ever asked yourself, sir, what sort of lives we have, living so close to ~~le~~ money & pleasure & freedom? Look at madam's room here: Wing's in it half the day, ~~and touching the~~ <'andling> pretty things, smoothing ~~the~~ lace cushions, <steppin' on velvet [word unclear]> smelling ~~the~~ flowers, <and> 'earing the fire crackle~~, & steppin' on velvet~~; when she ain't here she's in a ~~cold~~ black cupboard of a place, boiling 'ot in summer, bitter cold in winter—no cushions or carpet or fire there, & just light enough to put her eyes out mending 'er ladyship's ball-~~gowns~~ <dresses>. And s'posing, sir, of a winter night, when she's shivering up till nigh morning, waiting for her ladyship to come in from a ball, & wondering, maybe, what it wd be like to be dancing there 'erself in a room…. (*Untitled* 88)

'You see we're all made alike,' insists Alice Wing (*Untitled* 86), yet one woman shivers in a dark, unheated room, while another attends a society ball. Wharton, born into privilege, once again reminds us of her ability to expose the misery and exploitation of working lives, but here she does so in one of the most directly outspoken manners of her career. The maid has her ''ero', the butler Branwell, to come to the rescue, yet the reader is left to ponder the direction the unfinished play would have travelled. The maid's situation may have been only one intended focus of a four or five act play—her story safely 'hidden' by a return to higher society intrigues.

Or, *Untitled* may have been planned purely as a one-act drama—Wharton experimenting with her craft. Either way, what survives has—in spite of its flaws—a powerful, raw edge.

Untitled's trajectory from social privilege to social deprivation is mirrored in Lily Bart's journey in *The House of Mirth*, and a collaborative adaptation of Wharton's best-selling second novel would provide another theatre project for the writer in 1906. With this production, the author was working with combined Broadway royalty—Fitch and Frohman. Work on the playscript was divided very precisely—Wharton, at Fitch's stipulation, responsible for 'every word of the dialogue', while Fitch took charge of the scenario and dramatic movement of the play (*BG* 161). The *New York Times* reported that the play, 'follow[ing] closely the outline of the book' was 'received with approval by the audience' on its opening night at the Detroit Opera House on 17 September 1906, with 'an excellent performance' by Fay Davis as Lily, and 'Mrs. Wharton and a party of friends' in attendance.[27] Before the play transferred to New York, however, the situation changed. In a more fevered re-run of rumours of artistic differences that had arisen with Mrs. Campbell over the translation of *Es Lebe das Leben*, Wharton was once again the subject of gossip, with newspaper reports of drama offstage. A headline in the *New York Times* just a few days later shouted: 'WHARTON AND FITCH CLASH', reporting a dramatic 'quarrel' between the two over the dramatisation:

> He started in to remodel his work. He began to inject action into the study. Mrs. Wharton, looking at the matter from a literary point of view, objected.
>
> "You will ruin it, she declared."
>
> "As a dramatic production it is already dead," responded the playwright.
>
> "You will cut the heart out of it."
>
> "I will put some life into it."
>
> The dialogue waxed warmer and warmer.
>
> "Mark one thing," was Mr. Fitch's parting shot. "I will never dramatize another work of yours—never."[28]

The next day the paper published a letter from Fitch, under the heading: 'NOT TRUE, SAYS CLYDE FITCH', asking the editor to 'contradict absolutely' the earlier dispatch, insisting 'there was no occasion for any disagreement' and that both playwrights were 'only too happy to accept the verdict of The Detroit Free Press, which described the play as one of intense interest and the real drama of real life'.[29] Even so, the play's

October opening at the Savoy Theater in New York was poorly reviewed and promptly closed.

In *A Backward Glance*, the writer succinctly attributes the play's failure to W. D. Howells' line that the American public wanted 'a tragedy with a happy ending'—and this was a currency in which Wharton was not prepared to trade: '…I knew that (owing to my refusal to let the heroine survive) it was foredoomed to failure', she claimed (147). Reports from the time, however, suggest a different, more complex theory. On 28 October 1906, the *New York Times* ran a fascinating feature, 'Mrs. Wharton's Views on the Society Drama'. 'Author of "The House of Mirth", a best selling Novel but an unsuccessful Play, believes that the Comedy of Manners is impossible on the American stage today', read the headline.[30] The report was from Lenox where '[a]t an informal, though exclusive, little luncheon at which Mrs. Wharton was present … the situation of authors who may desire to see their work staged was thrashed out', with the article's focus on Wharton's postmortem of her failed production. By the time *The House of Mirth* opened in New York, 'the keynote of the play was out of tune'. The cause of this?: 'The avenging fates that order the destiny of plays made to fit the eye of the producer, which may be the only optical capacity of the American theatregoer.' In its journey from Detroit to New York there was a rapid revision even to the point of instructing Fay Davis 'to interpret hysterics at the end of the third act— "to strengthen the play"'. A comparison of characters in the novel and 'as they strutted upon the stage had left Mrs. Wharton in a coma of amazement'. In a strategy that Wharton would later use in her travel writing, America—specifically American theatre here—was held up to France and found to be wanting. The feature made it clear that 'plays demanding the most accurate interpretation, not of the leisure class, but of society in the highest application of that much-abused word, are not given the same care of production in America' as in France. Instead, 'the grip of the commercial necessities', including 'insufficient rehearsals' and 'insufficient acting' led Wharton to an understanding of 'why the play of manners is at present impossible on the American stage'. Not for the last time the writer who worked so hard for commercial success and enjoyed its benefits attacked its demands. The consequences of the failure of *The House of Mirth* were dramatically portrayed in the article as a potential body blow to the advancement of American theatre itself:

the artistic sacrifices so ruthlessly made in the performance of the play might, if they had been successfully protested against, have initiated in the American theatre an entirely new departure in stage quality. …

… the mystery to all her friends is that the producer overlooked these possibilities that were so largely to his advantage.

The trouble, say Mrs. Wharton's friends and admirers, is that "The House of Mirth" was the real thing in its own field, and the theatre reduced it to a claptrap drama of unreality.

Although it failed, "The House of Mirth" may remain in the history of the dramatic season as a pioneer play…

It suggests a text for the long-talked-of new theatre. May it lead the promoters in prayer to their new salvation—for Mrs. Wharton herself cannot set a standard in the American art of the stage. ('Mrs Wharton's Views on the Society Drama' SM2)

Wharton was presented as the lone trailblazer, who could not rescue American theatre from itself by herself. It was an extraordinary piece, the author seemingly complicit in a simultaneous charm offensive and blame game, with the most pointed critical observations attributed to unidentified 'friends' and admirers (though the 'claptrap' terminology tellingly echoes Wharton's observations in 'The Theatres' review above). One week later there was an interview with Clyde Fitch in the same paper to discuss *The House of Mirth*—the 'literary' play. No reference was made to the previous feature, but Fitch defended Frohman as producer and attributed the failure of *The House of Mirth* chiefly to the American theatregoer 'and the unpopularity of purely literary plays'.[31] Wharton had been complimentary about Fitch, but nevertheless had made it clear the play was under his 'personal supervision' ('Mrs Wharton's Views on the Society Drama'). Above all, however, her finger of blame was firmly pointed at the producer (unnamed but most *New York Times* readers would surely have known it was Frohman). It was a public accusation, made by Wharton, but not directly by Wharton, carefully mediated by those reported friends and admirers. Neither Fitch nor Frohman worked with Wharton again.[32]

Wharton had collaborated successfully with Ogden Codman, Jr. on *The Decoration of Houses* (1897), but the collaborative nature of theatre work by contrast had resulted in aborted productions, an unsuccessful stage version of *The House of Mirth* in New York, and differences of opinion over the translation of *Es Lebe das Leben* with Campbell. When it came to fiction, there could certainly be frustrations, for example over A. B. Wenzell's illustrations for *The House of Mirth* with which the author became unhappy to the point of removing them from her own copy, but Wharton's vision remained paramount, she was in control. The same could not be said of her work for the theatre—the playwright was not in control of the realised project—and her work in this genre had also exposed her to somewhat unsavoury public gossip. Such frustrations over issues of control may in part explain why Wharton was evidently still writing plays after 1906, but does not appear to be actively pursuing them to production. And after the *New York Times* article, Frohman may have been in no rush to work with *Wharton* again. Her move to France is almost certainly another reason for this. By 1907 Wharton was dividing her time largely between Paris and Lenox; in 1910 she rented an apartment in Paris, in 1911 the Mount was sold. French theatre, as described above, was a very different field from that of New York, and Wharton never sought an entrée into French playwriting. She did not abandon the idea of successful US productions altogether—and we will see that one of her reasons for setting aside her play-in-progress *Kate Spain* almost thirty years later was that the idea had been used by another writer, making hers unviable—but after 1906, and with the tremendous success of her second novel the year before, her primary foci for commercial success turned away from the stage.

In Wharton's unfinished play *The Arch.*, twenty-eight-year-old Rose has scandalised society by divorcing her first husband and taking a second—a successful architect, George Adrian. As the play opens, she has been married to her second husband for one year. Although George has been offered a partnership in New York, Rose refuses 'on principle' to be driven from the town.[33] Wharton highlights the classic double standards—the husband's rehabilitation into society is almost complete, while his wife receives few visitors and has struggled to regain access to her young son. George has a valuable architectural commission from society's moral arbiters—the Lyarts. Christina Lyart has accepted George back into the fold, but shuns his wife. Rose, however, stands by her actions: 'I am not ashamed of being divorced—nor is George ashamed of having married a divorced <woman>. Why should we have made any change in our lives? We get we get on very well without the Lyarts!' (*The Arch.* 99).

That which could so easily have been a simplistic black and white treatment of divorce within the confines of the stage, however, is swiftly subverted. Rose, it transpires, is not without her own prejudice. When a friend asks her in turn to receive a divorced woman, Mrs Caspian, in her home, the request is met with 'horrified silence' and 'injured dignity'. This case, it appears, is different. To her friend's question: 'Then what becomes of your theory of divorce as an expression of moral freedom, an escape from social hypocrisy?' (*The Arch.* 101), Rose has no answer. Mrs Caspian is tiring of her second husband. 'Can't a woman...<be> mistake<n> more than once?' enquires Fred Vanderfleet. 'The second time, she must ~~bear~~ <abide by> the consequences!' comes the retort (101). Wharton casts a full chorus of hypocrites, among them Mrs Vanderfleet, an elderly widow who may be morally outraged at Rose's actions, but still determined to net the aged Stuart Bayne for her young daughter, even though he is a married man.

Once again, Wharton refuses to offer a tragedy with a happy ending. Rose proclaims: 'I have ~~no pride~~ <none> except ~~him~~ in being ~~having married~~ <the wife> of the man I love. The laws of my country gave me that right, & I took it. As for social laws—Hillbridge laws—I simply don't care a fig for them!' (*The Arch.* 104). The devotion, however, does not remain mutual when the married moral purist, Christina Lyart, confesses her love for Rose's husband. A confrontation was planned between the two women, which Wharton ominously labels 'Big scene'. The divorced woman is to blame it seems: 'It is all Rose's fault—her preaching the gospel of divorce—her example—her talk of individual freedom &c—Rose repudiates the blame, but is inwardly aghast at what she has done' (*The Arch.* 108). Rose and her husband 'look at each other in blank horror.... At last she says desperately. "Oh, what have I done? All our lives are in ruins, & yet I can't kill myself, because of the boy"' (*The Arch.* 108). What follows is the most (melo)dramatic dénouement of Wharton's career:

> Rose (dully.) I can't kill myself ... because there's the boy ...
> Adrian (turning quickly.) But I can, you mean? (He sees the revolver on the table & catches it up.) My God, you're right—(He shoots himself & drops dead.)
> At Rose's scream Lyart dashes in, & draws back, seeing Adrian's body.)
> Lyart. George! (Slowly he understands.) Mrs Adrian ... Is he dead?
> ~~Rose (Kneeling by him) He's dead...~~
> Christina rushes in ~~& sees Adrian~~ <at the sound.>
> Christina. ~~Oh—~~<What is it? What has happened?> (She ~~pushes~~ sees Adrian's dead body.) Ah ...(
> Rose (Kneeling by her husband.) He's dead ...
> Christina (with a scream) No—no—no! (She flings herself on the body, pushing Rose aside)
> (Rose. (rising slowly to her feet & turning toward Lyart.) Oh, spare her ... spare her!

Lyart (looks at her intently for a moment. Then he moves toward his wife, who is cowering over Adrian's body.) Christina, come—my wife …
She looks up at him, horror struck, dazed, & he draws her slowly to her feet, keeping her hands in his, as the curtain falls. (*The Arch*. 108)

Through, among other motifs, its discourse on divorce, laced with hypocrisy, a young divorcée with a son caught up in a custody dispute, an old family friend in love with the divorcée's husband, an artistic husband driven to despair and suicide, there are decided resonances of *The Custom of the Country*. Celeste Michele Wiggins suggests *The Arch*. is an overlooked source for the 1913 novel, with the play providing the '"emotional and psychological ingredients" for [that] much larger satirical piece on this issue of marriage and divorce'.[34] Once again, however, the manuscript is undated, thwarting attempts to fix the genesis of the play to the turbulent years of construction (1907–1913) of *The Custom of the Country*. Wharton was clearly still actively engaged in playwriting in this period (see, e.g., dating of *The Necklace* below). The ambivalence of the depiction of Rose Adrian certainly lends itself to notions of a writer working through a shifting narrative stance towards the character portrayal, something that would manifest itself in the mutating positioning of narrator to female protagonist in *The Custom of the Country*. In the early scenes, Rose is presented as a woman adopting an individual, honourable moral code; by the end, she is charged with causing all the miseries through her loose, corrupting standards, specifically her 'preaching the gospel of divorce' (*The Arch*. 108)—a judgement Rose appears to accept (she 'is inwardly aghast at what she has done' [108]). No creation by Wharton would polarise to quite the extreme of Undine Spragg—read on a scale from repulsive monster to a victim of society and a patriarchal system. While Rose is certainly no Undine (e.g., she actually *wants* her son—and not as a bargaining tool), the play's projected, shifting position in relation to the beliefs and actions of *The Arch*.'s female protagonist may suggest a developing precursor to one of Wharton's most memorable fictional creations. Whatever the year of composition, however, this overlooked manuscript, for all its roughness and embracing of melodrama, offers an intriguing discourse on divorce, its consequences, and the potential for another memorable female characterisation for which Wharton's *fiction* is so renowned. There is no extant typescript of *The Arch*., and indeed the play may have been abandoned before reaching this stage of the writer's production process. Nevertheless, the nature of the surviving manuscript draft clearly evidences that considerable time and energy were invested in *The Arch*. Pencilled manuscript sheets, pencilled corrections, ink corrections, additional ink manuscript sheets, glued-in sections written in ink (and one in pencil), red pencil markings, and a blue strike-through suggest at least two different workings of the manuscript and four proof-readings carried out at different times.

From the beginning to the end of her career, Edith Wharton's talent always came laced with pragmatism. Here was a woman who would not hesitate to pit one publisher against another, sell her work to the highest bidder, or threaten to sue when an editor attempted to renege on a favourable deal. In the fabric of the work itself, that practical and commercial efficiency can at times be seen through the way in which an idea might be recycled or assume different forms. This process is in evidence in a number of the plays. 'Pomegranate Seed', testimony to the author's long fascination with the Persephone myth, would give the title to both verse play and short story (as well as to works written by her fictional female authors in *The Touchstone* and 'Copy'); 'The Children's Hour' was also trialled as both play and short story; while the infamous Lizzie Borden case inspired at least two works—'Confession' and *Kate Spain*, while we see the reworking of material in *The Shadow of a Doubt* for *The Fruit of the Tree*.

The Necklace, meanwhile, displays Wharton at her most pragmatic, the writer working on the story in two, possibly three genres. The two biographers who note this work identify *The Necklace* solely as a novel, dating its aborted composition between 1917 and early 1920.[35] Ideas for *The Necklace*, however, germinated several years earlier. On the verso of page seven of a holograph plot summary in the Beinecke archive can be found a rare date, the author writing in pencil: 'The Necklace Berlin. 1913—'.[36] The 1913 plot summary of *The Necklace* may have been originally intended for a prose story—though its scale is more suggestive of an extended short story than a novel, while references to 'scenes' are multi-purpose, equally adept to novel, short story or play. If the summary was initially designed for a novel or short story, however, it was subsequently revised, for in its complete form, it presents the scenario of a play. Notably, Wharton inserts a reference to '2d act' on page six (114) while there is an explicit, genre-identifying conclusion: 'the play ends in a scene of ghastly gaiety' (115). The author may have contemplated different genres for the story (and several changes of title from 'The Necklace', 'The Pearl Necklace', 'The Letter') but it is as a play that the surviving material was developed. The Beinecke archive holds two manuscript drafts of the dramatised version of

The Necklace, the second draft a much fuller manuscript, comprising two complete acts and the opening of the third.

In Guy de Maupassant's short story of the same title, a woman condemns herself to poverty replacing a friend's 'valuable' pearl necklace, which transpires to have been only paste. Wharton's necklace, meanwhile, is a ruse to disguise an affair. As her lover is spotted jumping from her bedroom window, a married woman attempts to conceal the true nature of the situation from her husband by posing as the victim of a burglary—her pearl necklace (swiftly hidden in a convenient vase) the apparent spoils. In many respects this is bread and butter Wharton, the scene opening on a drawing room (in Long Island), the bridge game underway, the social niceties masking an unhappy marriage. Yet one can see very clearly in *The Necklace*—often precisely *because* of its rough and unfinished nature—Wharton's fierce commercial instincts coming to the fore. This is a play that promises a somewhat sensationalist drama, this time explicitly tapping into and sustaining some of the popular stereotypes of adulterous intrigue—'A married woman', 'a lover (X)', 'the husband', 'a young girl' (*Necklace* 113–15). Once names are added, they—as with the majority of the plays—often undergo change. *The Necklace* unapologetically throws into to the mix many of the basic ingredients of a popular, unpretentious 'hit': marital deception, a jealous husband, a torn lover, a staged crime. It also, however, contains marked errors and confusions. Though points would presumably have been clarified as work progressed, confusion over names, variant spellings, missed underlines evident in the drafts collectively betray an uncustomary slackness—perhaps the scars of a hasty transition from previous genre incarnations, and/or a sign of a writer with too many projects on her work schedule. The August 1913 dating of the plot summary is revealing. That month the writer diagnosed herself as '…simply dead tired, from having always, these last months, a little too much to do' (*Letters* 304). Having completed 'the hard grind at [her] last chapters' of the long-delayed *The Custom of the Country* (*Letters* 303), the prospect of Germany was her reward, Wharton spending ten days in Berlin as part of her tour of the country in August 1913. En route, however, the exhausted writer—by her own account—collapsed (*Letters* 306). Yet, even on holiday, she continued to work.

Wharton's commercial interests would be well served by the theatre in the 1920s and 1930s, when a number of successful stage adaptations of her work brought significant financial rewards. Early in 1921, the writer had appointed Cadwalader Jones as her representative in 'theatrical and cinematographic matters' (cited Lee 594), but Wharton took a keen interest in the stage adaptations of her work, often encouraged by their mutual friend, the playwright Edward (Ned) Sheldon. There were discussions in February 1921 of a stage adaptation of *The Age of Innocence* by Zoe Akins, which did not come to fruition. A stage production of Wharton's Pulitzer Prize novel finally opened in New York in November 1928, adapted by new playwright Margaret Ayer Barnes, under the close guidance of Sheldon who advised on every scene. A lucrative Broadway season was followed by a successful four-month tour. ('Hurrah for Detroit! What a cheque!' exclaimed a delighted Wharton from France, as Minnie Jones continued to forward theatre receipts and royalties.[37]) Discussions concerning a stage adaptation by Akins of *The Old Maid* continued over years from 1927, before the play finally opened in 1935 to a successful run on Broadway and subsequent tour, winning a Pulitzer for its playwright. The following year saw the stage adaptation of *Ethan Frome*, by father and son team of Owen and Donald Davis. This time the public was not, it appeared, seeking a tragedy with a happy ending, and the play opened to excellent reviews in January 1936. Wharton followed its progress and success with interest, and agreed to write a preface when the play was published later the same year. In a glowing preface, Wharton thanked the playwrights for bringing to *Ethan Frome* 'a new lease of life'. In the draft version, her praise of the playwrights moves through varying degrees, from 'incredible skill' to 'unfailing skill' before settling on the final version of 'great' skill.[38] These productions brought particularly welcome financial rewards when the Depression years had engendered a dramatic fall in Wharton's earnings from her fiction. In May 1932 she would enquire of John Hugh Smith: 'What of the dollar, & prospects in general? The price of serial fiction (my main support) has dropped *three fourths*' (*Letters* 549). By April 1936, however, the financial outlook had brightened considerably and Wharton could write to Lapsley that she was 'sustained ... by the regular click of coin in [her] savings-box as the *three* plays (2 Old Maids & one Ethan) continue their fruitful rounds' (*Letters* 592).

Negotiations over dramatisations of her fiction in this period reignited Wharton's own enthusiasm for playwriting. In 1935 she began *Kate Spain*, a play inspired, like her story 'Confession', by a fascination with the infamous Lizzie Borden case. Borden, accused of the frenzied hatchet murders of her father and stepmother in Fall River, Massachusetts, in August 1892, was tried in a blaze of publicity. Eventually acquitted, she would live the rest of her life under a cloud of suspicion. The writer completed one act of *Kate Spain* by March of 1935, only to learn from Sheldon that the macabre subject had already 'been used' (*Letters* 584), and she would subsequently set the play aside. Wharton's biographers suggest that the play was written before the story 'Confession', which was included in *The World Over* (1936), first published in *Story-Teller* in March 1936 with a title that appeared to strip the narrative of all shade and ambiguity, 'Unconfessed Crime'.[39] Wharton's letter to Cadwalader Jones on 5 March 1935, though, offers a timeline in which the story predates the play: 'When I sent him [Ned Sheldon] the other day the story "Confession," suggested by the Lizzie Borden case, I wrote him that I was contemplating a play on the same subject, but I felt that it was more than likely that it had already been used' (*Letters* 584). While the initial motivation was likely financial, Wharton's enthusiasm for the project was evident. To her sister-in-law, she wrote that she had become 'so absorbed in writing the first act of the Lizzie Borden play that [she was] not sorry to have done it'. In a comment entirely at odds with the stern, inflexible public image that had settled around her, the septuagenarian, Pulitzer winning author concluded not only was the play 'good practice' but she was open to responses to her 'dialogue and construction' (*Letters* 584).

Wharton may have completed only one act of *Kate Spain*, but available evidence—as well as knowledge of her customary working practices—suggests that she had imaginatively mapped out the arc of the entire play. (It is labelled 'A Play in Three Acts', while the cast of characters includes a head-waiter and ladies at a hotel in Switzerland to whom the scene could not shift until later stages of the drama.) Wharton was not afraid of melodrama or sensationalism—the projected conclusion of *The Arch*. emphatically reminds us of that—but one of the more intriguing aspects of *Kate Spain* is the 'modern', way in which the writer begins at the very point at which other dramatists might have finished. Wharton's final decade often has the ability to surprise. The brutal father is dead, the trial concluded, the 'sensation' over before the action—or non-action—of *Kate Spain* begins. The first line of dialogue reads: 'Well—that's over.'[40] The play had moved far beyond the initial Lizzie Borden 'inspiration' to more interesting, layered propositions regarding the aftermath, suspicion and ambivalence, and the intrigue of changing power relations between mistress and blackmailing maid. There will be a bold revelation at the end of the act, but Wharton takes a potentially melodramatic scenario and largely strips it of melodrama. The tyrannical father and his murder are dispensed with, and she gives the audience the muted after-effects of an incident without embellishment (unlike the special effect sled-ride, crucial to the climax of the Davis' adaptation of *Ethan Frome*).

While identical principal characters appear in both versions—Kate Spain, Cassie Donovan (travelling under the names of Kate Ingram and Cassie Wilpert in the story), Severance, and the tabloid journalist Jimmy Shreve—play and story part company in their focus. 'Confession' gives us a male narrator, Severance, who recounts falling in love, as he recuperated at a hotel in the Alps, with a fellow guest revealed as the infamous Kate Spain. They marry; he never opens the letter with her 'confession'. The short story opens years after the trial and indeed is told after Kate's death. The focus is on the man, who tells 'his' story, while the relationship between the women is pushed to one side. The surviving act of the play, by contrast, is immediate, gripping, female focused, and raw. The trial has just concluded, Kate has been released from jail, and even though other characters enter proceedings the opening act has the intensity of a two-hander, with the focus on the dialogue between the women, the mind games, and indeed psychological torture to which Kate is subjected, realising she will never escape the stranglehold of her maid (who conveniently dies in the short story after a confrontation with Severance).

As noted above, there are moments in her plays when Wharton can be seen to make exacting demands of her actors, particularly on their entrance, requiring the simultaneous portrayal of a complex, contradictory myriad of emotions or appearances—all with the first step on stage. The initial descriptions of Kate and Cassie, by contrast, tap into stereotypes of the elegant, distressed lady and plodding domestic servant respectively. 'Kate Spain is about thirty-two, rather tall, very thin, with black hair and wide very pale gray eyes. Her mouth is beautiful, but the lips are white, and drawn into lines of misery.... Cassie is stout, with a red mottled complexion, thin brown hair, rather prominent bold eyes, and a thick white throat with a crease in it' (138). Once again, however, Wharton then undermines the stereotype—Kate is not the innocent she appears, while the audience learns what has made Cassie the way she is: product of 'a miserable life... a poor factory girl when father engaged her...He got her at lower wages because she wasn't trained to be a servant...He always promised to raise her, but he never did...' (*Kate Spain* 147). In the closing lines of the extant first act, Cassie produces evidence (the burnt remnants of a blood-stained dress or apron) that indicates Kate did indeed murder her father: 'Keep calm, won't you? (A pause.) To get that away from me, my dear, you'll have to commit another murder. (Kate falls back unconscious on the sofa.) Curtain' (*Kate Spain* 158). The maid whose strong trial evidence was in large part responsible for her mistress's acquittal is to blackmail her way to a new life. The play was clearly intended to open up, as we see from the characters listed in Switzerland, but the completed first act offers a compelling, intense inner drama of mind games and a stalking of mental vulnerabilities. By the time of *Kate Spain*, the author was seeing possibilities for her stage-craft that were not always apparent in her earlier theatre work.

Indeed there are indications that Wharton became attached to this project, and may even have planned a return to it, despite those concerns that the subject had already 'been used'. A fascinating interview in 1936 carried an unexpected headline: 'Edith Wharton in Profile/In First Interview of Long Career, America's Famed Novelist Talks of Growing Interest in Theater.' After the success of recent stage productions of her work, wrote journalist Loren Carroll, '…Mrs. Wharton's attention has turned more and more to the theater. … In her last book of short stories "The World Over" is one story she feels would make a good play. It is "The [sic] Confession"' ('Edith Wharton in Profile'). This was two years after Wharton had insisted in her published memoir that she had never taken her dramatic impulses very seriously. Wharton may have been contemplating a return to the project, or—ever pragmatic—may simply have been drawing attention to the story in the hope that another dramatist might seek the rights, thereby adding to that 'regular click of coin in [her] savings-box'. Either way, nothing further came of the idea and other ongoing commitments—not least *The Buccaneers*—consumed available writing time.

Wharton's playwriting career had come full circle—her last play, like her first, would never reach the professional stage. The evidence insists, however, that Wharton was interested in playwriting from the beginning to end of her professional life, with its mixed results inhabiting a significant, formative, and influential role in her career. In her plays Wharton made bold choices—in her appropriation and subversion of stereotypes, her openness to experimentation, her harnessing of controversial plotlines, on occasions her embrace of economy and quiet sobriety of method in what would otherwise have been a sensationalist drama. And she made at times what are still considered unexpected choices with a determined movement down the social scale. Wharton's playwriting leaves its mark on her fiction in its settings, its dialogue, immediacy, its often scenic visual impact, and the release of a narrative voice unfettered by the constraints of the stage.

Plays like *The Arch.* and *The Shadow of a Doubt* offered potential dress rehearsals, early incarnations of plots and characters that would be reenvisaged, or simply recycled for her fiction—the boldness of the euthanasia plot of *The Shadow of a Doubt* would be partially masked when it resurfaced as one of multiple storylines in *The Fruit of the Tree*. At present, *The Shadow of a Doubt* is the one complete original play by Wharton that we have. The professional interest the play attracted on its reappearance in 2016 spoke volumes to Wharton's creative gift. The BBC commissioned and broadcast a full dramatisation on Radio 3, directed by Emma Harding, while there have been at least three staged readings of the play by professional theatre companies in the US to date, indicating the play is so much more than a curiosity piece. Wharton's work in this genre is again being taken seriously on its own merits. While newspaper coverage, for example that of February 1901, cited earlier, suggests *The Man of Genius* was finished, the only extant typescript is incomplete. *The Tightrope* playscript, meanwhile, appears not to survive, but we know it was finished and was being read in theatre circles, so it is highly possible that complete scripts of both *The Man of Genius* and *The Tightrope* may yet resurface, which in turn may finally give even fuller realisation to *The New York Times*' 1902 announcement, 'MRS. WHARTON, PLAYWRIGHT'.[41]

Notes

1. 'The Lounger', *The Critic: An Illustrated Monthly Review of Literature, Art and Life*, 38.3 (March 1901), 195–97. Subsequent references to this work are included in the text.
2. Edith Wharton, *The Custom of the County* (New York: Charles Scribner's Sons, 1913), 21. Subsequent references to this work are included in the text (*CC*).
3. Edith Wharton, *The Reef* (New York: D. Appleton and Company, 1912), 46–59.
4. Edith Wharton, *The Age of Innocence* (New York: D. Appleton and Company, 1920), 132. Subsequent references to this work are included in the text (*AI*).
5. David Olivieri (Edith Jones/Wharton), *Fast and Loose*, in Laura Rattray (ed.), *The Unpublished Writings of Edith Wharton*, Vol. 2 (London: Pickering and Chatto, 2009), 29. See also the opening of Chap. 6, with its stage directions as a setting: 'A large studio on the third floor of a Roman palazzo; a room littered & crowded & picturesque in its disorderliness, as only a studio can be…' (22).

6. 'Novelties in Theatres...Mrs. Wharton as a Playwright', *New York Times (1857–1922)*, 19 December 1902, ProQuest Historical Newspapers: The New York Times with Index, 6. The article's final heading reads: 'MRS. WHARTON, PLAYWRIGHT. A Brilliant Little Play at the Matinee of the Empire Dramatic School.'
7. Edith Wharton, *The Shadow of a Doubt* (Lady Uske, Act III), in Laura Rattray and Mary Chinery, '*The Shadow of a Doubt:* A Play in Three Acts by Edith Wharton', *Edith Wharton Review*, 33:1 (2017), 113–257; 227. Subsequent references to this work are included in the text.
8. Edith Wharton, 'A Further Glance', 24, Edith Wharton Collection. Yale Collection of American Literature, Beinecke Rare Book and Manuscript Library, Yale University. Box 19, folder 600. Subsequent references to this work are included in the text ('FG').
9. Wharton, 'A Little Girl's New York', *Harper's Magazine* (March 1938), 356–64; 362.
10. Letter from Walter Berry to Edith Wharton, 31 January 1900, cited in Lee 181.
11. See letters from Berry to Wharton, 15 February 1900 and 31 January 1900, Beinecke, Box 23.
12. See letter from Berry to Wharton, 27 February 1900, Beinecke, Box 23.
13. See letter from Berry to Wharton, 22 February 1901, Beinecke, Box 23.
14. For an excellent, detailed examination of the thwarted production history of *Manon Lescaut*, see Mary Chinery, 'Re-forming Manon: A New History of Edith Wharton's 1901 Play, *Manon Lescaut*', *Edith Wharton Review*, 35:1 (Spring 2019), 47–74.
15. 'Plays and Players', *Boston Herald*, 2 February 1901, 17, America's Historical Newspapers: *Boston Herald*; 'The Stage', *Detroit Free Press*, 10 February 1901, A7, ProQuest Historical Newspapers: Detroit Free Press.
16. Cynthia Griffin Wolff, *A Feast of Words: The Triumph of Edith Wharton*, rev. ed. (Reading, MA: Addison-Wesley, 1995), 413. Subsequent references to this work are included in the text.
17. Wharton, 'The Theatres', New York *Commercial Advertiser*, 7 May 1902, reprinted in Wegener (ed.), *Edith Wharton: The Uncollected Critical Writings*, 78–80; 80. Subsequent references to this work are included in the text.
18. Edith Wharton, *The Man of Genius*, in Rattray (ed.), *The Unpublished Writings of Edith Wharton*, Vol. 1, 3–66; 65. Subsequent references to this work are included in the text.
19. 'At the Theatres', *The Atlanta Constitution*, 10 March 1901, 15. Online.
20. Letter from Walter Berry to Wharton, 22 February 1901. Beinecke, Box 23.
21. 'Theatrical Gossip', *The New York Times*, 8 March 1901. ProQuest Historical Newspapers: New York Times.

22. 'Kill to End Suffering', cited in Jennie Kassanoff, *Edith Wharton and the Politics of Race* (Cambridge: Cambridge University Press, 2004), 74. Subsequent references to this work are included in the text.
23. For more on this point, see Mary Chinery and Laura Rattray, '*The Shadow of a Doubt*: Discovering a New Work by Edith Wharton', *Edith Wharton Review*, 33.1 (2017), 104–8.
24. John Corbin, 'Topics of the Drama', *New York Times (1857–1922)*; 23 Nov 1902, 10. ProQuest Historical Newspapers: New York Times.
25. Edith Wharton, 'Translator's Note to *The Joy of Living*', reprinted Wegener (ed.), *Edith Wharton: The Uncollected Critical Writings*, 235.
26. Edith Wharton, *Untitled*, in Rattray (ed.), *The Unpublished Writings of Edith Wharton*, Vol. 1, 67–89; 70. Subsequent references to this work are included in the text.
27. '"THE HOUSE OF MIRTH.": Drama Made from Mrs. Wharton's Novel Is Produced at Detroit', *New York Times (1857–1922)*, 18 September 1906, ProQuest Historical Newspapers: The New York Times, 9.
28. 'WHARTON AND FITCH CLASH: Authoress Objects to His Dramatization of "House of Mirth"', *New York Times (1857–1922)*, 23 September 1906, ProQuest Historical Newspapers: The New York Times, 9. My thanks to Mary Chinery for sending me this newspaper article reporting on the 'quarrel' and Fitch's letter to the editor in response.
29. 'NOT TRUE SAYS CLYDE FITCH', Clyde Fitch Letter to the Editor, *New York Times (1857–1922)*, 24 September 1906, ProQuest Historical Newspapers: The New York Times.
30. 'Mrs Wharton's Views on the Society Drama': *New York Times (1857–1922)*, 28 October 1906, ProQuest Historical Newspapers: The New York Times with Index, SM2. Subsequent references to this work are included in the text.
31. 'Clyde Fitch Discusses "The House of Mirth"', *New York Times (1857–1922)*, 4 November 1906, ProQuest Historical Newspapers: The New York Times with Index, SM2.
32. Both Fitch and Frohman died prematurely—Fitch in 1909 after an operation for appendicitis and Frohman in 1915 in the sinking of the Lusitania.
33. Edith Wharton, *The Arch.*, in Rattray (ed.), *The Unpublished Writings of Edith Wharton*, Vol. 1, 93–115; 99. Subsequent references to this work are included in the text.
34. Celeste Michele Wiggins, 'Edith Wharton and the Theatre' (PhD dissertation, Case Western Reserve University, 1996), 123–24.
35. Wolff dates the novel at 1917–1918 (287), while Lewis dates the work from October 1919, continuing into 1920 (427).
36. Holograph summary and *The Necklace* in Rattray, *The Unpublished Writings of Edith Wharton*, Vol. 1, 113–15; 117–33. Subsequent references are included in the text.

37. Letter from Wharton to Mary Cadwalader Jones, 26 October 1929, Beinecke, Box 28, folder 856. Writing from Pavillon Colombe, Wharton continued 'Your letter came this morning, & I wish it had arrived two days ago, before dear little Grossie left for Hyères, for my literary success is nothing, in her eyes, compared to my theatrical royalties, & the said eyes wd. have goggled at this figure.'
38. Wharton, Preface to dramatisation of *Ethan Frome*, Ms Beinecke, Box 5.
39. Benstock suggests, 'Although Sheldon praised the draft of the first act, she rewrote it as a short story' (444), while Lee writes 'An unfinished murder-mystery play, "Kate Spain," based on the Lizzie Borden case, was turned into a story called "Confession"' (178).
40. Edith Wharton, *Kate Spain*, in Rattray (ed.), *The Unpublished Writings of Edith Wharton*, Vol. 1, 137–58; 138. Subsequent references to this work are included in the text.
41. 'Novelties in Theatres…Mrs. Wharton as a Playwright', 6.

CHAPTER 4

Travel Writings

> On his table lay the note: Lily had sent it to his rooms. He knew what was in it before he broke the seal—a grey seal with Beyond! beneath a flying ship. Ah, he would take her beyond—beyond the ugliness, the pettiness, the attrition and corrosion of the soul. (*HM* 249)

As Margaret Ayer Barnes worked on a stage adaptation of *The Age of Innocence* in 1928, Wharton, via her ever-supportive former sister-in-law Mary Cadwalader Jones, expressed concern at the way in which her central male protagonist Newland Archer was being scripted. Barnes reported to fellow playwright Edward (Ned) Sheldon, who closely advised on the adaptation: 'Our Archer appears a monstrous changeling in the cradle of Mrs. Wharton's hero!'; 'Mrs. Jones said it nearly killed Mrs. Wharton to have us say that Archer had never been abroad—but they will compromise on a grand tour of Europe before the opening of the play.'[1] Overseas travel and openness to travel are important markers for Wharton's characters of ease, fluency, education, culture, privilege, and sophistication—for both sexes, but especially her men. For Ralph Marvell and Newland Archer, experience of travel broadens individual views, if not necessarily conventional guiding mindsets or behaviour. Poverty precludes overseas travel in *Ethan Frome*, but the time Ethan spent on a notably 'slight' engineering job in Florida offers a tantalising phase of possibility and escape, one increasing his 'faith in his ability as well as his eagerness to see the world'.[2] It is not a universal panacea in Wharton's fiction, however. Travel for other

© The Author(s) 2020
L. Rattray, *Edith Wharton and Genre*,
https://doi.org/10.1057/978-1-349-59557-0_4

characters has no absorptive, enlightening effect. Ralph's cherished Italian scenes on his honeymoon are, for his limelight-seeking bride, just 'dirty and ugly', Europe 'all too dreadfully dreary', entirely devoid of appeal (*CC* 153). Similarly the honeymoon with May in Europe is a moment of realisation for Newland that his wife does not have the capacity for its transformative possibilities—'travelling interested her even less than he had expected' (195), though an early indication of Newland's own limitations comes as he surveys the 'bits of wreckage' (*AI* 67) of Countess Olenska's home and is bewildered by art works and arrangements that fall outside his knowledge, suggesting a Europe he does not know. Europe in Wharton's fiction can offer freedom, culture, the intellectual life, but its allure can also be illusory and dangerous. Ellen, though enriched by her European life, is also exposed early to its dangers, marked as 'different' by her travels, which will forever define her and in turn facilitate a disastrous marriage. Europe promises an escape that proves to be no escape at all for the fleeing adulterous couple Lydia Tillotson and Ralph Gannett in 'Souls Belated' (1899), while twenty years in Italy will not wash away the social sins of Mrs Lidcote in 'Autres Temps' (1911) on her return to New York.

Ten months before her death, Wharton wrote from Pavillon Colombe to her friend Mary Berenson: 'I wish I knew what people mean when they say they find "emptiness" in this wonderful adventure of living, which seems to me to pile up its glories like an horizon-wide sunset as the light declines. I'm afraid I'm an incorrigible life-lover & life-wonderer & adventurer' (*Letters* 598). Unlike her American-branded protagonist Undine Spragg of Apex, Edith Jones spent more of her formative years in Europe than in the country of her birth. To conserve income in the economic recession following the Civil War, the Jones family headed for Europe in 1866, spending six years in France, Italy, Germany, and Spain—a residence that sealed Wharton's life-long love affair with Europe. Returning to America was a jolt, Wharton recalling in *A Backward Glance* how the squalor of the New York docks dismayed her 'childish eyes, stored with the glories of Rome and the architectural majesty of Paris' (44). The family would return to France in 1880, seeking a better climate for her father's health. In fact both of Wharton's parents would die in France: her father in Cannes in 1882; her mother in Paris in 1901 after nearly a year 'paralysed & unconscious', Lucretia's death finally arriving as a merciful release.[3] The acquisition of a husband brought the twenty-three-year-old Edith Jones a passport to more adventurous travel, destinations she could not have easily visited as a single woman—and Teddy, before the ravages of illness took their toll, indulged her. (Wharton opens the chapter 'Friendships and Travels' in *A Backward Glance* with the strikingly directed statement, 'At the end of my second winter in New York I was married; and thenceforth my thirst for travel was to be gratified' [90].) In 1888 the couple lavished $10,000 on an Aegean cruise lasting close to three months on the yacht *Vanadis*—Wharton's detailed account of the trip admirably identified and recovered by Claudine Lesage, and published in 1992. Travel would later also afford the opportunity to displace a problem— Teddy dispatched on a world tour in 1910. After years of living in Newport, New York, and her estate 'The Mount' in Lenox, Massachusetts, combined with both extensive travel and extended residences abroad, Wharton made her permanent home in France. Her divorce would be finalised in a Parisian court to avoid publicity in April 1913, where journalists were not permitted access to court reports and proceedings (Lee 399). In a 'Talk to American Soldiers', which would prove part of the genesis for *French Ways and Their Meaning* (1919), Wharton made a very moving, public avowal in spring 1918: 'I believe if I were dead, and anybody asked me to come back and witness for France, I should get up out of my grave to do it.'[4]

Though she would make her home in France, it was in fact Italy that proved the inspiration for more of Wharton's early work, including her travel writing. After her marriage in 1885 she travelled to Europe almost every year, each visit incorporating several months in Italy. In *A Backward Glance* Wharton recalls that it was when she was abroad on her travels with her husband that she 'really felt alive' (91). The country was a tangible presence in the years she was emerging as a professional writer. Her now little-read first novel *The Valley of Decision* (1902) is set in Italy, as are the two books that followed, *Italian Villas and Their Gardens* (1904, discussed in Chap. 5) and *Italian Backgrounds* (1905), largely comprised of articles published between 1895 and 1903. Italy provided the setting for a sequence of early short stories, among them 'The Muse's Tragedy' (1899), 'Souls Belated', 'The Duchess at Prayer' (1900), 'The Confessional' (1901), 'A Venetian Night's Entertainment' (1903), 'The House of the Dead Hand' (1904), and 'The Letter' (1904), and for a number of her early poems, notably '"The Last Token"' (1878), 'The Last Giustiniani' (1889), 'The Tomb of Ilaria Giunigi' (1891), and 'Margaret of Cortona' (1901) which, as seen earlier, so inspired the wrath of the Catholic Church.[5]

Travels to Italy, and writing about travels in Italy, had long been a conventional pastime for the elite. In the nineteenth century, as Sirpa Salenius outlines, Italy was one of the primary destinations of the American Grand Tour of Europe, with 'the conformity of the tour ... further reinforced in the second half of the century with the publication of such "official" guidebooks as those written by Karl Baedeker and John Murray, which replaced the earlier personal and sentimental travel narratives.'[6] 'These guidebooks', continues Salenius, 'whose aim was to provide objective and factual information to travellers, dictated the places to visit, sights to see, and art works to be admired' (Salenius 5). In *A Backward Glance*, Wharton, describing the New Yorkers of her parents' generation, exclaims that 'the self-respecting American on his travels frequented only the little "colonies" of his compatriots already settled in the European capitals, only their most irreproachable members!' (62). As Virginia Ricard observes, Italy 'was a place to be visited, and possibly to be settled in, but on no account to be more intimately connected with'.[7] Wharton, by contrast, as Ricard explains, sought a different Italy, making a point in *A Backward Glance* of distinguishing herself from the readers of 'agreeable volumes of travel and art-criticism of the cultured dilettante type' of her parents' generation who had been willing to follow set itineraries and to neglect any work of art conceived after the late Middle Ages (cited in Ricard 71). Lee underlines that during a period of twenty years, from 1885 to 1905, Wharton set herself a demanding programme of study in the fields of art, architecture, and literature (cited in Ricard 71). She also acquired three friends and mentors with expert knowledge of, and passion for, the country: Charles Eliot Norton, Harvard's first professor of art history (and father of Wharton's friend Sally); French writer Paul Bourget, author of *Sensations d'Italie* (1892) and with whom Wharton travelled in Italy at the turn of the century; and Vernon Lee (Violet Paget), author of *Studies of the Eighteenth Century in Italy* (1880) among other titles. There were sentimental attachments too. Recalling her father's illness and their visit to Florence and Venice she muses in *A Backward Glance*, 'it must have been then that he gave me "Stones of Venice" and "Walks in Florence", and gently lent himself to my whim of following step by step Ruskin's arbitrary itineraries' (87). Before she was done, however, Wharton would be forging her own Italian path.

Market-savvy from the outset of her career, Wharton used her knowledge of the busy transatlantic tourist traffic as part of her publishing sales pitch. Having separately published six essays on Italy that would make their way into the volume that became *Italian Backgrounds*—spanning 'A Tuscan Shrine' to 'Picturesque Milan', appearing in *Scribner's Magazine* in January 1895 and February 1903 respectively—Wharton suggested book publication to William Brownell in a letter dated 16 August 1903:

> Why shouldn't we publish this autumn my collection of Italian sketches? I had forgotten all about them; but as my first article on Italian villas is coming out in the Century in Nov., it seems to me it might be a happy moment ... I believe the book would sell well, for there is such a great rush to Italy every autumn now on the Mediterranean steamers, & people so often ask me where these articles can be found. (*Letters* 86)

Publication would, nevertheless, be held back, partly to avoid overlapping with *Italian Villas and Their Gardens* which came out as a volume in November 1904, after magazine serialisation. With three chapters added to those already published, *Italian Backgrounds* appeared in April 1905.[8] Wharton's original suggestion of 'Italian Impressions' for its title was rejected by Brownell for not being 'cathedral enough', so she proposed instead 'Italian Backgrounds' to mean that 'the most interesting Italy is the one in the background, behind the official guide-book Italy.'[9] Following her debut novel, *The Valley of Decision*, and *Italian Villas and Their Gardens*, *Italian Backgrounds*, as Lee recognises, 'has the look of a mature book of her forties, but in fact was compiled over ten years and was a fusing-together of twenty years of looking, learning and loving', taking shape during adventurous journeys of the 1890s (Lee 92, 93).

Italian Backgrounds is a handsome volume, with its dark green cloth, gilt titles, and tooling to the cover and spine, and illustrations by E.C. Peixotto (which drew praise, if bordering on the inane, from the *Spectator* reviewer: 'The very pretty illustrations add much to the attractiveness of all these studies; their light and bright delicacy is in itself truly Italian.'[10]) Between its attractive covers, however, lies one of Wharton's most empowering texts. Certainly this is a cultural guide through which to educate—and Wharton is at pains in the opening chapter, 'An Alpine Posting-Inn', to distinguish her informed travels from those of 'Americans going "right through," with their city and state writ large upon their luggage'.[11] Yet it is also an inherently rebellious, even subversive volume, Wharton letting her readers in on the secrets, taking them on the journey with her and then inviting them to make a journey, real or imagined, of their own. This is no Baedeker, by the letter guide, but a volume that opens up a cultural history, and ways of reading that history, one with secrets still to discover, and that encourages its readers to stray from a well-trodden path. Wharton's Italy is 'the land of unsuspected treasures' (*IB* 29). 'One of the rarest and most delicate pleasures of the continental tourist is to circumvent the compiler of his guide-book', she writes, encouraging new approaches and unconventional routes (*IB* 85).

In a manuscript fragment, 'Italy Again', written three decades later, Wharton wryly observed, 'The cultivated amateur of my youth was encouraged to dash off impressionistic sketches of travel', having been led to 'obscure corners' and 'unnoticed landscapes' by 'charming little amateur books'.[12] *Italian Backgrounds*, however, does so much more: it explicitly validates other ways of looking, other ways of reading—looking to the side, in the margins, beneath and beyond. The writer who records hieroglyphic worlds in her fiction illuminates here possible ways to read and understand a country, a model by which looking beyond the foreground, beyond the obvious, reveals more:

> In the Italian devotional pictures of the early Renaissance there are usually two quite unrelated parts: the foreground and the background.
> The foreground is conventional.... It is only in the background that the artist finds himself free to express his personality. Here he depicts not what some one else has long since designed for him, in another land and under different conceptions of life and faith, but what he actually sees about him...
> As with the study of Italian pictures, so it is with Italy herself. The country is divided, not into *partes tres*, but in two: a foreground and a background. The foreground is the property of the guide-book and of its product, the mechanical sight-seer; the background, that of the dawdler, the dreamer and the serious student of Italy. (*IB* 173–74, 177)

Reading the country is explicitly likened to reading a book: 'Italy, to her real lovers, is like a great illuminated book' (*IB* 179). And—quite unexpectedly for a volume illuminating historic treasures, a piece of travel writing, and travel largely before the modern age of travel (the motor car will play a major role in many of the later texts)—*Italian Backgrounds* can be viewed in a number of respects as the closest Wharton will ever come to a modernist treatise. Here is a volume honouring individual adventure, 'the parentheses' (170), the 'intervals between … systematized study' (170), 'escapes from the expected' (86), 'miles unmeasured' (86), 'the margins' (179), the 'exhilaration' of discovery (179): 'there is no short cut' (177) as its author invites, even demands, reader participation. The writer who would later be saddled with old grande dame associations turns out to be far too liberal and progressive for the *Times Literary Supplement* reviewer, who complained of *Italian Backgrounds*: 'It appears that she is so free from prejudice as to be able to admire the best work of every style and period. We feel this to be a little more than human, and it must be owned that we resent it.'[13]

'Deconventionalize' urges Wharton in the final chapter of *Italian Backgrounds* written especially for the volume, her own version of 'Make it new!':

> The famous paintings, statues and buildings of Italy are obviously the embodiment of its historic and artistic growth; but they have become slightly conventionalized by being too long used as the terms in which Italy is defined. They have stiffened into symbols, and the life of which they were once the most complete expression has evaporated in the desiccating museum-atmosphere to which their fame has condemned them. To enjoy them, one must let in on them the open air of an observation detached from tradition. Since they cannot be evaded they must be deconventionalized; and to effect this they must be considered in relation to the life of which they are merely the ornamental façade. (*IB* 177–78)

During the period Wharton worked on her Italian texts, she also wrote eight chapters of her subsequently abandoned novel, *Disintegration*. This manuscript promised one of her most innovative experiments in the use of multiple, roving perspectives. The reader is presented with the perspective of a young girl (Valeria Clephane) abandoned by her mother, that of a family friend (George Severance), and of social observers, and Valeria's father (Henry Clephane), through conversation with Severance. (The perspective of the 'offending' woman, Alice Clephane/Wing is denied). Over the course of the eight extant chapters, the shifts prove both an ambitious plot and focus-altering device: 'were not events beginning to ~~declare~~ <show> that there might have been two sides to the story?' poses the narrative (107)—and Wharton presents at least four. Different ways of looking, different ways of reading were evidently high on the writer's agenda, and they filtered admirably through the varied genres she was manoeuvring during this time.[14]

As more women travelled without male companions, conduct books, aimed specifically at female travellers, flourished. Scholars have suggested that many women travellers to Italy may well have identified with the country's political struggles, its fight for unification and independence likely to 'have resonated with the feminist desires of British and American women', as Debra Bernardi phrases it, only adding to Italy's appeal.[15] Sarah Bird Wright reminds us there was a tradition of popular women travel writers, citing Harriet Beecher Stowe with a ready audience for her *Sunny Memories of Foreign Lands* (1862), while the following decades, she notes, 'brought travel accounts by dozens of women: Mary Blake (on Mexico and Europe); Anna Dodd (on France and England); Julia Dorr (on England); Susan Hale (on Spain); Adelaide Hall (on Europe and the Mediterranean); and Eliza Skidmore (on Alaska, Malaya and Japan)'.[16] At the turn of the new century, Wharton's sister-in-law, Mary Cadwalader Jones, published her own travel book—the eminently pragmatic and gendered, *European Travel for Women: Notes and Suggestions* (1900), with a chapter devoted to Italy. Jones' volume is packed with practical advice for the woman traveller in Italy: how to insure a parcel, buy train tickets, which window to use at the ticket office, the arrangement of toilet facilities between train carriages, how and how much to tip, taxi fares, church opening hours, how to engage a gondolier in Venice (the last also 'useful as a body-guard to keep off the swarms of guides and beggars, and he will do so with an eloquence of vituperation which you could never hope to equal'.[17])

Wharton, by contrast, seldom presents herself as a 'woman traveller' in her travel writings. There are rare exceptions, when she journeys to countries (rather than individual locations) off the tourist trail. In Morocco, for example, it is her very status as a woman that will gain her admittance to the harems, whereas in *The Cruise of the Vanadis* '[the] early established rule that no female, human or animal, is to set foot on the promontory' of Mount Athos and its monasteries means Wharton must remain on board, while her male companions (her husband and their friend James Van Alen) go ashore.[18] During that early *Vanadis* cruise, a journey which included Algiers, mainland Greece and its islands, and Smyrna on the Asia Minor coast, she writes of the risks posed by a number of their destinations, notably in Smyrna, as narrated by the US consul and his wife, with accounts of twenty-one murders committed in a single month, Europeans threatened and blackmailed, robberies, and the consul unable to venture out without an armed escort. These are not perceived as explicitly gendered threats however—the targets are affluent merchants and European residents and visitors, and Wharton is clunkily egalitarian in judging the murderers 'made up of the dregs of different nations', not all Greeks as 'the Turks' all claimed (*CV* 150). A rare (if unstated) fear of sexual violence as a woman traveller is admitted privately by the writer in a letter during a 1914 visit to Tunisia (about which no separate travel book was forthcoming), when Wharton, disturbed in the middle of the night, put out her hand in the darkness only to touch a man bending over her: 'I should be very glad to die, but it's no fun struggling with you don't know what in the dark', she wrote, describing the experience as a 'hateful thing' that 'murdered sleep for a long time to come' (*Letters* 324, Lee 448)—a heart-stopping, 'what if' moment recognisable to women across time.

Wharton's published travel writing, however, primarily promotes an intensely American narrative of individualism and independence of spirit which mutes any gendered discourse. Instead there is the advocation of straying from the familiar path, an empowering venture into the unknown. Even so, gender is not entirely removed from the equation, as evidenced by Wharton's extraordinary account in her 'A Tuscan Shrine' chapter of *Italian Backgrounds*, which is in itself an expert exposition on individual perspective. Here we see Wharton unapologetically doing her own thing, on her own terms, correcting the misattribution of a set of terracottas in San Vivaldo, and in the process confounding her critics. She was the 'non-expert' woman, mocked by men (including Bernard Berenson), but the (male) art establishment is proved wrong and Wharton, after all, seen to be right—though she has, with pointed irony, to rely on the male director of the Royal Museums at Florence, Professor Ridolfi, to confirm her case, Wharton quoting extensively from his letter in professional validation. *He* has the final word of the chapter, not she, declaring that the works previously attributed to the seventeenth-century artist, Giovanni Gonnelli, are indeed the work of an artist of the school of the Robbias a century before (*IB* 105–6).[19]

The charge has been levelled at Wharton that she loved Italy, but not Italians. Robin Peel asserts that 'Wharton's love of Italy did not include a love of Italians, from whom she had that disdain so striking in Anglo-Saxon rhetoric of the late Victorian and Edwardian period',[20] while Lee suggests she 'came to feel that she was more worthy of Italy than the Italians', noting that '[t]his was not an unusual boast for a cultured American traveller' (95). The private arena of personal correspondence certainly allowed prejudices to roam unguarded, as evident in her view of Naples and its people, recounted in one of her exuberant letters to Anna Bahlmann, a depiction of diametrically opposed extremes: 'more gorgeous, more noisy, more brilliant than anything you can conceive of—& also filthier, & more detestable' (*My Dear Governess* 71). And yet those diametrics bookend in the same letter of 27 March 1887 a warm, stereotype-challenging description of an elderly woman who shows the couple round a villa for which she has a key and stops their preconceptions in their tracks before they leave by kicking off her shoes, climbing 'with amazing ease' to the top of a high mandarin tree to procure two bunches of fruit for the couple. The gift bearer tellingly begins the account as 'an old peasant woman' but ends (though still nameless) elevated to 'an old lady' (*My Dear Governess* 72). Wharton's European education would take many forms, and however cultured, sensitive and open to new experience she proved, a set of prejudices common to the affluent leisured classes was undeniably also packed in her European luggage.

Such prejudices are not transferred wholesale to her published work, however. While Maureen E. Montgomery suggests that Wharton's 'claims of [Italian] immersion are compromised' by her holding of the country's people 'at a distance', she persuasively argues that 'Wharton's representations of Italians lack the debasement that characterizes the travelogues of her contemporaries.'[21] Noting practical guides that 'alerted Americans to the childishness of Italians with their "simple tricks" and persistent "cupidity"', to 'thieves and beggars' (as evidenced in Cadwalader Jones' guide above), and American travellers engaged 'in visceral reactions to the working classes and beggars of Italy that take "distancing gestures" ... to a new level', Montgomery underscores the idea that '[f]or Wharton, the impediments to travel reside more in the shortcomings of the stock travel guide or the imagination of travelers than in the local people' (Montgomery 123). Meanwhile in her striking essay, 'Pathways to a Personal Aesthetic: Edith Wharton's Travels in Italy and France', Maureen E. St Laurent makes a case for Wharton's inclusivity, suggesting that her 'concern for the material reality informing all artistic production' results not in 'artistic elitism', but 'rather an aesthetic of the margins and of the marginalized, particularly those on the socio-economic margins', leading the writer 'to a realistic assessment of who bears the cost, yet earns little glory in the creation of a culture's greatest productions'.[22] As we have seen in a number of her plays and poems with their movement down the social scale, Wharton looks beyond to acknowledge those often left in the shadows, the background and on the margins.

Montgomery argues that in *Italian Backgrounds* Wharton can be seen to go 'a long way toward avoiding the worst elements of a colonialist discourse that seeks to debase the "other"' (126). In a balanced essay, she nevertheless views the author as engaged 'in a problematic aestheticization of contemporary Italians by preferring to relate and relegate them to a past when Italian art flourished', with them 'embody[ing] for her all that is admirable about the rich cultural history of Italy' (Montgomery 126). The past is certainly pervasive in the Italian travel writings, though it does not receive unquestioning veneration—and indeed Wharton was unusual in, and praised for, her urging of attention to Italian art beyond the mid Renaissance (and she chooses the eighteenth century in which to set her Italian novel, *The Valley of Decision*, a century she describes as 'all in nuances'[23]) The *Nation* reviewer observed: 'We are warned against dividing ourselves into the two camps of Gothic and classical art; rather to keep our minds open to the appreciation of all that is good of whatsoever time,' while the *Spectator* opined, 'She is perfectly right in her opposition to that narrow view of art which ceases to admire at the mid-Renaissance.'[24]

The 'rich low murmur'[25] of the past remained an important sounding bell for Wharton throughout her personal and professional life—and we see the past particularly amplified in her travel writing on Greece. Wharton worked on two accounts of her travels in and around Greece—neither of which would be published in her lifetime.[26] Most important is the still rarely discussed account of her 1888 cruise on the Vanadis, the bound and typed pages recovered by Lesage from a municipal library in Hyères,[27] while thirty-eight years later Wharton set out to recreate much of the Vanadis route on a chartered yacht, the Osprey, sketching her impressions in a set of notes now housed in the Beinecke Library at Yale. Accompanying her on the 1926 journey were Daisy Chanler, Logan Pearsall Smith (brother of Mary Berenson), Robert Norton, John Hugh Smith, and Harry Lawrence of the Medici Society (and Chanler and Pearsall Smith would go on to publish their own accounts of the journey.[28]) In *A Backward Glance*, Wharton enthuses: 'Only twice in my life have I been able to put all the practical cares out of my mind for months, and each time it has been on a voyage in the Aegean' (100). Misremembering the first cruise as a four-month voyage (her precisely dated account reveals the journey began on 17 February and came to an end on 7 May), it was a daring and rebellious act that met with opposition from both sides of the twenty-six-year old's family (*BG* 97–98).

The focus of the minimal critical discussion conducted on *The Cruise of the Vanadis* speaks loudly to (subsequently challenged) understanding of Wharton biography in the 1990s, around the time of the volume's belated publication. In her introduction, Lesage describes the account as Wharton's 'maiden "Odyssey" into literature' (*CV* 24), but we know she had been writing from the moment she was physically able, and that she had built both a private and professional publishing record before 1888. Wright, the first scholar to give sustained attention to Wharton's travel writings, proposes that '[t]he *Vanadis* diary and its epigraph [from Goethe's *Faust*] suggest that travel not only met a deeply felt inner need on the part of Edith Wharton, but also offered a means of escape from what had turned out to be a disappointing marriage' (*Edith Wharton Abroad* 16). Though a private yacht on which one's husband is one of only three travellers for almost three months could scarcely be perceived as an 'escape' from marriage, subsequent revelations of the Bahlmann correspondence ultimately skewered the idea that the Wharton marriage was a disappointment from the beginning. These were still the very early years of the marriage, and in *A Backward Glance* Wharton credits her husband with making the journey happen in the face of that family opposition, when she said she 'really want[ed] to go' (98). Louis Auchincloss, meanwhile, recycles the myth of Wharton as an overbearing companion: 'One occasionally has a glimpse of the author's sometimes rather domineering personality in her admissions that her rigorous schedule of exhaustive sightseeing may have caused a bit of a strain on her two more easygoing male companions, and we note that she found the captain surly and indifferent', Auchincloss misquoting Wharton's 'inefficient' for 'indifferent' ('Foreword', *CV* 16). What we see instead—for example in the visits to the catacombs of Syracuse which are of no interest to Wharton, but of great interest to the men—is a companionable, accommodating trio. And Auchincloss neglects to mention Wharton's delight with the rest of the crew of sixteen ('with the sole exception of the Captain, who was surly and inefficient, they gave us entire satisfaction and it would be hard to find anywhere a nicer or more willing set of men' [*CV* 221]). What is ultimately another intriguing, even exciting travel text has been partially obscured by the broad, lingering shadows of Wharton mythology.

In *A Backward Glance* Wharton describes the Aegean cruise as a voyage 'almost unheard of' in 1888, a 'mad' scheme in the eyes of the couple's families (98). The writer's account of Mount Athos in *The Cruise of Vanadis* is 'thought to be the first by an American' (*Edith Wharton Abroad* 18)—though in reality she is not able to give a first-hand depiction of the male-only domain and its monasteries and hermitages. It is a frustration that (even though she will not portray it in such terms) leads Wharton to strike a blow for women's rights as she orders the launch 'as near the forbidden shores' as possible, which in turn prompts a scene that borders on the comic as a group of caloyers clamber hurriedly down the hill to prevent her landing (*CV* 174–75). The Whartons and Van Alen certainly travelled in immense luxury. The crew of sixteen comprised the captain, mate, two engineers, two firemen, the boatswain, five able seamen, two stewards, and two cooks, plus their own maid and valet—the timely death of a distant relative ultimately covering the Whartons' share of costs for a 'taste of heaven' (*BG* 100)[29]—but many of the expeditions onshore inevitably involved long, uncomfortable journeys for a 'lady' traveller, often made on donkey. At times, *Wharton* is the curiosity, for example in Astypalia, where crowds gather, grasping the folds of her dress 'in their excited curiosity', to the point where the travellers have to beat a retreat to the shelter of the café, while their friend apologetically explains that the sight of a steamer was new to the inhabitants of the island (*CV* 119). At other points, the travellers venture into the unknown only to replicate the structures of New York society, arriving with letters of introduction, making visits to bankers, being hosted and escorted by diplomats and dignitaries, including the US Minister to Greece. In a moment that is both culturally crass and unintentionally comic, a Sunday service is held in the saloon of the yacht at which the entire crew is present, with prayers read at a table covered with the American flag.

Wharton's *Vanadis* account intertwines both the literary and factual. An additional companion on the cruise for this extraordinarily accomplished young woman, well versed in ancient Greek literature, history, and culture, took the form of Homer's *The Odyssey*, specifically Macmillan's 1883 third edition of a translation by S. H. Butcher and A. Lang, which survives in Wharton's library at the Mount, her copy signed and dated 1888.[30] References to Homer, Shelley, Goethe punctuate *The Cruise of the Vanadis*, yet the account is at times particularly notable for a vivid, precise, factual, almost documentary quality, which distinguishes it from much of the author's later travel writing. There is a rare staccato to Wharton's prose here, with brief paragraphs, statements, and frequent times and dates. The account may have been a daily recording, or recreated from contemporaneous notes at a later date, though the staccato quality perhaps argues against the latter. Certainly the expedition assumes an energetic pace and is expertly planned, though on occasion those plans are blown off course by the natural and man-made inconveniences of illness, yacht repair, or bad weather. It must be remembered of course that Wharton appears to have made no attempt to have the account published. Even so, she thought enough of it to have it typed and bound, though we cannot be sure when. Thanks to Lesage's keen eye, we know the watermark of the paper is dated 1896, however, and that the typescript was discovered in the town where Wharton rented and later bought her last home. It is possible the author had the account typed as late as 1926, part of the preparation for her 'recreation' of the trip on the Osprey—but again this can only be speculation.

Criticism on *The Cruise of the Vanadis* has been swift to read its author as 'essentially a novice', 'a youthful apprentice', the diary conveying 'a carefree "amateur" approach', with the text her 'apprenticeship' in travel narrative.[31] This approach is closely linked to a stale, broader endeavour to read the author's travel writing essentially as part of Wharton's journey of 'self-discovery', about her 'striving for self-definition'.[32] It has been suggested that '[u]nsteadiness in the narrative voice and the intended audience of the journal marks the apprentice seeking her way, the narrator now engaged in interior monologue, now proceeding diary-like to tell of handkerchiefs purchased and hours of lunch, now addressing an off-stage interlocutor' ('Dog-Eared Travel Book' 151). Again the early dating of the typescript—or at least the cruise that inspired it—may encourage such readings, but they do not appear to withstand close inspection. I suggest *The Cruise of the Vanadis* does not harbour an unsteady narrative voice; on the contrary it offers up and champions another narrative of individualism and independence of spirit. In this at times essayistic, subjective, very modern account nowhere are the individualism and independence more effectively showcased than in Wharton's reaction to the Cathedral of Monreale: 'The interior is, of course, magnificent, but to eyes accustomed to St. Mark's it lacks depth and variety of colour; it seems to me that for this bright climate it is too much lighted. Of course I know that in saying this I am running counter to the opinion of the highest authorities; but this Journal is written not to record other people's opinions, but to note as exactly as possible the impression which I myself received' (*CV* 67). As Wright recognises here, Wharton offers 'no apologies for disagreeing with "authorities"' (*Making of a Connoisseur* 14). The narrative voice states its case and unapologetically holds its ground, unwilling to bow to outside authority. At points the narrative does indeed span interior monologue, diary-like precision, an offstage interlocution—with none of these deemed mutually exclusive. Again, it is one of Wharton's travel narratives that pushes the boundaries, and refuses to conform, in the case of *Vanadis* presenting at times almost as modernist collage effect with those shifts. While important work has addressed the at-times unorthodox modernism of Wharton's fiction in recent years, it is in her travel writing and (as explored in Chap. 6) her critical writing where the author often appears at her most modernist. And on occasion Wharton explicitly draws attention to the artificiality of the whole process and its performance—for example outside Trypiti where a woman appears and parades in holiday dress to cater to the visitors' desire to see 'some of the old costumes on the island' (*CV* 101). *Italian Backgrounds* validates margins and parentheses; *The Cruise of the Vanadis* transports to thresholds between East and West in both its physical and imaginative geography, as Wharton's travel writing, like Lily Bart's stationery seal with its flying ship and motto, journeys in many senses of the word 'Beyond!' And intriguingly in *The Cruise of the Vanadis* there is much *not* to wonder at in the beyond. Almost half a century later, Wharton remembers 'the wonders of the cruise', its 'inexhaustible memories' (*BG* 98), while in its closing paragraphs the 1888 account matter-of-factly states that the cruise 'from first to last, was a success' (*CV* 221). Yet the text of the cruise is also notably marked by the language of let-down: disappointing', 'disappointed', and 'disappointment' used a total of sixteen times through the narrative. On such occasions, the text envisions the decline of Greek civilisation in the very sites of the country's ancient glories, text and traveller here refusing to be seduced by a romantic allure.

Between 1908 and 1920, firmly established as an internationally acclaimed novelist, Wharton published four more travel texts, all with Scribner's: *A Motor-Flight Through France* (1908); *Fighting France: From Dunkerque to Belfort* (1915), and *French Ways and Their Meaning* (1919), both rooted in the First World War and its aftermath; and *In Morocco* (1920), also drawing on a war-time visit to the country. All of the titles were part of a sustained love letter to France that also left a powerful imprint on Wharton's fiction. The works from 1915 on, though still under-read, are the more familiar of the travel texts, if generally consulted to illuminate the author's war work and thinking during the years of the hostilities and immediately beyond. Wharton, as generations of scholars have underscored, was a pragmatic, hard-headed businesswoman, and each of these travel writing titles earned a double pay day, with sections of each volume appearing first in magazines and journals. When it came to travel writing, however, financial returns were markedly low compared to her novels, and travel books were a particularly expensive production, often requiring illustrations. As we have seen with Wharton's poetry, the economic pay-off was rarely the sole consideration, but article and serialisation fees in respect of the travel writing certainly provided a welcome subsidy and additional exposure. Wright records that while 'Scribner's offered an advance of only $2000 for *In Morocco* (1920), which earned about $300 in its first year, the firm paid $15,000 in serial rights' (see *The Making of a Connoisseur* 68). In one of the more unusual sales of the author's work, *French Ways and Their Meaning* was 'ordered to be placed in all ships' libraries by the U.S. Department of the Navy' (Lee 462), Wharton thereby officially demarcated as transatlantic educator and guide.

While *Italian Backgrounds* conveyed a nineteenth-century aesthetic in terms of slow, leisurely travel (though not, I have argued, in the book's content), Wharton's 1908 travel text immediately advertises its modernity with its title, a volume fusing the author's love affair with the country with her love of the motor car. While only three years separate publication, *A Motor-Flight Through France* literally accelerates proceedings into the new century, the tempo of the text defined by the exhilarating allure of mobility and speed. And again, Wharton is ground-breaking in this regard. As Gary Totten reminds us, 'Wharton's effusive description of the car's speed … predates F. T. Marinetti's emphasis on automotive speed in the Futurist Manifesto of 1909 and his later statement in 1916 that "[t]he intoxication of great speeds in cars is nothing but the joy of feeling oneself fused with the only *divinity*."'[33] Wharton's car is in the fast lane, seventeen years ahead of the ultimate American modernist depiction of the automobile—Fitzgerald's *The Great Gatsby* (1925) conveying both the extraordinary glamour and allure of mobility and speed, with an invention that in part makes the Roaring Twenties possible, but always with the technologies of speed threatening to lead to disaster, and a road of fatalities. The car in *A Motor-Flight Through France* brings convenience, luxury, freedom from fixed railway timetables and 'the beaten track', liberation from 'bondage' as it is phrased in the text's opening,[34] echoing a motif of imprisonment that overshadows protagonists of her fiction. At this point in her life and career, Wharton embraced the motor car without reservation—though, as we will see, the car takes her not to the future, but to the past. Contemporary reviews clocked the text's speed, at times tutting disapproval, the *Nation*'s reviewer protesting that 'the motor is waiting, and Mrs. Wharton and her reluctant readers must rush on'; 'Nowhere does she remain for more than the briefest of impressions, and again and again she is whisked past the very places she longs to see. And the reader, most of all, is left lamenting.'[35]

Totten's article, which explores the fascinating dialectic of history and technology in *A Motor-Flight Through France*, determines that 'Wharton's automobile not only shapes her travel experiences and narratives ... but also allows her to imagine new travelling identities available for automobiling women' (Totten 133). He observes that Wharton becomes 'an active and confident motorist in her text', 'disrupting gendered notions about women's incompetent' automobility (Totten 138). Yet the writer of *A Motor-Flight Through France* does not identify as a woman traveller, or present this as a gendered expedition. And invisible through much of this is the chauffeur—in Wharton's case her employee Charles Cook—who undertakes the driving, the passengers merely back seat drivers, even while dictating the direction of travel. The text is defined more by class, than by gender. And unlike *Italian Backgrounds*, which was within genuine reach of an aspirational middle class, the required ownership of or access to an automobile makes the French motor-flight almost exclusively a journey of the most privileged. (Julian Barnes observes in his introduction to the Picador Travel Classics edition of the text that there is 'much textually suppressed domestic support on these motor-flights'[36]). Wharton's homage to the car, her use of the collective '[f]reeing us' from the bondage, having 'given us back the wonder, the adventure and the novelty' of travel, inevitably confines the 'us' to the affluent elite (*MF* 1).

Wharton never indulges in 'vulgar' name dropping to identify her fellow travellers on the journeys she describes in *A Motor-Flight Through France*, but Teddy was a constant, while her brother Harry joined them on the first flight from Boulogne, and Henry James accompanied the couple on their spring 1907 journey taking in Poitiers, the Pyrenees, Provence, the Rhône Valley, and back to Paris. Neither, tellingly, does Wharton reference James' own earlier travel text, *A Little Tour in France*, published as a volume in 1884. *A Motor-Flight Through France* offers no leisurely or meandering introduction; instead the text moves straight into gear with its opening statement: 'The motor-car has restored the romance of travel.' The car takes Wharton to the past, and at the text's opening it is an American past speaking to an American traveller (and reader), conjuring up images of a frontier history, forefathers, 'our posting grandparents' (*MF* 1), a vehicle to 'adventure' (three uses: *MF* 1, 6, 65), and 'novelty' (*MF* 1). Wharton undertakes the reverse journey of the American pioneers, yet, unlike Henry James and his passionate pilgrims, ultimately remains a pioneer, her position and the language of a shared heritage here aligning her to an American readership and traveller.

Correspondence in which Wharton expresses dissatisfaction with and/or alienation from America is often highlighted by scholars, for example the familiar letter to Sally Norton of 5 June 1903, in which she describes herself as feeling 'out of sympathy with everything' in the country of her birth, and its reference to 'wretched exotics' (*Letters* 84–85). It is sometimes forgotten, however, that there are other letters in which Wharton expresses homesickness, while in a letter to Bahlmann in June 1896 she poignantly takes stock: 'Time was, as you know, when I should have been glad to make my home in Europe, but it was made in America, & I have fitted myself into it tant bien que mal, & taken its creases more than I realized until I left it again' (*My Dear Governess* 158–60). Wright observes that by *A Motor-Flight Through France* Wharton 'is an authoritative guide to the country that, as a nation, is in the ascendant in her psyche' (*Making of a Connoisseur* 160), and indeed one of the textual strategies of this volume is to hold up America to France, and find the former wanting. Even so, as that strategy itself attests, Wharton is able to translate the journey for an American readership, those 'creases' making her a qualified guide. In *A Motor-Flight Through France*, once again reading a country is likened to reading a book and it is a book that France, sometimes in a flurry of drive-by impressions, appears to transform from monochrome to colour, 'the passing from a black-and-white page to one illuminated. And every day now would turn a brighter page' (*MF* 73–74). There may be 'countless Frances within France' (*MF* 54), but characteristics that are seen to unite them include appreciation of the past, respect for the land, continuity, 'the long process of social adaptation which has produced so profound and general an intelligence of life' (*MF* 28), a physiognomy that 'if not vividly beautiful, is vividly intelligent' (*MF* 76).

Fighting France: From Dunkerque to Belfort has generally been read both by war and Wharton scholars as propaganda, war writing, reportage (often as an effective illumination of the author's war work), or simply filed under the all-encompassing 'non-fiction'. The form of *Fighting France*, however, with its overlooked full title announcing the journey's point of departure and destination, *From Dunkerque to Belfort*, is that of travel writing, and indeed the opening chapter, 'The Look of Paris', describing a journey motoring north from Poitiers, could almost be the continuing instalment of *A Motor-Flight Through France*. The journey will even revisit a number of the sites of the 1908 text, though this time scarred by the ravages of war. (The later work was originally seen as four individual essays in *Scribner's Magazine* in 1915, with a fifth published in *The*

Saturday Evening Post in November, and a final new essay 'The Tone of France' added to the volume.) In the immediately pre-war opening of *Fighting France*, Wharton includes descriptions of sights travelling north from Poitiers, the cathedral at Chartres, impressions of Paris, the 'great city, so made for peace and art and all humanest graces',[37] with a number of fixed, hallmark sights that would be instantly recognisable to her readers—the Arc de Triomphe, the Champs Elysées, the Eiffel Tower et al.

An air of unreality pervades the text almost from the beginning, however. In *A Backward Glance*, Wharton recalls that 'Everything seemed strange, ominous and unreal, like the yellow glare which precedes a storm. There were moments when I felt as if I had died, and waked up in an unknown world. And so I had. Two days later war was declared' (*BG* 338). Even so, as Olin-Ammentorp observes, Wharton's 'enthusiasm for trips to the front equaled her enthusiasm for travel in times of peace' (34). In a letter to Charles Scribner in June 1915, Wharton described her travels to the front as 'eight days of wonderful adventures' (cited Olin-Ammentorp 34)—and she was far from alone among writers, artists, and soldiers still to see action in expressing excitement and a sense of adventure, notably in the early stages of the war. Just as social connections played a role in securing publication of Edith Jones' poems in the *Atlantic Monthly* at the start of her career, so they facilitated Wharton's trips to the front line and the securing of the necessary travel permits. Even so, this was not some society lady's self-indulgent trip: Wharton's contribution—as with her wider relief work—was totally full-blooded, committed, and engaged. In her preface to *The Book of the Homeless*, Wharton writes with great sensitivity, 'we workers among the refugees are trying, first and foremost, to *help a homesick people*. We are not preparing for their new life an army of voluntary colonists; we are seeking to console for the ruin of their old life a throng of bewildered fugitives'[38]—and Alan Price has argued that '*[n]o other artist* [my italics] did so much to alleviate suffering among the refugees from Belgium and the occupied provinces of northern France.'[39]

In a variation of her earlier pioneer motif, Wharton trailblazes in *Fighting France*, heading as close to the heart of the conflict as she is permitted, with unprecedented opportunities to witness events at the front, conveying supplies in her car to hospital and troops: 'Here we were, then, actually and literally in the first lines!', she exclaims in the text (*FF* 132). In her excellent introduction to the centenary edition, Alice Kelly recognises that 'readings of *Fighting France* frequently dismiss the text as naïve propaganda, criticising her evasive presentation of the war dead through oblique modes or by not mentioning them all.'[40] Wharton skilfully harnesses the tropes of travel writing, notably descriptions of landscape and buildings—in this text often devastated landscape and buildings, rather than devastated bodies—to convey the ravages of destruction and this new world, in a way not dissimilar to the later First World War art of Paul Nash. And, again, harnessing the conventions of a travel text, but adapting them to correlate to a confused, transformed world, *Fighting France* gives way to an increasing sense of disorientation and unreality. As a travel text it provides a persuasive, again modernist metaphor for a world that has descended into unprecedented confusion: Wharton illuminates a journey that begins with defined routes and plans, only for both traveller and reader to become lost, with the signposts literally removed from the roads in a country at war. Signposting and certainties are gone. A decade earlier in *Italian Backgrounds*, that absence presented unprecedented opportunity to stray from the received cultural, tourist map; by 1915 in *Fighting France* it presents a disturbing otherworld.

In concluding *Fighting France*, Wharton eulogises her vision of the French national spirit:

> This, then, is what "France is like." ... All France knows today that real "life" consists in the things that make it worth living, and that these things, for France, depend on the free expression of her national genius. If France perishes as an intellectual light and as a moral force every Frenchman perishes with her; and the only death that Frenchmen fear is not death in the trenches but death by the extinction of their national ideal. (238)

'[W]hat "France is like"' is a topic to which Wharton would return in *French Ways and Their Meaning* (1919), recalling in *A Backward Glance* that she was asked to write it 'after our entry into the war, with the idea of making France and things French more intelligible to the American soldier' (357). The work appeared first in *Hearst's International Cosmopolitan* from October 1918 to June 1919, with material also drawn from *Ladies' Home Journal* and *Scribner's Magazine*, while Olin-Ammentorp identifies the talk Wharton delivered to American soldiers in spring 1918 as 'the seed' for the volume (261). Wharton presents herself as the guide, the explicator of cultures and indeed national identity. 'Reverence', 'Taste', 'Intellectual Honesty', 'Continuity' give their names to four of the chapters, qualities 'singled out, as typically "French" in the best sense of that many-sided term'.[41] In her preface Wharton described it as 'essentially a desultory book, the result of intermittent observation, and often, no doubt, of rash assumption … written in Paris, at odd moments, during the last two years of the war' (*FWTM* v). (It was a line she took with much of her literature during the war, asking André Gide, for example, in a letter of August 1917 to read *Summer* 'with indulgence', as it had been written in 'fits and starts' due to her work with refugees [*Letters* 397]). By the time of writing, however, the author had long been resident in France, was the recipient of the country's highest honour in recognition of her war work, and France had provided the major setting for a number of works of fiction, including *Madame de Treymes* (1907), *The Reef* (1912), and *The Marne* (1918) and a significant setting in *The House of Mirth* and *The Custom of the Country*. Her qualifications for the role of explicator to the American reader appeared secure.

The critical consensus on *French Ways and Their Meaning* suggests a combination of Wharton seen to be condemning America and publicly justifying her decision to make her life in France. In their important volume, *Wretched Exotic: Essays on Edith Wharton in Europe*, Katherine Joslin and Alan Price write that Wharton 'condemned American society at the top of her voice in *French Ways and Their Meaning*', and that the text 'constitute[s] her most open defense of her choice to live in France'.[42] The *New Republic* reviewer called the text 'the apologia pro patria sua', asking 'Can it be possible that America will survive this apologist and France this defender?'[43] The text is read as part of an ongoing 'self-discovery' motif: Shirley Foster argues that in *French Ways and Their Meaning* the author 'not only precludes the possibility of disagreement but establishes for herself a new identity in a new homeland' (144), that the author perhaps saw in France 'a more readily accessible locus for a new and freshly-oriented selfhood' (133), while Wright suggests that Wharton's 'praise is overdone but necessary to justify her expatriation' (*Making of a Connoisseur* 102).

One of the most striking features of *French Ways and Their Meaning*, however, is just how closely Wharton aligns herself with 'Americans' and indeed defines herself as 'American'. Both alignment and identification are insistent and explicit through the text, as 'we', 'us', 'our', 'We Americans': 'We Americans have hitherto been geographically self-contained' (32), 'we Americans deprive ourselves' (29), 'why should we Americans be conservative?' (35), 'the very qualities we have had the least time to acquire' (19), 'we Americans apply ourselves' (9), 'unintelligible to us' (17), 'our Constitution' (34). And once again in her travel writing, Wharton draws on the pioneer motif, conjuring up images of the American frontier: 'We are a new people, a pioneer people, a people destined by fate to break up new continents and experiment in new social conditions' (*FWTM* 18–19), '[t]he stern experience of the pioneer' (*FWTM* 84). There is no doubt that Wharton cherished the country she made her home through the second half of her life. (Her library holds the first four volumes of George Santayana's *The Life of Reason* from 1905, with Wharton writing a single-word annotation next to Santayana's observation, 'In some nations everybody is by nature so astute, versatile, and sympathetic that education hardly makes any difference in manners or mind': 'France' [cited Lee 674–75][44]) The writer was assimilated in France, but remained American in her attitudes, and her persistent alignment with America in her travel writings powerfully dispels the blanket anti-Americanism that critics often see in Wharton. Her close, perhaps closest, French friends, Paul and Minnie Bourget, certainly saw innate Americanness. In her daybook Minnie Bourget complained, for example, of the 'American efficiency' of Wharton's approach to her war work: '[a]n indispensable, well-oiled operation … but the whole thing lacks heart' (cited Lesage 6); she was seen to be too focused on 'the business of charitable works … and the constant calling for the *produced effect*' (cited Lesage 169), Minnie concluding critically '[a]nd what about the causes?' (Lesage 169). Minnie, writes Lesage, 'thought that Edith's assessment of the conflict was just too "impersonal," that she viewed the war as an American in France whose first thought was for the Allies, not for the French' (160). As late as 1924, Paul Bourget recorded in his daybook, 'Our poor little Edith is always agitated. She cannot rest. It's that American activeness operating in a lifestyle that is meant to be one of reverie and leisure. Strange inability to adapt hereditary faculties' (cited Lesage 214).

Related to these questions of Americanness is the lecture 'L'Amérique en guerre', which Wharton gave in French to an audience of approximately 400 in Paris in February 1918, part of a series 'France and Its Allies at War: The Witnesses Speak'. Recovered and translated a century later by Virginia Ricard and published, the lecture can now be seen as a revealing preparatory text for *French Ways and Their Meaning*. In the lecture Wharton shows her knowledge of American history, challenges stereotypes of Americans as rich and brutish, and expresses many positives about the country—her country, 'the great country it is today': 'those who sacrificed everything for their ideas are the ones who shaped the soul of my country most profoundly, more profoundly than those who faced similar dangers for material gain'; 'the settlers ... were innovators where municipal organization was concerned and many a democratic idea that had been smothered by the laws of the mother country prospered rapidly in the soil of the New World'; 'We know it is our duty to fight for the liberty of our Allies because we bought our own at so high a price.'[45]

In an interview about this important, newly discovered lecture, Ricard—when asked whether anything surprised her about it—succinctly observed:

> She seems to me to be more knowledgeable about American history than I would have thought and she clearly has a worldview, has thought about the meaning of the New World and the different forces at work in history and her own place in that history. I was surprised at how clearly she comes out on the side of free public education, religious freedom, freedom of the press, Wilson's League of Nations, what she calls "centripetal forces" and more generally the "boundless ambitions" of the young—read new ideas.[46]

Certainly America falls miserably short in *French Ways and Their Meaning* when held up to France, but Wharton prepares an authoritative, understanding explication for such a thesis in this lecture 'L'Amérique en guerre', which in many ways might also be seen as an answer to Minnie's complaint above, an explanation for why she is the way she is: 'I wanted to describe our origins. I wanted above all to help you understand why our point of view, our ways, and our habits do not always resemble yours. How could it be otherwise? Think that while you were building Versailles, we were cutting down virgin forests ... Between these two pasts, one entirely improvised, the other founded on a long tradition of culture, there is no common measure' ('America at War'). 'We take shortcuts and byways', argues the speaker, 'whereas you tread the paths traced by a long and glorious tradition' ('America at War'). Short-cuts of any variety are anathema to Wharton (a mantra we will see repeated in her literary criticism). She references—and condemns—'short-cuts' and their consequences on five separate occasions in *French Ways and Their Meaning*, notably: 'America, because of her origin, tends to irreverence, impatience, to all sorts of rash and contemptuous short-cuts; France, for the same reason, to routine, precedent, tradition, the beaten path' (32); 'As long as America believes in short-cuts to knowledge, in any possibility of buying taste in tabloids, she will never come into her real inheritance of English culture' (55).

French Ways and Their Meaning draws to a close with a bold, unashamed advocacy of culture, of the rich world of the imagination and its transformative impact:

> as long as enriching life is more than preserving it, as long as culture is superior to business efficiency, as long as poetry and imagination and reverence are higher and more precious elements of civilisation than telephones or plumbing, as long as truth is more bracing than hypocrisy, and wit more wholesome than dulness, so long will France remain greater than any nation that has not her ideals. (149)

Much of *French Ways and Their Meaning* is about a route to being a better American—taking the best of all qualities, appreciating and benefitting from cultural exchange. However much America is seen to be wanting, Wharton continues to ally herself with the United States, and indeed her travel writing, rather than underscoring a new identity, compellingly (re) aligns her with the country of her birth.

Near the close of *French Ways and Their Meaning*, Wharton recalls a moment from her Vanadis cruise decades before, when bad weather forced the yacht to take shelter in a small harbour on the Mainote Coast in a place that was not considered particularly safe (and she then goes on to compare the French spirit to the guidebook's seemingly contradictory description of the Mainotes: 'generous and brave, yet fierce and vindictive' [*FWTM* 147–48]). Wharton's final travel book, *In Morocco*, brings her full circle to largely uncharted territory for the American traveller. Though not published until Autumn 1920 (much of the text serialised the summer before), *In Morocco* was very much embedded in the war years, describing a wartime visit. Its author was part of an official party visiting Morocco for a month between September and October 1917 sent by the French government at the invitation of General Hubert Lyautey, 'Resident-General' of the country. As Wharton takes pains to inform the reader both in the preface to the first edition and the opening paragraph of her study, Morocco is '*a country without a guide-book*'.[47] Once again, the car is a major player—here a 'military motor'—but the romanticism with which Wharton imbues this mode of travel in *A Motor-Flight Through France* is seriously punctured in the later text. As Totten phrases it, '[t]yre punctures and mechanical problems are no longer opportunities for idling and contemplation but annoying inconveniences that threaten the pleasure of the journey', while the author also 'worries that an improved highway system will lead to the despoiling of authentic Moroccan culture by the imminent tourist hordes' (Totten 142).

In the preface to the 1927 edition of *In Morocco*, Wharton returns to the metaphor of previous travel books, 'To visit Morocco is still like turning the pages of some illuminated Persian manuscript all embroidered with bright shapes and subtle lines.'[48] This time, however, it is a text that Wharton partially struggles to decipher. The volume's dedication to the general and his wife, identified here only as 'Madame Lyautey', is revealing (the dedication all in upper case, but with the general in largest font): 'Thanks to whose kindness the journey I had so long dreamed of surpassed what I had dreamed' (*IM* v). A sensation of dreaming and states in-between wake and sleep will be evoked repeatedly in the text: 'in Morocco the dream-feeling envelopes one at every step' (85), 'the boundary between fact and dream perpetually fluctuates' (39), 'an air of dreamlike unreality' (157), 'how can it seem other than a dream?' (157). The author is there by invitation, and *In Morocco* stands almost as an extended thank you letter to her hosts, with the occasional polite criticism. At times the text hovers between mystery, exoticism, enchantment—and a narrative of benign colonialism, that, in Schriber's apt phrase, 'constructs ... the inferiority of Moroccans'[49] and the beneficence of French control. Even her horror at the lives of women in the harem ultimately exudes the air of one of her drawing room scenes, a place of exquisite discomfort, of bored conversation, while the Sultan 'with the air of the business-man who has forgotten to give an order before leaving his office' heads to the telephone (*IM* 181). A similar approach is visible in a short travel essay Wharton wrote in French on Inès Lyautey's considerable charitable endeavours, 'Les Oeuvres de Mme Lyautey au Maroc' published in Autumn 1918 in *France Maroc*, a journal that Frederick Wegener, who first identified the essay, suggests 'served virtually as an official publication of the Protectorate'.[50] Wharton—describing in the essay visits to convalescent soldiers near Salée, to an impressive maternity hospital ('where young Frenchwomen ... come to give birth'), a nursery (where 'small French boys and girls' play) and a local dispensary where 'the Arab women' with sick children wait in gratitude—concludes that 'one must have nearly the same qualities to govern a colony well as to direct a charity well'.[51] Contemporary reviewers largely took *In Morocco* at face value: 'the story of Morocco from the dark backward and abysm of time has run in a recurring cycle', wrote the *Times Literary Supplement* reviewer, without any trace of cynicism.[52] It was left to Irita Van Doren in the *Nation* to observe that '[a]ll the properties of an Arabian Nights tale are here—camels and donkeys, white-draped riders, palmetto deserts, camel's hair tents, and veiled women', while Wharton 'accepts without question the general theory of imperialism'.[53] In her repeated evocation of 'adventure', however, Wharton draws again on the pioneer motif, the travels of *In Morocco* taking her into 'the vast unknown just beyond' (4).

1920 essentially marked the end of Wharton's published travel writings—though there would be many more journeys, and a scattering of unfinished writings in the genre and diary/notebook sketches, including evidence that the author began work on a projected travel book on Spain. It was a country she first visited as part of that six-year European residence as a child, Wharton recalling in *A Backward Glance* 'that the Spanish tour was still considered an arduous adventure, and to attempt it with a young child the merest folly' (31). Concluding that '[p]erhaps, after all, it is not a bad thing to begin one's travels at four', the author looks back at 'a jumble of excited impressions: breaking down on wind-swept sierras; arriving late and hungry at squalid *posadas*; flea-hunting, chocolate-drinking..., being pursued ... by touts, guides, deformed beggars, and all sorts of jabbering and confusing people; and, through the chaos and fatigue, a fantastic vision of the columns of Cordova, the tower of the Giralda ... and everywhere shadowy aisles undulating with incense and processions' (*BG* 31–32). As an adult, Wharton would resume her travels to Spain in the years prior to the First World War, referencing a trip with Rosa de Fitz-James and Jean du Breuil in the chapter 'Widening Waters' of *A Backward Glance*, and 'two more Spanish journeys' with the observation, 'Before the war motoring in Spain was still something of an adventure; the roads were notoriously bad, motor-maps were few and unreliable, the village inns dubious' (*BG* 330–31). In addition, Teresa Gómez Reus calculates that Wharton made at least five visits to Spain between May 1925 and April 1930, while also planning another journey with Berry in 1927, which would have to be cancelled due to his failing health. 'No other country would she tour with the same perseverance during these five years', concludes Gómez Reus.[54] Even so, the unpublished writing that may have been intended as part of a travel book on Spain is comparatively slight: four typescript pages of 'A Motor-Flight through Spain' in the Beinecke Library, with obvious echoes of the earlier work on France, along with a few manuscript pages of 'Back to Compostela'. In addition, Wharton kept a diary of her final Spanish trip with Walter Berry in 1925, now housed in the Lilly Library, University of Indiana, and facsimiles of the latter two texts have been valuably reproduced and made readily accessible by Patricia Fra López in her *Edith Wharton Back to Compostela*, published in 2011.[55]

In part Wharton's travels in Spain were coloured by nostalgia ('Spain was enriched for me by a rush of juvenile memories' she wrote in *A Backward Glance* [330]) and later by sentiment, returning after Walter Berry's death to places previously toured with 'the Love of all my life' as she called him in 'Quaderno dello Studente' ('QS' 213). Once again, however, Wharton—having reached her sixties and not always in the best of health—was a trailblazing figure. The journeys she made (in 1925 and 1928) to Santiago, Marta González observes, come from a time 'when there are very few references to the participation of public figures, more scarce even when we talk about women on the Way of St. James' ('Preface', in Fra López, *Edith Wharton Back to Compostela* 14). Ever eager to 'go to more out-of-the-way places' (*BG* 331) in Spain, Wharton's travels involved a number of long and strenuous journeys—by car, train, even mule, or horse when roads proved impassable by car. These relatively late journeys were also a return to adventure: 'Santiago de Compostela will always seem to be at the end of the western world', '[p]art of its magic lies in this remoteness', writes Wharton, the travellers missing several of 'the most interesting' monuments on their list 'because they were not to be found on any map, and the authors who sang their praises forgot to say if they & how & whence they were to could be reached and how—whether by motor, or on horse-back, or by a long difficult scramble on foot' (*Edith Wharton Back to Compostela* 153, 161–62). Many of Wharton's private writings in the last decade or so of her life portray an air of wonder: from the exclamations in 'Quaderno dello Studente' ('Love & Beauty have poured such glowing cups for me' ['QS' 215]) to the 'unimaginable beauty' of a 'memorable land' in her 1926 notebook recording the Osprey cruise, sentiments at times absent from the earlier Vanadis trip.[56] The 'Spain Diary', meanwhile, offers an itemised, staccato response of elation and disappointment, albeit very much weighted towards the former: 'Incomparable', 'Very beautiful', 'exquisitely decorated', 'remarkable', 'extraordinary', 'splendid', 'Divine', offset against 'very disappointing' (Oviedo's cathedral and cloisters), 'too vile' (hotel), 'too filthy' (Comercio), 'What riches—again in a dung-hill!' ('Last Spanish journey' in *Edith Wharton Back to Compostela* 75, 73, 71, 70, 81, 95, 101). And the diary underscores Wharton's omnipresent 'curiosity', a leitmotif for many of her published travel texts ('very curious' [church at Santa Cruz], 'curious little

Romanesque ch.', 'Curious great supporting buttresses', 'very curious effect' ['Last Spanish journey' 67, 88, 92]). Gómez Reus concludes that for Wharton 'Spain was a mystifying text, abounding in art and architecture, but in its composition so disjointed and inarticulate that it ended up being too incompatible with the structures of her literary imagination' ('Remember Spain!' 191). Whether Wharton's curiosity translated to understanding in her travels to Spain, there is ultimately insufficient, developed text categorically to judge. Either way, Spain would not become part of her published travel record.

Wright lists multiple theories for what she sees as 'Wharton's decision to focus on fiction rather than travel writing during the 17 years between 1920 and 1937': 'the question of financial return' (citing 'the more lucrative field of fiction'), 'time constraints, marketing forces, an immersion in Europe that ultimately proved enervating to her travel writing, and the taxing nature of travel writing itself', 'doubt about the reception her works of travel would find in postwar America', and inability to view European countries with a fresh eye 'after a decade as a permanent resident of France and frequent traveller throughout Europe' (*Making of a Connoisseur* 69–70). The fact, however, that these unfinished writings, with possibilities of development for publication, even exist in the archive, suggests that Wharton did not make an outright, determined decision to cease publishing in the field after 1920. And while the twenties saw the start of Wharton's highest financial returns, money as we see repeatedly, was a guiding, but not the sole motivator for this writer. Neither did Wharton solely 'focus on fiction': the generic range of her publications continued well beyond 1920, spanning life writings, critical writings, poetry, novels et al. Certainly the author was still embarking on the strenuous journeys that had always been essential to her research for travel writings—and Spain as a lesser-known destination for her readers avoided a potential scenario of familiarity breeding contempt. While critics often still focus on Wharton 'looking back' in her writing after the war—the memoir *A Backward Glance*, the New York of her parents' generation in *The Age of Innocence*, a return to the past in her final, unfinished novel, *The Buccaneers*—much more of her work from this period is in fact concerned with the 'now': Wharton addressing, for example, the 1920s, the jazz age, modernism, the current state of fiction in *Twilight Sleep* (1927), *The Writing of Fiction* (1925), the 'state of the novel' address in the Vance Weston novels as the burgeoning writer experiments with form. Perhaps the most persuasive theory is the most prosaic: Wharton simply ran out of time and found that she had said what she wanted to say about the countries outside America in which she was most fluent, especially Italy and France. We cannot know for sure.

What *is* certain, however, is a notable, very substantial, and at times still under-appreciated body of travel writing, which offers its readers less familiar aspects on, as well as a number of new insights into Wharton's career. Her travel writing is not the tired cliché of her journey of personal 'self-discovery'. Instead it opens up pathways, encouraging her readers not simply to follow lesser-known tracks, but to forge their own, advocating an empowering venture into the unknown. Wharton's work in this genre notably values parentheses, margins, different ways of looking and reading, with the boldness of her achievements in this field at times belittled and partially obscured by lingering biographical myths. Wharton's travel writing as a body of work offers up a life-affirming, glorious paean to culture, validating knowledge, a rich, full, civilised life, and denying shortcuts. Wharton did not promote herself as a woman traveller, but she was a trailblazer nevertheless: a woman in a man's world at times, at others a traveller in a country without a guide book. Travel writing afforded her an unapologetic voice of authority, intellect, and knowledge—though on occasion qualified by restraints of the time, as seen with the male professorial validation of her terracotta attribution in *Italian Backgrounds*. Wharton was brave in her travel writing, for example in an explicit call to 'Deconventionalize', at times boldly modernist, and she refused in her affirmation of culture to dumb down. Rather than her travel writing suggesting that Wharton established a new identity in a new homeland, this genre presents the writer (in Europe) at her most American: she is often the pioneer, prioritising individualism and adventure. The alignment and identification as an American are often insistent and explicit. Wharton cannot always fully read it (as per Morocco) but her travel writing at its best invites the reader to journey in all senses of the word 'beyond'.

Notes

1. Undated letter from Margaret Ayer Barnes to Edward Sheldon, cited in Eric Barnes, *The Man Who Lived Twice: The Biography of Edward Sheldon* (New York: Scribner's, 1956), 154–55.
2. Edith Wharton, *Ethan Frome* (New York: Charles Scribner's Sons, 1911), 76.
3. See letter from Wharton to Sally Norton, 3 June 1901. Beinecke, Box 29.

4. Wharton, 'Talk to American Soldiers', reprinted in Olin-Ammentorp, 261–72.
5. *Fast and Loose*, the novella Wharton wrote in the guise of David Olivieri when she was fourteen, also has scenes set in Italy, where Guy Hastings works as an artist and tries (and fails) to mend his broken heart.
6. Sirpa Salenius, 'Introduction: Women in the Garden of Italy', in Salenius (ed.), *American Authors Reinventing Italy: The Writings of Exceptional Nineteenth-Century Women* (Il Prato, 2009), 5. Subsequent references to Salenius' introduction are included in the text.
7. Virginia Ricard, 'Legendary Spell: Edith Wharton's Italy', in Salenius (ed.), *American Authors Reinventing Italy*, 72. Subsequent references to Ricard's essay are included in the text.
8. Wharton also cited illustrations as a reason for the delay. See her letter to Frederick Macmillan dated 23 February 1905, in Shafquat Towheed (ed.), *The Correspondence of Edith Wharton and Macmillan, 1901–1930* (Basingstoke: Palgrave Macmillan, 2007), 84–85. Subsequent references to this work are included in the text.
9. Letter from Brownell to Wharton, 24 August 1903; letter from Wharton to Edward Burlinghame, 31 September 1903, both cited in Lee 92.
10. 'Italian Backgrounds', *Spectator*, 95 (30 September 1905), 470–71, reprinted in *Edith Wharton: The Contemporary Reviews*, 106.
11. Edith Wharton, *Italian Backgrounds* (New York: Charles Scribner's Sons, 1905), 13. Subsequent references to this work are included in the text (*IB*).
12. 'Italy Again', cited by Mary Suzanne Schriber, 'Edith Wharton and the Dog-Eared Travel Book', in Katherine Joslin and Alan Price (eds.), *Wretched Exotic: Essays on Edith Wharton in Europe* (New York: Peter Lang, 1993), 148. Subsequent references to this work are included in the text. Lee dates the writing of the fragment to October 1934 (737).
13. 'Pictures from Italy', *Times Literary Supplement*, 7 July 1905, 215, reprinted in *Edith Wharton: The Contemporary Reviews*, 99.
14. The bulk of the surviving materials for 'Disintegration' appear to have been written in 1902, but the narrative was imagined before Wharton wrote *The Valley of Decision*, and Wharton may have continued the writing of 'Disintegration' beyond 1902. For a discussion of the timings, see *The Unpublished Writings of Edith Wharton*, Vol. 2, 65–66; 65–118.
15. See Salenius 5–19, and Debra Bernardi '"Sublimest Heaven" and "Corruptest Earth": Sexuality in Margaret Fuller's Italian Writings', in *American Authors Reinventing Italy*, 21–38.
16. Sarah Bird Wright (ed.), *Edith Wharton Abroad: Selected Travel Writings, 1888–1920* (London: Robert Hale, 1995), 10, n.3. Subsequent references to this work are included in the text.

17. Mary Cadwalader Jones, *European Travel for Women: Notes and Suggestions* (New York: Macmillan, 1900), 231.
18. Edith Wharton, *The Cruise of the Vanadis* (New York: Rizzoli, 2004), 173–74. Subsequent references to this work are included in the text (*CV*).
19. For an excellent summary of modern art historians' views, see Eleanor Dwight, *Edith Wharton: An Extraordinary Life* (New York: Harry N. Abrams, 1994). Dwight records: 'Wharton had the last laugh...and her opinion has been confirmed by modern scholars' (73), then notes, in a more complex summation: 'After Wharton's essay appeared in 1895, scholars gradually came to agree that these figures popularly attributed to Giovanni Gonelli had been made earlier....Modern scholars feel that many different artists participated in creating the figures, but that three groups, *Lo Spasimo*, *L'Ascensione*, and *La Maddalena ai Piedi*, three of the five Wharton had singled out, are similar to the known style of Giovanni della Robbia' (284). Subsequent references are included in the text.
20. Robin Peel, 'Wharton and Italy', in Rattray (ed.), *Edith Wharton in Context* (New York: Cambridge University Press, 2012), 285–92; 287.
21. Maureen E. Montgomery, 'Possessing Italy: Wharton and American Tourists', in Meredith L. Goldsmith and Emily J. Orlando (eds.), *Edith Wharton and Cosmopolitanism* (Gainesville, FL: University Press of Florida, 2016), 110–31; 123. Subsequent references to this work are included in the text.
22. Maureen E. St. Laurent, 'Pathways to a Personal Aesthetic: Edith Wharton's Travels in Italy and France', in *Wretched Exotic*, 165–79; 167–68, 169.
23. Edith Wharton, 'Maurice Hewlett's *The Fool Errant*', *The Bookman: A Literary Journal*, XXII (September 1905), 64–67; 65: Subsequent references to this work are included in the text. https://babel.hathitrust.org/cgi/pt?id=njp.32101077276960&view=1up&seq=80.
24. '*Italian Backgrounds*', *Nation*, 80 (22 June 1905), 508, and '*Italian Backgrounds*', *Spectator*, reprinted in *Edith Wharton: The Contemporary Reviews*, 98; 105.
25. Edith Wharton, *The Buccaneers* (New York: D. Appleton-Century Company, 1938), 249. Subsequent references to this work are included in the text (*B*).
26. For a discussion of the imaginative constructions of Greece in Wharton's work, see Myrto Drizou, 'Edith Wharton's Odyssey', in Jennifer Haytock and Laura Rattray (eds), *The New Edith Wharton Studies* (New York: Cambridge University Press, 2019), 65–79.
27. In her 2018 book, Lesage speculates that it was around the time of the auctions of the contents of Wharton's home, Sainte-Claire, in Hyères, in November 1941, that Mélanie Garcin, a secretary at the law offices of

Maître Boissonnet, to whom Royall Tyler had granted the authority to settle the remainder of Wharton's estate, gave the typescript of *The Cruise of the Vanadis* to the Hyères city librarian. See Claudine Lesage, *Edith Wharton in France* (Prospecta Press, 2018), 247. Subsequent references to this work are included in the text.

28. In her 1936 memoir, *Autumn in the Valley*, Daisy Chanler (publishing as 'Mrs. Winthrop Chanler') devotes chapter eight ('Aegean Cruise') to an account of the Osprey journey, quoting extensively from the diary she kept during those travels: 'It was like being shown a rainbow bridge to the land of dreams', she recalls (*Autumn in the Valley* [Boston, Little, Brown, and Company, 1936], 209). In a point-scoring chapter ('The Expatriates') of his reminiscences *Unforgotten Years*, which he begins while on the *Osprey*, but published after Wharton's death, Logan Pearsall Smith writes about Wharton and the cruise on which he was her guest, finding fault with his hostess, and patronising the cruise veteran with his advice. Appearing to mask misogyny as detached affection at several points in the chapter, Smith writes: 'To see this stately lady, conscious from birth of her dignity and position, and a little over-anxious, in my opinion, to assert them, placed in a position from which all dignity was absent, was a hardship which I was capable of bearing. A slight touch of friendly malice and amusement towards those we love keeps our affection for them, I find, from becoming flat' (*Unforgotten Years* [London: Constable, 1938], 247–48).
29. Notably, Wharton learns of the bequest from her father's cousin that will pay for the cruise only towards the end of the voyage; they embark on the cruise without financial guarantees (*BG* 100).
30. See Ramsden, 58. *The Odyssey* was also taken on the *Osprey* cruise. See Chanler, 211.
31. See *Edith Wharton Abroad*, 16; *Making of a Connoisseur*, 14, 160; 'Dog-Eared Travel Book', 150, 151.
32. See Mary Suzanne Schriber, 'Edith Wharton and Travel Writing as Self-Discovery', *American Literature*, 59:2 (May 1987), 257–67, and Shirley Foster, 'Making It Her Own', in Joslin and Price (eds.), *Wretched Exotic: Essays on Edith Wharton in Europe*, 129–45. Under that title of 'Edith Wharton and Travel Writing as Self-Discovery', Schriber suggests, 'When submitted to the art of composition, a number of journeys and a melange of esthetic, cultural, and geographical exploits became an act of self-discovery in which Wharton identified the intensity of her engagement with Europe and the degree to which Europe stimulated, excited, and energized her' (260), and 'Having set out first on physical journeys and then on imaginative reconstructions of them, Wharton recognized in the narrative version of herself a woman who had undertaken a spiritual quest and had found her most authentic self' (267). Subsequent references to these works are included in the text.

33. Gary Totten, 'The Dialectic of History and Technology in Edith Wharton's *A Motor-Flight through France*', *Studies in Travel Writing*, 17:2 (2013), 133–44; 133–34. Subsequent references to this work are included in the text.
34. Edith Wharton, *A Motor-Flight Through France* (New York: Charles Scribner's Sons, 1908), 1. Subsequent references to this edition are included in the text (*MF*).
35. '*A Motor-Flight Through France*', *Nation*, 87 (12 November 1908), 469, reprinted in *Edith Wharton: The Contemporary Reviews*, 163–64.
36. Julian Barnes, 'Introduction', *A Motor-Flight through France* by Edith Wharton (New York: Picador, 1995), 4.
37. Edith Wharton, *Fighting France: From Dunkerque to Belfort* (New York: Charles Scribner's Sons, 1915), 6. Subsequent references to this work are included in the text (*FF*).
38. Edith Wharton (ed.), *The Book of the Homeless (Le Livre des Sans Foyer)* (New York: Charles Scribner's Sons, 1916), xx.
39. Alan Price, 'Wharton Mobilizes Artists to Aid the War Homeless', in Joslin and Price (eds.), *Wretched Exotic*, 219–40; 219.
40. Alice Kelly, 'Introduction: Wharton in Wartime', in Kelly (ed.), *Edith Wharton Fighting France: From Dunkerque to Belfort* (Edinburgh University Press, 2015), 1–48; 21.
41. Edith Wharton, *French Ways and Their Meaning* (New York: D. Appleton & Co., 1919), 18. Subsequent references to this work are included in the text (*FWTM*).
42. Katherine Joslin and Alan Price, 'Introduction', in Joslin and Price (eds.), *Wretched Exotic: Essays on Edith Wharton in Europe*. 1–16; 12, 10. Subsequent references to this work are included in the text.
43. '*French Ways and Their Meaning*', *New Republic*, 20 (24 September 1919), 241, reprinted in *Edith Wharton: The Contemporary Reviews*, 273.
44. Ramsden records in his catalogue that Wharton's library holds four of the five volumes (lacking *Reason in Science*, 1906), each signed Edith Wharton, with markings throughout the first three volumes (109).
45. Edith Wharton, 'America at War', trans. Virginia Ricard, *Times Literary Supplement*, 16 February 2018, 3–5: https://www.the-tls.co.uk/articles/public/america-at-war-wharton/.
46. 'Interview with Virginia Ricard, translator of newly discovered Edith Wharton lecture "France and its Allies at War"', 20 February 2018: https://whartoncompleteworks.org/2018/02/20/interview-with-virginia-ricard-translator-of-newly-discovered-edith-wharton-lecture-france-and-its-allies-at-war/.
47. Edith Wharton, *In Morocco* (New York: Charles Scribner's Sons, 1920), vii, 3. Subsequent references to this edition are included in the text (*IM*).

48. Wharton, 'Preface', *In Morocco* (London: Century Publishing, 1984), 16.
49. Mary Suzanne Schriber, *Writing Home: American Women Abroad, 1830–1920* (Charlottesville: University Press of Virginia, 1997), 77, cited by Gary Totten, in 'Afterword: Edith Wharton and the Promise of Cosmopolitanism' in Goldsmith and Orlando (eds.), *Edith Wharton and Cosmopolitanism*, 256.
50. Frederick Wegener, 'Edith Wharton on French Colonial Charities for Women: An Unknown Travel Essay', *Tulsa Studies in Women's Literature*, 17:1 (Spring 1998), 11–21; 13.
51. Edith Wharton, 'Madame Lyautey's Charitable Works in Morocco' (translation: Louise M. Wills), *Tulsa Studies in Women's Literature*, 17:1 (Spring 1998), 29–36; 30, 31–32, 33.
52. '*In Morocco*', *Times Literary Supplement*, 7 October 1920, 649, reprinted in *Edith Wharton: The Contemporary Reviews*, 299.
53. Irita Van Doren, 'A Country Without a Guidebook', *Nation*, 111 (27 October 1920), 479–80, in *Edith Wharton: The Contemporary Reviews*, 300–1.
54. Teresa Gómez Reus, '"Remember Spain!" Edith Wharton and the Book She Never Wrote', *English Studies*, 98:2 (2017), 175–93; 180. Subsequent references to this work are included in the text.
55. See Patricia Fra López, *Edith Wharton Back to Compostela* (Universidade de Santiago de Compostela, 2011). Fra López states that Wharton began writing 'Back to Compostela' approximately five years after the 'Spain Diary', in 1930 (24). Subsequent references to this work are included in the text.
56. 'Osprey' Notes and Accounts (Yacht) [1926], Beinecke. With thanks to Myrto Drizou. In a letter to Vernon Lee on 28 February 1926, Wharton wrote: 'The B. Bs [Berensons] have probably told you that I am off next month with three or four friends on a cruise to Crete, Cyprus & the Aegean. It's an old dream—a hunger nearer—stilled since I cruised in the Aegean over 30 years ago, & vowed to do it again, some day, somehow.' Vernon Lee Papers, Special Collections, Somerville College, University of Oxford, courtesy of the Principal and Fellows of Somerville College, Oxford.

CHAPTER 5

Architecture and Design

> We must teach our children to care for beauty before great monuments and noble buildings arise.... If with your aid we can prove to the fathers and mothers that in surrounding the children with beauty we are also protecting them from ugliness—the ugliness of indifference, the ugliness of disorder, the ugliness of evil; having done this our cause is gained.[1]

In an exuberant, now little-read parody of Laurence Housman's (anonymously published) *An Englishwoman's Love-Letters*, Wharton's female protagonist writes to her 'Belovèd':

> One can see that your mother has not had many artistic advantages; the drawing-room curtains are *too awful*; and sooner or later that bed of red geraniums by the front door will *have to go*. I made no allusion to the curtains beyond saying that I could not live in a room with aniline colours; for your sake, Darling, I was patient and forbearing....[2]

Four years later, Lily Bart would volunteer a similar sentiment with her observation, 'If I could only do over my aunt's drawing-room I know I should be a better woman' (*HM* 10). Taste, proportion, harmony, simplicity, fitness would become watchwords of Wharton's architectural and design digest. Edmund Wilson suggests that the author's earliest fiction 'had somewhat the character of expensive upholstery', while 'in her novels she adopts the practice of inventorying the contents of her characters' homes', Wharton proving 'not only one of the great pioneers, but also the poet, of interior decoration' who 'piles up the new luxury of the era to an altitude of ironic grandeur' ('Justice' 19, 22, 23). Excess, showiness, ostentation, vulgarity mark and mar new-age imposters, not least the 'heavy gilt armchairs', 'florid carpet', 'salmon-pink damask' and 'highly varnished mahogany' of 'the Looey suites' of the Hotel Stentorian which house the Spragg family at the opening of *The Custom of the Country* (4). Harmony, understatement, individual but well-informed taste, on the other hand, are indicators of esteem—a philosophy that, in opposition to Wilson's perceived inventory, often underscores Wharton's minimalism in terms of writing and design. Ugliness for this author is invidious and far-reaching, leaving mental as well as physical scars. In *A Backward Glance* she identifies '[o]ne of the most depressing impressions' of her childhood as 'the intolerable ugliness of New York, of its untended streets and the narrow houses so lacking in external dignity, so crammed with smug and suffocating upholstery' (54–55). Wharton does not pull her punches. New York is remembered as a city 'cursed with its universal chocolate-coloured coating of the most hideous stone ever quarried, this cramped horizontal gridiron of a town ... hide-bound in its deadly uniformity of mean ugliness' (*BG* 55). In an early, reported speech to teachers of Newport public schools on 'Schoolroom Decoration', Wharton eloquently advocates for beauty: 'to put some beauty into the bare rooms of Newport is not only a good thing but a necessary thing, and necessary not only on artistic grounds but on moral grounds as well'; 'let us for ourselves and our children refuse anything less than the best' ('Mrs. Wharton Addresses the Teachers').

Wharton's first professional book publication was her 1897 design collaboration with Ogden Codman Jr., *The Decoration of Houses*. Described in *A Backward Glance* as the 'clever young Boston architect', Codman worked on a number of the Whartons' homes: their property in Newport, Land's End, from 1893, their Park Avenue house in New York, and later on the interior design of The Mount. Before embarking on *The Decoration of Houses*, Codman 'had greatly enhanced his reputation in 1895 by decorating ten bedrooms at "The Breakers"', Cornelius Vanderbilt's Newport estate.[3] Of the Land's End project, Wharton recalled 'we asked him to alter and decorate the house—a somewhat new departure, since the architects of that day looked down on house-decoration as a branch of dressmaking, and left the field to the upholsterers, who crammed every room with curtains, lambrequins, jardinières of artificial plants, wobbly velvet-covered tables littered with silver gewgaws, and festoons of lace and dressing tables' (*BG* 106–07). Finding a shared vision of interior decoration as 'simple and architectural' with a dislike of 'sumptuary excesses' (though Codman's other rich clients might take a different line), Wharton recalls in *A Backward Glance* that they 'drifted … toward the notion' of putting their views into a book (107).

At the end of the nineteenth century and beginning of the twentieth century, much of Wharton's professional work was rooted in collaboration—*The Decoration of Houses* achieving greater success and recognition than a number of the collaborative ventures for the stage, discussed in Chap. 3. Though Codman and Wharton would later give different accounts of their respective contributions to the project, Richard Guy Wilson's research of their surviving correspondence in his incisive essay 'Edith and Ogden: Writing, Decoration, and Architecture' indicates (along with 'the unalphabetical arrangement of the authors' names' on the published volume, suggests Wilson) that Wharton 'not only wrote most of the book, but also contributed many of the ideas'.[4] She certainly had the knowledge, as a largely self-taught authority on design, with expertise acquired through extensive reading, research, and travels in Europe, her friendships with figures such as Egerton Winthrop and Vernon Lee, and a fascination particularly with Italian architecture. (In *A Backward Glance*, Wharton would recall that after *The Valley of Decision* she was still better known for her understanding of Italian seventeenth and eighteenth-century architecture than as a novelist [129]). Wharton's frustrations at times with Codman's lack of productivity in the collaboration are clearly expressed in the correspondence, as evidenced in a letter of June 1897: 'Anytime in the last three months you could have made the whole bibliography in your office in an hour—I suppose now that will have to be left out too. I regret very much that I undertook the book. I certainly should not have done so if I had not understood that you were willing to do half…I hate to put my name to anything so badly turned out' (cited Wilson 152). Wilson detects in the letter 'a peevish tone' (152), but the author's charges—if true—were a perfectly legitimate cause for complaint, and an early indication of Wharton's driven, professional perfectionism. A *Scribner's Magazine* advertisement running in *Vogue* in September 1897 listed the volume as 'In Press', (with the title, 'House Decoration'), and with Codman's name first ('By Ogden Codman, Jr., and Edith Wharton').[5] On publication, however, that order had been reversed.

Annette Benert, Ailsa Boyd, Eleanor Dwight, Judith Fryer, Cecilia Macheski, Maureen E. Montgomery, Emily Orlando, Gary Totten, and Lisa Tyler are among those who have offered rewarding examinations of Wharton's fiction in the context of her interests in architecture and design.[6] Elsewhere *The Decoration of Houses* often remains overlooked by Wharton's literary scholars, perceived as an anomaly in the author's extensive back catalogue—though it is a volume that made, and continues to make, a significant impression in its field. 'It became the fashion to use our volume as a touchstone of taste' recalls Wharton in *A Backward Glance* (110). In his 2018 *Classical Principles for Modern Design*, 'practicing decorator' Thomas Jayne suggests, 'It's not an overstatement to say that it is the most important decorating book ever written ... *The Decoration of Houses* is like scripture: it is sometimes called the Bible of interior decoration.'[7] '[A] good case can be made for arguing that interior decoration as we know it to-day started with Edith Wharton, who in collaboration with Ogden Codman wrote *The Decoration of Houses*' opens *English Decoration in the Eighteenth Century* by John Fowler and John Cornforth (cited Coles 256). Pauline C. Metcalf calls it 'a book that has been, since its publication in 1897, the classic primer for traditional interior decoration',[8] while architectural historian Wilson deems *The Decoration of Houses* 'pathbreaking' (133), helping to 'change taste in decoration on both sides of the Atlantic' (158). 'For years', writes Wilson, 'the book was the bible of classical decoration, and it exercised a substantial influence on succeeding books' (158)—among them *The House in Good Taste* (1913) by Elsie de Wolfe, the actress cast in Wharton's *The Shadow of a Doubt* in 1901, who subsequently reinvented herself as a founding figure of interior design.

In reality, *The Decoration of Houses* was less innovative per se, than beautifully timed. The writer who would expertly convey a society in transition through her fiction brilliantly captured and presented before the reading public, with her co-author, a transformative period of design that was already underway. 'This book has come at an opportune moment', recognised muralist Edwin H. Blashfield, reviewing the volume for *Book Buyer* in March 1898.[9] Indeed Wharton and Codman freely acknowledge and welcome in their opening chapter 'the steady advance in taste and knowledge to which the most recent architecture in America bears witness'.[10] In a foreshadowing of a strategy employed in other genres, most notably her travel writing, America is held up to France and found wanting, while the writers explicitly identify themselves as American in their opening line: 'The last ten years have been marked by a notable development in architecture and decoration, and while France will long retain her present superiority in these arts, our own advance is perhaps more significant than that of any other country' (*DH* 1). 1893 was a spectacular, headline year for American architecture, with the World's Columbian Exposition in Chicago. Its 'gleaming "White City"', writes Macheski, 'advocat[ed] a renaissance of architecture and city planning based on the training of the Ecole des Beaux-Arts in Paris'—participating architects and artists having 'trained largely in Paris, as the United States had no school of architecture' (189). '[M]onumental classical planning, architectural composition, and decorative painting and sculpture were introduced to America on a vast and heroic scale', with newspapers and magazines 'full of stories about the fair and the artistic Renaissance which it heralded for America' (Coles 258). While there is no record of Wharton attending the Exposition, she would certainly have been aware of it and have read about it, and not only as her friend Paul Bourget was one of many visitors reporting on the event.

Wharton and Codman offered readers a number of similar themes and inspirations in *The Decoration of Houses*, but a different focus, with their interests applied not to huge public monuments but to the private home. Not for the last time, Wharton would validate and prioritise the domestic space. In his review, Blashfield (whose own work featured at the Exposition) immediately recognised the connection to the wider movement, but also the distinction in application: 'Societies have been formed in behalf of the allied arts as applied to the treatment of great public monuments. Mrs. Wharton and Mr. Codman have in turn stepped forward as the protagonists of harmony in the treatment of that lesser but perhaps even more important monument, the private house' (5). A number of reviewers suggested that the volume's handsome illustrations of French, Italian, and English interiors of 'just such magnificent places' gave the reader 'a false idea'[11] of its contents—an objection anticipated by the writers with a (not entirely persuasive) explanation for 'the seeming lack of accord': 'This has been done in order that only such apartments as are accessible to the traveller might be given as examples' (*DH* xxii). Reviewers on the whole, however, were highly responsive to the book's theses. A majority of reviews did not name in the body of the text Wharton or Codman, both publishing their first (professional) volume: the focus instead was on the arguments the work presented. It was a luxury Wharton was not often afforded in her career: fast forward two years and reviews of her first collection of stories, *The Greater Inclination*, would swiftly draw comparisons to Henry

James, while decades later reviewers cast her as the old-time grande dame, with its accompanying weight of responsibilities. The reception of *The Decoration of Houses*, by contrast, was a rare pre-expectation, pre-reputation moment for the writer.

Though Wharton would never present herself in these terms, she was again proving a trailblazer as one of the few women making a mark in the field. Not for her the extraordinary, but separatist 'Women's Pavilion' of the Chicago Exposition; Wharton inhabited her space on her own terms. Helena Chance suggests 'Wharton was a reformer, not an innovator in interior design in the early twentieth century, but she was significant in being one of the few women in Europe and the United States to have a substantial impact on taste.'[12] Crucially, Wharton and Codman were presenting their vision of interior design as a *profession*. In Chap. 6, male reviewers will be seen in full condescension mode almost thirty years later in response to *The Writing of Fiction*, but late nineteenth-century reviews of *The Decoration of Houses* did not noticeably patronise Wharton as a woman—perhaps of course because here she was paired with a man—though we will observe a different critical response to the male/female professional pairing in *Italian Villas and Their Gardens*. (The *Advertiser* reviewer of *The Decoration of Houses* did, nevertheless, fall back on gendered stereotypes with the observation, 'Many details are discussed which would not have been included if there had been but one author, or two authors of one sex' [review cited in Wilson 158]). As Lisa Tyler recognises, Wharton must have been 'aware of the gender implications', captured in her observation cited above about architects looking down on house decoration 'as a branch of dressmaking'. Tyler cites modern design historian Lucinda Havenhand: 'Interior design is perceived as feminine, superficial, and mimetic as opposed to a male, rational, and original architecture. Although the subtext is not said out loud, it is still clear: interior design is inferior to architecture.'[13] In *The Decoration of Houses*, the authors' insistence that 'All good architecture and good decoration (which it must never be forgotten *is only interior architecture*) must be based on rhythm and logic' brilliantly 'collapses the (historically gendered) distinction between interior decoration and architecture' (Tyler 154).

One of the most expansive reviews of *The Decoration of Houses* was for the *Bookman* and by none other than Walter Berry, whom Wharton credited with extensive 'modelling' work on the volume (*BG* 108)—a fact he neglected to mention in a review that combined précis, praise and primer for how to read the 1897 text. Repeating the authors' claim that '[n]o study of *house-decoration as a branch of architecture* has for at least fifty years been published in England or America' (*DH* xx), Berry deemed the volume 'a work of large insight and appreciation, one that is certain to exert lasting influence in the revival of a subject generally misunderstood and mistreated'.[14] *The Decoration of Houses* is a deeply knowledgeable, well-researched text; an extensive list of French, English, German, and Italian 'Books Consulted' dating back to the seventeenth century placed before the introduction immediately advertises the volume's credentials (subsequently masked by the relegation of the list to the end of the text in the modern reissue by Norton.) Wharton also made use of her social contacts, having asked leading American Renaissance architect Charles McKim to read the manuscript draft, on which he had reported favourably. *The Decoration of Houses* proves authoritative, at times didactic, but also—as we will similarly see in *The Writing of Fiction*, discussed in Chap. 6—in large part a pragmatic, engaged handbook.

Wharton and Codman lay out their thesis directly in the opening pages. Rooms may be decorated 'by a superficial application of ornament totally independent of structure, or by means of those architectural features which are part of the organism of every house, inside as well as out' (*DH* xix). Though the 'architectural treatment' (*DH* xix) held its own until the second quarter of the nineteenth century, since then 'various influences have combined to *sever* the natural connection between the outside of the modern house and its interior' (*DH* xix, my emphasis). House-decoration, to the authors' regret, has ceased to be a branch of architecture. '[A]rchitecture and decoration, having wandered since 1800 in a labyrinth of dubious eclecticism, can be set right only by a close study of the best models' (*DH* 2), with those models 'chiefly to be found in buildings erected in Italy after the beginning of the sixteenth century, and in other European countries after the full assimilation of the Italian influence' (*DH* 2). In a leitmotif that will resurface in Wharton's literary criticism, the authors propose that 'originality lies not in discarding the necessary laws of thought, but in using them to express new intellectual conceptions.... Most of the features of architecture that have persisted through various fluctuations of taste owe their preservation to the fact that they have been proved by experience to be necessary; and it will be found that none of them precludes the exercise of individual taste' (*DH* 9). In a blunter exposition one year earlier in a letter to the *Newport Daily News*, Wharton protested the loss of Newport's old houses: 'why have so many been demolished, and so many ruthlessly mutilated?'; 'The desire to do differently for the sake of doing differently is puerile.'[15] Key words resonate through *The Decoration of Houses*: twenty-six uses of 'proportion' or 'proportions' (with 'proportion' also the closing word of the volume); twenty uses of 'suitable' ('eminently suitable' [14], 'a suitable background' [25], 'suitable height' [54], 'a more suitable setting' [84], 'more suitable material' [82], 'a suitable place' [158]); sixteen references to 'harmony'; twelve references to 'proper ('the proper use of each moulding' [19], 'the science of restoring wasted rooms to their proper uses' [22]) 'restored to its proper place' [36], 'the proper arrangement of what the room was to contain' [51]); along with multiple references to 'fitness', 'order', 'purpose', 'common sense', 'simplicity' and a loss of 'taste' ('a perversion of taste' [27], 'general decline of taste' [82], 'the general downfall of taste' [92], 'strange lapses from taste' [101]).

One target for Wharton and Codman was Charles L. Eastlake's popular *Hints on Household Taste* (1868). A pointed footnote drew attention to the 'curious' fact that in Eastlake's 'well-known' volume, 'no mention is made of doors, windows or fireplaces' (*DH* 64). *The Decoration of Houses*, by contrast, devotes chapters to the structural building blocks of the profession—walls, doors, windows, fireplaces, ceilings, and floors. Wharton and Codman remind readers 'that walls are meant to support something, that doors are for entrance and exit, that windows should give light and may be looked from, that fire-places may contain fire and should not be draped with silks nor even with woollens' (Blashfield 6). There are chapters on 'Entrance and Vestibule', 'Hall and Stairs', on the drawing-room, boudoir and morning-room, on gala rooms, library, smoking-room and 'den', dining-room, bedrooms, the school-room and nurseries, with a final chapter on bric-à-brac ('though cheapness and trashiness are not always synonymous, they are apt to be so in the case of the modern knickknack' [*DH* 186]). Less is often more, rooms have a purpose, privacy is key, comfort matters, connections and organic unity are essential. In conclusion the authors write: 'There is no absolute perfection, there is no communicable ideal; but much that is empiric, much that is confused and extravagant, will give way before the application of principles based on common sense and regulated by the laws of harmony and proportion' (*DH* 198).

In many regards, not least with its discussion of drawing-rooms, gala-rooms, and private libraries—the type of rooms most readers do not own, *The Decoration of Houses* can easily appear as Wharton's most elitist text. Indeed Lee suggests '[i]t is hard to take *The Decoration of Houses* quite seriously now'—though her focus is not on those settings, but on the volume's perceived manner and tone: 'It has such high-handed prejudices.... It is so sure of being right.... It is so snooty' (134–35). Charles de Kay in the *New York Times* suggested the volume 'is to be warmly recommended to people who are about to finish their homes'[16], while Blashfield saw the 'authors address themselves to two classes, the moderately well-to-do and the wealthy' (7). Yet despite the highlighting of economies at points ('When a room is to be furnished and decorated at the smallest possible cost, it must be remembered that the comfort of its occupants depends more on the nature of the furniture than of the wall-decorations or carpet' [*DH* 25–26]), the primary focus is on very wealthy households and houses dependent on servants for their smooth running. As Wharton learned in Newport, not everyone was interested in, willing, or able to contribute to her vision. As 'Secretary of the association for decorating the Newport schools', she had to write again to the editor of the Newport *Daily News* to make another appeal for funds to continue the work of decorating its public schoolrooms: despite the fact that '[t]he work done has apparently met with general approval', 'to our great disappointment, we have received but few contributions from citizens of Newport'.[17] At the same time, however, *The Decoration of Houses* was an aspirational text and Wharton and Codman fervently believed in the trickle-down effect: 'When the rich man demands good architecture his neighbors will get it too' (*DH* xxi–xxii); 'Every good moulding, every carefully studied detail, exacted by those who can afford to indulge their taste, will in time find its way to the carpenter-built cottage' (*DH* xxii). As Virginia Ricard recognises, drawing links between 'The New French Woman' and *The Decoration of Houses*, 'Wharton sets out to instruct the general public about the uses of accumulated architectural knowledge usually considered the preserve of the happy few. Taste and beauty are available to all.' However 'great' the houses, 'the real purpose of the book is to democratize the art of building—and living—nobly, just as the purpose of "The New Frenchwoman" is to make a partly forgotten past available to all'.[18] Coles recognises in turn 'Wharton's complex feeling that our art and architecture should not merely consist of acquisitions and possessions, but be a reflection of the quality of our life and aspirations—what we ask of ourselves and are willing to live by and live up to' (275). Ultimately, like much of her travel writing, *The Decoration of Houses* is a bold paean to culture, to living a full, civilised, meaningful, connected life.

Italian Villas and Their Gardens (1904) proves in many ways what Richard Guy Wilson deems a 'natural successor' to *The Decoration of Houses*[19]—with the creation of an extraordinary home, The Mount at Lenox, falling largely in-between. Wharton outlined her approach in a letter to Vernon Lee: 'This year, finalmente, I am going to do the long deferred articles on Italian villa-gardens; not from the admiring ejaculatory, but, as much as possible, from the historical & architectural standpoint; & I shall want all the help & advice you are willing to give me.'[20] 'The book is not about horticulture ... but a treatment of gardens as architectural assemblages', highlights Wilson (*Edith Wharton at Home* 102–03), while Helena Chance suggests Wharton's 'views on garden design were shaped by theories similar to those in interior design and architecture, which were reactions against inauthentic, eclectic approaches to historicism, with a mixing of styles and "inappropriate" use of materials and plants' (203). *The Speaker: the liberal review* recognised in Wharton's volume '[t]he Italian garden ... conceived as a kind of open-air house' (the otherwise illiberal reviewer suggesting 'This book is a good example of the thoroughness and intelligence often now to be found in the work of American women').[21] The project was originally commissioned as a series of articles for *The Century Magazine*, running in 1903 and 1904, accompanying Maxfield Parrish's watercolours. (In December 1903, *Vogue* suggested '[t]he illustrations ... are considered the most beautiful pictures of the kind that have ever appeared'[22]). In *A Backward Glance*, Wharton credited the 'unexpected popularity of "The Decoration of Houses", and also of "The Valley of Decision", which was now rewarding [her] for the long months of toils and perplexity [she] had undergone in writing it' for the commission, 'armed' with which she set out with Teddy for Italy and began her work 'in all seriousness' (*BG* 129).

And indeed it was 'in all seriousness'. '[H]aving been given the opportunity to do a book that needed doing, I resolutely took it', recalled Wharton (*BG* 139). Her approach to the project underscored her perfectionism, professionalism, and authority. Eleanor Dwight notes that between January and June 1903, the Whartons visited more than seventy villas and gardens; by the time they reached Florence and had viewed twenty-six villas, 'many unknown or almost inaccessible', she wrote to *Century* editor Richard Watson Gilder asking (successfully) to be paid more (Dwight 103, 107). Research was exhaustive, Wharton having 'immersed herself in ground-plans, guide-books, architectural treatises, diaries and travellers' accounts, from the fifteenth to the nineteenth centuries, in four languages' (Lee 112), and the volume, like *The Decoration of Houses*, would include an impressive bibliography. One of the reasons the work was so extensive was Vernon Lee, who eased the path for Wharton, generously made introductions, accompanied her on many visits, and alerted her to unknown villas. Lee earned her dedication in the volume: 'To Vernon Lee who better than any one else has understood and interpreted the garden-magic of Italy' (*IVG* v). Wharton warmly acknowledged Lee in *A Backward Glance*, calling her 'the first highly cultivated and brilliant woman [she] had ever known' (*BG* 132), and appreciating 'the open doors and a helpful hospitality' she found as a result of Lee's generous interventions in the research for *Italian Villas and Their Gardens* (*BG* 135). Wharton wrote to Sally Norton from Florence in March 1903, 'Miss Paget (Vernon Lee) has such a prodigious list of villas for me to see near here, & is taking so much trouble to arrange expeditions for us, that I think we shall have to stay here longer than I expected—perhaps ten days' (*Letters* 80). The research was hard work, at times involving arduous carriage excursions to reach otherwise fairly inaccessible villas. In an undated letter to Lee, Wharton explained that her previous two villa excursions had 'brought back a sun-stroky kind of state that I get into now & then in Italy', leaving her exhausted. Even so, Wharton enthused, 'I can't thank you enough for telling me about the Villa Bombicci & still more about V. Pucci'—both referenced in the published volume.[23]

Wharton boldly laid claim to the 'new'. Her recollection of *Italian Villas and Their Gardens* in *A Backward Glance* exudes confidence, individualism, and a sense of democratic purpose: 'At that time little had been written on Italian villa and garden architecture, and only the most famous country-seats, mostly royal or princely, had been photographed and studied. ... I wished that my new book should make known the simpler and less familiar type of villa' (*BG* 135). In a manner reminiscent of *Italian Backgrounds*, Wharton claimed for her focus less familiar, different, individual pathways. Arranged by geographical regions, with separate chapters on Florentine, Sienese, Roman, 'near Rome', Genoese, and Lombard villas, with a final chapter on villas of Venetia (in which Wharton reiterated her case, 'Writers on Italian architecture have hitherto paid little attention to the villa-architecture of Venetia' [*IVG* 231]), the ambitious volume covered around eighty villas and their gardens, with twenty-six drawings by Parrish, supplemented by nineteen photographs, and a scattering of drawings by other artists (C. A. Vanderhoof, E. Denison, Malcolm Fraser).

Once again Wharton offered a vision of cohesion, connection, seeing things in the whole. A desire for 'harmony' pervades the text ('harmony of design' [8], 'perfect harmony between the material at hand and the use made of it' [94], 'in harmony with the surroundings' [197]), with repetitions of 'garden-magic' and Wharton's much-vaunted 'simplicity' and 'proportion'. The garden 'must be studied in relation to the house, and both in relation to the landscape' (*IVG* 6). (It was perhaps a revealing slip in a November 1904 letter to Lee, announcing the imminent arrival of the volume, when Wharton wrote 'I am sending you this week my "Italian ~~Gardens~~ Villas & their ~~Villas~~ Gardens"'[24] '*Villa*, in Italian, signifies not the house alone, but the house and pleasure-grounds', informs Wharton in the volume [*IVG* 54], the technically redundant dual listing of both villas and gardens of the title likely included for the benefit of a garden-loving readership. Wharton looks away from 'the haphazard and slipshod designs of the present day' (*IVG* 250) to find inspiration from the Italian 'landscape-architect' of the sixteenth to the end of the eighteenth century and his 'deeper harmony of design' (*IVG* 8): '[I]n the blending of different elements, the subtle transition from the fixed and formal lines of art to the shifting and irregular lines of nature, and lastly in the essential convenience and livableness of the garden, lies the fundamental secret of the old garden-magic', writes Wharton (*IVG* 7–8). The old Italian garden 'was meant to be lived in—a use to which, at least in America, the modern garden is seldom put' (*IVG* 11); garden and landscape 'formed part of the same composition' (*IVG* 6); gardens combine beauty with utility. An Italian garden 'does not exist for its flowers', a factor partly explained by 'so hot and dry a climate', resulting instead in 'a wonderful development of the more permanent effects to be obtained from the three other factors in garden-composition—marble, water and perennial verdure—and the achievement, by their skilful blending, of a charm independent of the seasons' (*IVG* 5). The 'inherent beauty' of the garden is to be found in 'the grouping of its parts—in the converging lines of its long ilex-walks, the alternation of sunny open spaces with cool woodland shade, the proportion between terrace and bowling-green, or between the height of a wall and the width of a path' (*IVG* 8).

Italian Villas and Their Gardens offered both scholarly, analytical, authoritative text and a practical handbook for gardeners at home (and the author incorporated a number of these ideas in her own Italian gardens at The Mount completed in 1907). Wharton was not advocating a literal transplantation, however. Acknowledging that the 'cult of the Italian garden has spread from England to America', the author pithily observes 'a marble sarcophagus and a dozen twisted columns will not make an Italian garden' (*IVG* 12). Instead she argues that if 'the old Italian gardens ... are to be a real inspiration, they must be copied, not in the letter but *in the spirit* [my emphasis]': 'a piece of ground laid out and planted on the principles of the old garden-craft will be, not indeed an Italian garden in the literal sense, but, what is far better, *a garden as well adapted to its surroundings as were the models which inspired it*' (*IVG* 12). This was an empowering, enabling text, sharing with readers 'the secret to be learned from the villas of Italy' (*IVG* 13), a secret that held the potential to improve the quality of life.

On submitting the first *Century* article, however, the author found her seriousness, professionalism, and authority under attack. Wharton's text was deemed 'too dry and technical' (*BG* 138); the editor 'pleaded' for her to introduce in the next article 'a few anecdotes, and a touch of human interest' (*BG* 138). Could she not write as though for a 'young lady from the West'? (cited Lee 112). Wharton held her ground: 'As to changing the character of the articles, that seems to me almost impossible. If I had understood that you wished the "chatty" article on Italian gardens, of which so many have been written, & forgotten ... I should have told you at once that I was not prepared to undertake the work' (cited Dwight 108). While the author read the situation as editorial 'fear their readers would be bored by the serious technical treatment of a subject associated with moonlight and nightingales' (*BG* 139), there was also a decided gender bias here. The male artist's pictures were 'admired' (*BG* 138), while the female expert's authority was seen to require levity and dilution—an early reminder that we have often underestimated the level of sexism Wharton encountered in her career. And even today the author's responses to challenges from editors and others are at times swiftly read as any combination of the haughty, highhanded or peevish, rather than as a strong-minded, resolute professional defending her position and holding the line.[25] Recalling the disagreement three decades later, Wharton presented herself as the determined fighter on behalf of her 'colleagues' (*BG* 138) against censorship and American magazines' 'fear of scandalizing a nonexistent clergyman in the Mississippi Valley' (*BG* 139)—a passage the *Ladies' Home Journal* notably excised from its serialisation of *A Backward Glance*, as outlined in Chap. 7. Wharton depicted her stance as a debt to be paid by the writer of means: 'Not being obliged to live solely by my pen I thought I owed it to less lucky colleagues to fight for the independence they might not always be in a position to assert' (*BG* 138–39). But again, though she would never frame it as such, this was also a case of the resolute, independent woman, the female professional having to stand up and be counted in a man's world.

Wharton's independent stance came at a significant price. Her 'punishment' (*BG* 138), as she termed it, was that the company 'refused (when the volume came out) to publish the plans of certain little-known but important gardens ... which [she] had taken great pains to procure, because, according to the publishers, the public "did not care for plans"' (*BG* 138–39). Wharton's expertise, scholarship, and professionalism were compromised. She recalled in *A Backward Glance* that 'when "Italian Villas" became, as it soon did, a working manual for architectural students and landscape gardeners, [she] was often reproached for not having provided the book with plans' (*BG* 139). Several reviewers explicitly criticised their omission. The *Nation* review concluded, 'it is to be regretted that plans, however meagre (mere thumbnail sketches would have served), have not been included among the illustrations. Without them, the descriptions, though well written, are sometimes hard to follow; with them, all would have been clear and simple.'[26]

Ultimately *Italian Villas and Their Gardens* was less of a collaboration between Wharton and Parrish than a distant arranged marriage. Wharton appeared eager for a genuine partnership, hoping to visit villas together—but Parrish (a hugely popular American artist, who had previously illustrated Wharton's short story 'The Duchess at Prayer' for *Scribner's Magazine*) proved elusive. 'Where *is* Mr. Parrish? Not a word from him yet!', she wrote to Gilder from Florence in March 1903 (*Letters* 83). The author herself did not think the images and text were compatible. While describing them as 'brilliant idealisations of the Italian scene' (*BG* 138), she suggested 'the Parrish pictures ... should have been used to illustrate some fanciful tale of Lamothe-Fouqué's, or Andersen's "Improvisatore"' (*BG* 139), and a number of reviewers played out an unhappy duel between written text and images. 'Mr. Parrish has performed his part of the task in a delightful and satisfactory way', judged the *Critic*; 'When, however, we turn from the illustrations to Mrs. Wharton's text, we are met by a distinct disappointment.' With a decidedly sexist undercurrent, and one suggesting transgression, the review determined, 'she prefers to make her book a book of instruction in the facts and principles of Italian garden design, rather than to assist Mr. Parrish in reviving the "vague enjoyment" which is the first impression produced by the gardens on every sensitive person.'

'That such instruction is needed', the review concluded, 'we would not for a moment deny; but Mrs. Wharton should have seen the propriety of finding another time and place for her lesson.'[27] Wharton, however, would not relegate herself to the assistant role; rather her approach was authoritative, precise and, for the *Critic* reviewer, evidently 'improper'.

Italian Villas and Their Gardens has been credited as 'pioneering'[28] and as 'one of the most influential works on the Italian garden ever published in the United States',[29] helping to 'fuel the rage for Italian gardens in America' (*Edith Wharton at Home* 105). It was not, however, entirely original. Aside from Lee, Charles A. Platt (whom Wharton did not reference) had published two articles on Italian gardens in *Harper's New Monthly Magazine* in July and August 1893, released as a volume, *Italian Gardens*, the following year. Platt's statement that '[t]he evident harmony of arrangement between the house and surrounding landscape is what first strikes one in Italian landscape architecture—the design as a whole'[30] has a familiar ring to the Wharton reader, but Platt's thesis was made a decade earlier. In an insightful essay exploring the correspondence of Wharton and her niece, landscape architect Beatrix Farrand, Mia Manzulli claims that one of Farrand's early articles, 'The Garden in Relation to the House' (1897) anticipates *Italian Villas and Their Gardens*, with Farrand (then still Beatrix Jones) asserting that 'the "arts of architecture and landscape gardening are sisters, not antagonists."'[31] The two page article is in fact Jones' abstract of a paper titled 'The Garden in Relation to the House', given by H. E. Milner 'the well-known English landscape gardener', at a meeting of the Royal Institute of British Architects regarding 'the treatment to be adopted in laying out private grounds, particularly in regard to their more immediate relation to the house'.[32] Milner was evidently expressing broadly similar views regarding cohesion, proportion, and house-garden-landscape connected perspective, but focused on the English garden and its very different historical precedents and results. Jones' responses to the paper, in turn, are limited to the closing paragraph, but the points, again, are made, indicating that some of the broader, conceptual discussions were already in play. Wharton, however, looked to Italy for inspiration. Meanwhile, Platt undeniably preceded her, but Wharton's study was 'longer, more comprehensive, and knowledgeable' (*Edith Wharton at Home* 105), 'discussed many more gardens than Platt (approximately eighty as opposed to his twenty)' and was 'carefully researched' (Davidson 66) compared to Platt's text which 'contained not a single date or architect' (Russell 15) and was 'more of a "coffee table" book of beautiful photos with brief descriptions that emphasized the horticultural beauty of the gardens' (Chance 204).[33] Wharton may not have crossed the line first, but she took the discussion to another, elevated level, ensuring her volume was 'the most scholarly analysis of the design principles of Italian gardens from the Renaissance onward published in English at that time' (Chance 204).

After 1904, Wharton would never publish another volume on architecture or design. Partly, she had said much of what she wanted to say, and both *The Decoration of Houses* and *Italian Villas and Their Gardens* had been impeccably timed, the former capturing the wider moment of change, applied to the private home, while the other both capitalised on and educated an American audience's enthusiasm for Italian garden design. While scholarly, both volumes also tapped into an ongoing American fascination with self-help and self-improvement, Wharton advocating and illuminating pathways to beauty and a subsequently improved quality of life. One year later *The House of Mirth* would give Wharton a second, best-selling novel, and the many demands on her writing time would vie for attention. Partly too, as with her stage work, the writer took a step away from collaboration, which brought with it certain creative frustrations—and also meant losing a share of the profits. (In September 1902, on the verge of moving into The Mount, Wharton wrote to Brownell to thank him—very precisely—for a royalty cheque for $2, 191 81/100 which, 'even to the 81 cents, is welcome to an author in the last throes of house-building' [*Letters* 70]). Manzulli notes that Beatrix Farrand's biographer Jane Brown speculates Farrand 'stopped writing gardening articles after 1907 either because she found writing difficult or because she was wary of competing with her aunt', with 'further articles of significance ... not published until the late 1930s' (Manzulli 40). With Farrand on the path to becoming a celebrated landscape architect, it is also possible that *Wharton* did not produce another volume as *she* did not wish to be in competition with or be seen to trespass on her niece's turf. There would be rare short pieces—in 1914, the review of *The Architecture of Humanism: A Study in the History of Taste* by her friend Geoffrey Scott, architect and authority on Italian architecture of the Renaissance; in 1924, an introduction to *Gardening in Sunny Lands: The Riviera, California, Australia* by 'Mrs. Philip Martineau'—and brief unpublished work (notably 'Gardening in France', an unfinished account of her restoration of the gardens at Pavillon Colombe), but no other dedicated volumes.

Wharton was also moving more determinedly from theory to practice. There had been her hands-on approach to the design of The Mount, followed by its grounds—with Francis V. L. Hoppin, Codman, Farrand, and Wharton all professionally involved. In *A Backward Glance*, the author recalled that she was 'often taxed by [her] friends with not applying to the arrangement of [her] own rooms the rigorous rules laid down in "The Decoration of Houses"' (*BG* 110–11). Wilson, Boyd, and Scott Marshall are among those who have written eloquently about the creation of The Mount, Wilson noting that the interiors 'both follow and depart' from those rules (*Edith Wharton at Home* 66), while Marshall judges 'much of the genius of Edith's design of The Mount is in the skilful blending of the best of French, English, and Italian classical design elements to create a new American vocabulary'.[34] Wharton created three extraordinary gardens in her lifetime at her homes: the garden at The Mount, followed by those at Pavillon Colombe outside Paris, and Château Ste Claire, Hyères. Some of the publicity she attracted, notably in the US society columns, was for her (and—invisible—her gardeners') horticultural prowess. In August 1906 *Vogue* noted that among those winning prizes at the Lenox Horticultural Society was 'Mrs. Edith Wharton, the novelist' who 'took first premium with twelve varieties of perennials', while a year later the magazine reported that a 'garden party was given by Mrs. Edith Wharton, in her new Italian gardens at the "Mount"'.[35] In August 1909, *The Washington Post* reported, with barely disguised glee, in its 'Snapshots at Social Leaders':

> The famous goldfish pool, where Edith Wharton, the authoress, had a bower at The Mount in Lenox, the country place of her husband, Edward R. Wharton, has been destroyed to make room for a trout pond.
> Mrs. Wharton is away in Italy writing another novel. She went abroad last winter, and this year Albert R. Shamuck, former president of the Automobile Club of America, has a lease of the property.[36]

On 3 July 1911, just returned to The Mount a few months before its sale, Wharton delighted in the beauties of its grounds, writing to Fullerton, 'Decidedly, I'm a better landscape gardener than novelist, and this place, every line of which is my own work, far surpasses the House of Mirth' (*Letters* 242). Indeed in certain circles of her acquaintance Wharton would be remembered as much, or even more, as a gardener than a writer. One of the French translators of *The Age of Innocence*, Madame Saint-René

Taillandier, suggested for Percy Lubbock's *Portrait of Edith Wharton*, 'Which of us all who knew her, however slightly, can recall her name without the vision of a garden, perfect in its beauty?'[37] Younger writer, friend and fellow gardener Louis Bromfield believed her two gardens in France were 'to those who knew … as great works of art as the best things she had ever written'.[38] Wharton would display a gamut of emotions writing about her gardens in her private correspondence and diary entries. References in her letters span the jovial and unashamedly self-indulgent (suggesting to Farrand she wants to 'wallow in flowers … all the year round' [cited Manzulli 46]) to the effusive, amusingly competitive (teasing Bromfield that she wants to 'swank' to him about her roses), to expressions of technical expertise and dry enquiries for addresses of specialist growers to her knowledgeable friends, alongside the philosophical: 'the garden is the last moral life-preserver left. I pity those who haven't it', she agreed with Bromfield in a letter of June 1933.[39] Gardening affiliations for Wharton could supersede all considerations of politics, class, position. In a delightful recollection, Bromfield describes introducing an ill, frail, elderly Wharton to a 'strange, wild' dahlia grower, 'a communist, not in the dull doctrinaire way, but in a primitive, fundamental fashion' ('Tribute' 110, 111) only for the two seemingly incompatible bedfellows immediately to hit it off, to become for a time 'brother and sister' talking of 'flowers, of soil, of fertilizers, of experiments, of climates' ('Tribute' 113). Of that afternoon, Bromfield recalled that he had 'never seen her happier' ('Tribute' 113). In a record of Wharton's last journal, covering the final months of her life from November 1936, references to her writing subside as she increasingly struggles with ill health, but pottering, strolling, walking in her beloved gardens at Sainte-Claire feature prominently.[40] In November 1926, returning to Sainte-Claire after eight months away, Wharton recorded a brief entry in 'Quaderno dello Studente' (the journal discussed in Chap. 7): 'Oh, the joy of being alone—alone; of walking about in the garden of my soul!' ('QS' 212).

In her 1936 volume, *Autumn in the Valley*, Daisy Chanler would ethereally imagine Wharton's Sainte-Claire garden as 'somehow an image of her spirit, of her inmost self. It shows her love of beauty, her imagination, her varied knowledge, and masterly attention to detail; like her, it is somewhat inaccessible. Her garden is a symbol of the real Edith' (114–15).[41] In the chapter 'And After' of *A Backward Glance*, Wharton suggested that settling into Pavillon Colombe after the war offered a return to 'peace and order', when she finally had 'leisure for the two pursuits which never palled, writing and gardening' (*BG* 363). And the author was phenomenally successful at both. In Wharton's papers at the Beinecke, a typed outline of the Sainte-Claire estate prepared after the author's death, with a purchase price of $85,000, highlights the gardens as 'among the most celebrated in France ... stocked with rare flowers'.[42] A beautifully photographed feature 'A Riviera Garden' in *Country Life* in 1928 praised Wharton's skill 'both as a designer and as a gardener', her ambitious planting, Sainte-Claire's accommodation to the landscape beyond, its rock garden with subtropical plants 'said to be even more complete than the famous collection at the Prince of Monaco's on the borders of Monte Carlo': 'It is difficult to describe such a garden ... as it contains so much and is so intimate, apart from any consideration of the natural ground,' concluded the journalist.[43]

Indeed Allan R. Ruff, in his study of the gardens and friendship of Wharton and Lawrence Johnston (creator of the celebrated garden at Hidcote Manor in Gloucestershire), suggests that a fundamental reason 'why neither ... left an account of their garden ... was ... because each garden was its maker's own private world into which he or she alone could escape from the exigencies of daily life.... To have written about it would have admitted other, unknown people, and broken the spell of an intimate, private world' (222). Any doubts about the importance of Wharton's gardens to her wellbeing are surely dispelled by her anguished responses to the near destruction of her gardens at Sainte-Claire in the unforgiving winter of early 1929. The loss was described in her diary as 'torture' (Lewis 487); she wrote to Lapsley, 'Oh, Gaillard, that my old fibres should have been so closely interwoven with all these roots and tendrils' (cited Lewis 487); while to Lee she revealed, 'The ruin of my garden is so total & so tragic that I can't bear as yet to look at it, & wd. leave tomorrow, if I could.'[44] The vagaries of the weather feature prominently in Wharton's writing about gardens—and her own gardens did not escape them. In her introduction to Martineau's *Gardening in Sunny Lands*, Wharton compares 'the first months of planning and planting in the Riviera' to a 'long honeymoon'. In the second year, however, 'the flower-lover' will 'learn his lesson' when in the south 'conditions are so different and the caprices of the elements so incalculable'.[45] The few, unpublished essays the author produced on her gardens give an indication of what has been lost to a wider readership, but also sound a note of caution. An extraordinary, undiluted emotional investment that transfers beautifully to poetry (and we see in Chap. 2 that Wharton turned to poetry, and specifically a poem set in a garden on the day of Walter Berry's death, 'Garden Valedictory') or at times to fiction (e.g., Charity Royall's responses to nature conveying her burgeoning sexuality in *Summer*) may not transfer successfully to writing about garden design. At moments Wharton's rare, brief essays on her gardens are wonderfully evocative, but at others emotionally overblown. Of the latter, 'Spring in a French Riviera Garden', evoking a magical transition from winter to spring, appears weighed down by an overly-laboured, heavy lyricism ('what a rush of hurrying flower-feet is in the air! The tireless Laurustinus leads the way, already thrusting its snowy corymbs among last year's blue-black berries; the Photinias are crowning their stately growth with burnished terminal shoots'; 'the species Irises are weaving their enchantment; ... the exquisite lilac-blue of *Reticulata Cantab* lies like a fragment of sky on the brown earth.'[46]) More successful is Wharton's unfinished account of the restoration of her gardens at Pavillon Colombe, 'Gardening in France', published for the first time in 2000 in Bratton's edition of the Wharton-Bromfield correspondence. The terrain is still 'horticultural heaven', but the tone is more muted (Wharton opens with the wry observation that 'It used to be said that good Americans went to Paris when they died; but the saying should be qualified by adding that garden-loving Americans go to the suburbs of Paris') and the descriptions less excessively ornate, conveying, literally, a more down-to earth account of the restoration and composition of the garden ('Gardening in France' in Bratton, 135–39; 135).

Wharton's published record of writing on architecture and design remains therefore largely an early-career accomplishment: one looking to Europe for its inspiration, but to America for its application and impact. (A record of her last journal reveals that on the day of her death—11 August 1937—Wharton had been due to lunch with Ogden Codman, also a long-time resident of France—but the neat full circle of a meeting at the very end of her life with the collaborator on her first professional published book did not come to pass.[47]) As other scholars have noted, significant protagonists in Wharton's fiction would be architects: from *Summer*'s Lucius Harney (in whom Orlando detects a 'queer' shadow of Codman [224]) to *The Age of Innocence*'s Dallas Archer, whom Wilson deems 'part of the classicism of the American Renaissance' (175). Manzulli observes, in turn, that while 'Wharton's female characters are rarely writers, they are, on occasion, gardeners', among them 'amateur botanist' Justine Brent of *The Fruit of the Tree*, and Halo Tarrant 'whose artistry is reflected in the gardens that she creates and rehabilitates in *The Gods*

Arrive' (45). Always overlooked in the architectural tally is Wharton's unfinished play, *The Arch*. (discussed in Chap. 3), which headlines an architect as its leading male protagonist—George Adrian—but we do not see him at work. In an interesting gender twist, we do, however, learn '[o]f what a clever draughtsman' a young woman, Effie Vanderfleet, 'is getting to be', having 'made such a beautiful plan for Mr Bayne's new house' (*The Arch*. 107). Here, Wharton simultaneously captures changing times and shifting gender roles, but also re-cements them—the praise is all part of a mother's ongoing ruse to net the rich Stuart Bayne as a husband for Effie. Meanwhile, Wharton herself was seen in a number of ways to be transgressive in her writing on architecture and design: authoritative, professional and expert, she refused to produce the 'chatty' work on Italian gardens, to play the supporting role to a male collaborator, or indeed to apologise for her expertise. She would in turn enjoy greater success than her protagonists. If her writings on architecture and design are not entirely original, they nevertheless raised the discussions in America to another level. Adopting a scholarly, authoritative approach, Wharton resisted dumbing down, but also introduced a very pragmatic, can-do sharing of knowledge, empowering the reader, indeed showing an early faith in her reader that editors sometimes lacked. Taste, proportion, harmony take the reader a considerable way to Wharton's destination, whatever the field. Like much of her travel writing, Wharton's work in architecture and design offers an undaunted extolment of culture, of a rich, meaningful, connected life. So too, we will see a number of her design theories echoed in her literary criticism in the next chapter: '[O]riginality', write the authors near the outset of *The Decoration of Houses*, 'lies not in discarding the necessary laws of thought, but in using them to express new intellectual conceptions' (*DH* 9).

Notes

1. 'THE NEWS—NEWPORT/EDUCATION THROUGH THE EYES/ Mrs. Wharton Addresses the Teachers on Art in the Schoolroom'. Newspaper clipping [October 1897], Edith Wharton Collection, Yale Collection of American Literature, Beinecke Rare Book and Manuscript Library, Yale University (folder 1525). Subsequent references to this work are included in the text.

2. Edith Wharton, 'More Love-Letters of an Englishwoman', *Bookman: A Literary Journal*, XXI (February 1901), 562–63; 562: https://babel.hathitrust.org/cgi/pt?id=njp.32101077276861&view=1up&seq=908.
3. William A. Coles, 'The Genesis of a Classic', in Edith Wharton and Ogden Codman, Jr., *The Decoration of Houses* (New York: W. W. Norton & Co, 1998), 256–75; 260. Subsequent references to this work are included in the text.
4. Richard Guy Wilson, 'Edith and Ogden: Writing, Decoration, and Architecture', in Pauline C. Metcalf (ed.), *Ogden Codman and the Decoration of Houses* (Boston, MA: Boston Athenaeum, Godine, 1988), 133–84; 148. Subsequent references to this work are included in the text.
5. Advertisement, Charles Scribner's Sons, *Vogue* 10:13, (23 September 1897): C4, Proquest The Vogue Archive.
6. See, for example, Annette Benert, *The Architectural Imagination of Edith Wharton* (Madison, NJ: Fairleigh Dickinson UP, 2006); Ailsa Boyd, 'From the "Looey suite" to the Faubourg: The Ascent of Undine Spragg', *Edith Wharton Review*, 30:1 (Spring 2014), 9–28; Dwight, *Edith Wharton: An Extraordinary Life*; Judith Fryer, *Felicitous Space The Imaginative Structures of Edith Wharton and Willa Cather* (Chapel Hill: University of North Carolina Press, 1986); Cecilia Macheski, 'Architecture' in Rattray (ed.), *Edith Wharton in Context*, 189–98; chapter three, 'Interiors and Facades', Maureen E. Montgomery, *Displaying Women: Spectacles of Leisure in Edith Wharton's New York* (New York: Routledge, 1998); Emily Orlando, 'The "Queer Shadow" of Ogden Codman in Edith Wharton's *Summer*', *Studies in American Naturalism*, 12:2 (2017), 220–43; Gary Totten, 'The Art and Architecture of the Self: Designing the "I"-Witness in Edith Wharton's *The House of Mirth*', *College Literature*, 27: 3 (Fall 2000): 71–87; Lisa Tyler, 'Wharton, Hemingway, and the Architecture of Modernism: Gendered Tropes of Architecture and Interior Decoration', in Lisa Tyler (ed.), *Wharton, Hemingway and the Advent of Modernism* (Baton Rouge: Louisiana State University Press, 2019), 151–66. Subsequent references are included in the text.
7. Thomas Jayne, *Classical Principles for Modern Design: Lessons from Edith Wharton and Ogden Codman's The Decoration of Houses* (New York: Monacelli Press, 2018), 7.
8. Pauline C. Metcalf, 'Preface', in Metcalf (ed.), *Ogden Codman and the Decoration of Houses* (Boston, MA: Boston Athenaeum, Godine, 1988), ix.
9. Edwin H. Blashfield, 'House Decoration', *Book Buyer*, 16 (March 1898) 129–33, reprinted in *Edith Wharton: The Contemporary Reviews*, 5–7; 5. Subsequent references to this work are included in the text. Three years later Wharton, in turn, would write a highly favourable *Bookman* review of *Italian Cities* by Blashfield and Evangeline W. Blashfield (his wife), published by Scribner's.

10. Edith Wharton and Ogden Codman Jr., *The Decoration of Houses* (New York: Charles Scribner's Sons, 1897), 1. Subsequent references to this work are included in the text (*DH*).
11. 'Hints for Home Decoration', *Critic*, 32 (8 January 1898), 20, reprinted in *Edith Wharton: The Contemporary Reviews*, 4–5; 5.
12. Helena Chance, 'Interior and Garden Design', in Rattray (ed.), *Edith Wharton in Context*, 199–208; 203. Subsequent references to this work are included in the text.
13. Lucinda Havenhand, 'A View from the Margin: Interior Design', *Design Issues*, 20.4, 33. Cited in Tyler 154.
14. Walter Berry, '*The Decoration of Houses*', *Bookman*, 7 (April 1898), 161–63, reprinted in *Edith Wharton: The Contemporary Reviews*, 8–10; 8.
15. 'To the Editor of the Daily News', *Newport Daily News*, 8 January 1896, reprinted in *Edith Wharton: The Uncollected Critical Writings*, 54–57; 57, 56.
16. Charles de Kay, 'How To Arrange A House', *New York Times (1857–1922)*, 27 March 1898, ProQuest Historical Newspapers: The New York Times with Index, IMS14.
17. 'More Money Needed/Continuation of the Work of Decorating Public Schoolrooms Desirable', Letter to the Editor of the *Daily News*, undated clipping, Beinecke, folder 1530. Wharton writes:

> The persons who responded so generously to our first appeal are almost all summer visitors, who have many other obligations in their winter homes, and who, while taking a general interest in the welfare of Newport, have no special reason for concerning themselves with the development of her schools. The permanent residents, especially those whose children attend the schools, are those to whom we naturally looked for aid; but, to our great disappointment, we have received but few contributions from citizens of Newport. This is the more disappointing as we have been given to understand that the work of the association is favorably regarded here; while we have taken special pains to make it known that any contribution, however small, will be of service in buying casts and photographs.

The letter includes a list of contributors to school decoration, a list notable for Wharton's friends and members of the social elite, including Mrs Astor $20, Mr Walter Berry $10, Mrs Cornelius Vanderbilt $100.00, Mrs F. W. Vanderbilt $50, Mr Egerton Winthrop $50.00.

18. Virginia Ricard, 'Edith Wharton's French Engagement', in Jennifer Haytock and Laura Rattray (eds.), *The New Edith Wharton Studies* (New York: Cambridge University Press, 2019), 80–95; 88.

19. Richard Guy Wilson, *Edith Wharton at Home: Life at The Mount* (New York: Monacelli Press, 2012), 102. Subsequent references to this work are included in the text.
20. Letter from Wharton to 'Miss Paget', 31 December [1902], Vernon Lee Papers, Special Collections, Somerville College, University of Oxford, courtesy of the Principal and Fellows of Somerville College, Oxford.
21. 'Italian Gardens', *The Speaker: the liberal review*, 26 November 1904, British Periodicals 206–07. The review opens:

    > This book is a good example of the thoroughness and intelligence often now to be found in the work of American women. "There are a million more women than men in Great Britain," it has been said, "and most of them are writing gardening books." The reviewer, in consequence, is not apt to expect much of a book about gardens written by a woman, but in this case he gets a great deal. Miss Wharton has not written about Italian gardens because she wanted to write a book and because they seemed to her an easy subject to make a book out of, but because she both admires and understands them. Her object is to show why they are admirable, and she does so with great clearness and precision.

22. 'Books and Magazines', *Vogue*, 22: 23 (3 December 1903), 755, ProQuest The Vogue Archive.
23. Letter from Wharton to 'Miss Paget', 'Thursday' [no date], Vernon Lee Papers.
24. Letter from Wharton to 'Miss Paget', 11 November 1904, Vernon Lee Papers.
25. Regarding the disagreement between author and editors over the 'dry', serious tone of *Italian Villas and Their Gardens*, Lee suggests Wharton responded 'haughtily' (Lee 112).
26. '*Italian Villas and Their Gardens*', *Nation*, 79 (24 November 1904), 423, reprinted in *Edith Wharton: The Contemporary Reviews*, 89.
27. 'Pen and Pencil in Italy', *Critic*, 46 (February 1905), 166–68, reprinted in *Edith Wharton: The Contemporary Reviews*, 92–94.
28. Vivian Russell, *Edith Wharton's Italian Gardens* (London: Frances Lincoln, 1997), 17. Subsequent references to this work are included in the text.
29. Rebecca Warren Davidson, 'Opposites Attract: The Garden Art of Charles Platt, Maxfield Parrish, and Edith Wharton', *Edith Wharton and the American Garden* (Lenox, Mass: The Mount Press, 2009), 61–74; 61. Subsequent references to this work are included in the text.
30. Charles A. Platt, *Italian Gardens* (New York: Harper & Brothers, 1894), 6.
31. Mia Manzulli, '"Garden Talks": The Correspondence of Edith Wharton and Beatrix Farrand', in Clare Colquitt, Susan Goodman and Candace Waid (eds.), *A Forward Glance: New Essays on Edith Wharton* (Newark: University of Delaware Press, 1999), 35–48; 41. Subsequent references to this work are included in text.

32. Beatrix Jones, 'The Garden in Relation to the House', *Garden and Forest*, 10: 46 (7 April 1897), 132–33; 132. Online.
33. For a comparison of Platt's *Italian Gardens* with Wharton's *Italian Villas and Their Gardens*, see Davidson 66–72.
34. Scott Marshall and John G. Waite Associates, *The Mount, Home of Edith Wharton: A Historic Structure Report* (Mount Ida Press, 1997), 37, cited in Ailsa Boyd, '"The Decoration of Houses": The American Homes of Edith Wharton', *The Journal of the Decorative Arts Society 1850–The Present*, 30 (2006), 74–91; 85.
35. 'Society', *Vogue*, 28: 8 (23 August 1906), iii, ProQuest; 'Society', *Vogue*, 30: 5 (1 August 1907), 124-B, ProQuest The Vogue Archive.
36. 'Snapshots at Social Leaders: Events and Gossip...', *The Washington Post (1877–1922)*, 29 Aug. 1909, ProQuest Historical Newspapers: The Washington Post, E7.
37. Percy Lubbock, *Portrait of Edith Wharton* (New York: Appleton-Century-Crofts, 1947), 154. Subsequent references to this work are included in the text.
38. Louis Bromfield, 'A Tribute to Edith Wharton', reprinted in Daniel Bratton (ed.), *Yrs. Ever Affly: The Correspondence of Edith Wharton and Louis Bromfield* (Michigan State University Press, 2000), 108–22; 109. Subsequent references to this work are included in the text.
39. Letters from Wharton to Louis Bromfield, 30 July 1932 and 12 June 1933, in Bratton (ed.), *Yrs. Ever Affly: The Correspondence of Edith Wharton and Louis Bromfield*, 29, 49.
40. See 'Dernier journal d'E.W.', Wharton Papers, Beinecke. Box 63, folder 1776.
41. For a discussion of Wharton's restoration of her gardens both at Pavillon Colombe and Sainte-Claire at Hyères, see chapter ten 'Edith Wharton and Her French Gardens' of Allan R. Ruff's study, *An Author and a Gardener: The Gardens and Friendship of Edith Wharton and Lawrence Johnston* (Oxford: Windgather Press, 2014), 197–225. Subsequent references to this work are included in the text. For a study of the landscape and planting at Sainte-Claire, see Dwight, 236–250.
42. Louis Auchincloss Material, Edith Wharton Papers, Beinecke. Box 64, folder 1792.
43. E. C. 'A Riviera Garden: Sainte-Claire Le Château, Hyères', *Country Life* (Archive: 1901–2005); 3 November 1928; 64, 1659, Country Life Archive, 610–13.
44. Letter from Wharton to Vernon Lee, 19 February 1929, Vernon Lee Papers.

45. Edith Wharton, 'Introduction to *Gardening in Sunny Lands: The Riviera, California, Australia*', reprinted in Wegener (ed.), *Edith Wharton: The Uncollected Critical Writings*, 246–47. On weather conditions in the Riviera, Wharton writes, 'Where the midday sun is so much hotter, proportionately great is the evening chill. Tender blossoms coaxed forth by a week of summer warmth will be cruelly nipped by a sudden blast off the snow-covered Alps; plants that crave sun in the north languish for half-shade in the south; others that under rainy skies thrive in a comparatively light soil need a damp crevice to nurse their roots through the southern summer' (246).
46. Edith Wharton, 'Spring in a French Riviera Garden', in Dwight, *Edith Wharton: An Extraordinary Life*, 246–47.
47. 'Dernier journal d'E.W.', Wharton Papers, Beinecke, box 63, folder 1776.

CHAPTER 6

Critical Writings and Literary Theory

If no art can be quite pent-up in the rules deduced from it, neither can it fully realize itself unless those who practise it attempt to take its measure and reason out its processes. (*WF* 119)

Is it because these were men, while George Eliot was a woman, that she is reproved for venturing on ground they did not fear to tread?[1]

In many regards the 1920s heralded for Wharton what Shari Benstock terms her 'Age of Acclaim' (385). That acclaim brought awards in a series of firsts. In 1921 she became the first woman to win the Pulitzer Prize for fiction for her novel *The Age of Innocence*, while in June 1923 she was awarded an honorary doctorate of letters by Yale University, again the first for a woman, with Wharton hailed at the degree ceremony as a writer who held a 'universally recognized place in the front rank of the world's living *novelists* [my emphasis]'.[2] In January 1925 she was the first female recipient of the gold medal of the National Institute of Arts and Letters for 'distinguished' service, followed in 1929 by the gold medal from the American Academy of Arts and Letters—on this occasion as the second female recipient (see Benstock 385–86). Wharton was elected to the National Institute in 1926 and to the Academy in 1930, while in 1927 she was nominated for, though did not win, the Nobel Prize. The cataclysmic rupturings of the First World War may have ensured that life would never be the same at the dawn of a new decade, but writing—the pulse beat at the heart of Wharton's routine—continued its regular rhythm, with the 1920s also heralding the era of her greatest marketability and financial returns.

Indeed it was in the twenties that Wharton was really established as one of America's best-selling and most highly paid authors. From 1920 to the end of 1924, estimates suggest that Wharton's work earned her around $250,000, the modern equivalent of nearly $3,000,000 (see *Letters* 418). New income streams opened up, notably with the sales of film rights, including those of *The Glimpses of the Moon* (an adaptation on which her younger contemporary F. Scott Fitzgerald worked), *The Age of Innocence* and *The Children* (filmed as *The Marriage Playground*). Published in 1928, *The Children*, a Book-of-the Month Club choice, earned Wharton $95,000, marking the peak of her commercial success. The author's move to Appleton was highly advantageous, the publisher offering a package that combined the serialisation of her work in mass circulation magazines on lucrative terms, with large advances, and coverage of both the US and UK markets, with British copies imported wholesale from the American print run. Wharton, in turn, observes Shafquat Towheed, 'added much needed critical esteem to Appleton's openly populist list', ensuring '[t]he cultural capital that [she] had accrued over nearly two decades with Scribner's in New York and Macmillan in London could finally be transformed into the substantial cash advances which she had always wanted' (43–44).

Yet the 1920s also ushered in Wharton's Age of Vulnerability. That vulnerability was inherent even in the Pulitzer acclaim as an award conferred on the novel which fulfilled the prize criteria of best presenting 'the wholesome atmosphere of American life and the highest standard of American manners and manhood' (cited Lee 590), and then in Wharton's case somewhat marred by the public revelation that Sinclair Lewis had in fact been the jury's first choice. The award (and lucrative advertising tag) would be satirised as the 'Pulsifer Prize' in her 1929 novel *Hudson River Bracketed*. Wharton's reputation came increasingly under threat. She was set up—and at times rigidly and unhelpfully set herself up—in strict opposition to her younger contemporaries, and was seen to represent an older tradition, for good or ill. Such diametrics would be baldly displayed in a 1925 review that described *The Mother's Recompense* as 'old-fashioned', with Wharton 'content to practice good craftsmanship without enlarging' the scope of the novel, in contrast to the 'brilliant experimentalism' of Virginia Woolf's *Mrs Dalloway*, published the same year.[3] Two months earlier, Wharton introduced herself to Scott Fitzgerald and his generation as a representation of 'the literary equivalent of tufted furniture and gas chandeliers' (*Letters* 481). In a memorable broadside against James Joyce two years earlier, Wharton had deemed *Ulysses* 'a turgid welter of pornography (the rudest schoolboy kind) & unformed & unimportant drivel'. '[U]ntil the raw ingredients of a pudding *make* a pudding', she continued, 'I shall never believe that the raw material of sensation & thought can make a work of art without the cook's intervening', before adding an all-encompassing sideswipe: 'The same applies to Eliot' (*Letters* 461). In a defensive follow-up in the same letter to Bernard Berenson, the author protested: 'I *know* it's not because I'm getting old that I'm unresponsive. The trouble with all this new stuff is that it's à thèse: the theory comes first, & dominates it. And it will go the way of "unanimisme" & all the other isms' (*Letters* 461).

In *A Backward Glance* Wharton would profess a phlegmatic approach to readers and reviewers: 'If one has sought the publicity of print, and sold one's wares in the open market, one has sold to the purchasers the right to think what they choose about one's books' (212), yet her private comments at times told a different story. In 1925 Woolf's essay on 'American Fiction' for *The Saturday Review* included Wharton (alongside Henry James and Joseph Hergesheimer, misnamed by Woolf as Henry Hergesheimer) as an example of an American writer too like English writers ('they do not give us anything that we have not got already'), being preoccupied with 'English good manners' and 'obsessed with surface distinction' (cited in Lee 611) in contrast to Sinclair Lewis, Sherwood Anderson, Willa Cather, and Ring Lardner. Woolf's dismissal evidently rankled: 'Mrs. Virginia Woolf writes a long article...to say that no interesting American fiction is, or should be, written in English; and that Henry Hergesheimer [*sic*] and I are negligible because we have nothing new to give—not even a language! Well—such discipline is salutary' (cited in Lee 611). In a letter to Daisy Chanler in June 1925, Wharton bewailed the 'densities of incomprehension' displayed by reviewers of *The Mother's Recompense* (*Letters* 483), while in October 1928 to Royal Cortissoz she expressed outright dismay at the reviews of *The Children*: 'the uncomprehending drivel (laudatory or other) that I have so far read ... really plunged me in the deepest literary discouragement I have ever known' (*Letters* 518). Reviews made for increasingly uncomfortable reading. In a letter to her younger contemporary Zona Gale (in which Wharton once again presented her self-deprecating calling card: 'I thought you all regarded me as the Mrs.—well, fill in a respectable deceased Victorian name—of America'), the older figure surmised: 'having all through my early career been condemned by the reviewers of my native land for "not knowing how to construct" a novel, I am now far more utterly banned by their descendants for "constructing."'[4]

It was in this watershed decade, when her position simultaneously appeared never more secure and yet never more precarious, that Wharton would choose to produce her most substantial and significant thesis on the theory and art of writing with a series of articles which would ultimately form the basis of the volume *The Writing of Fiction* published by Scribner's in October 1925 (the last book she would publish with them).[5] When it came to *A Backward Glance* in 1934, Wharton explained that she would not be addressing there 'any general theory of technique' as she had 'to the best of [her] ability, analyzed this process' in her 1925 volume (199). *The Writing of Fiction* was the culmination of a long and productive engagement with the genre, Wharton producing a substantial, varied body of work in the field. While *The Writing of Fiction* would initiate a later run of critical writing, there were significant, if somewhat sporadic early essays and reviews, including 'The Vice of Reading' (*North American Review*, October 1903), 'George Eliot' (*Bookman*, May 1902), and on poetry and the theatre, referenced in earlier chapters, including 'Mr. Paul on the Poetry of Matthew Arnold' (*Lamp*, February 1903), 'The Sonnets of Eugene Lee-Hamilton' (*Bookman*, November 1907), 'The Theatres' (New York *Commercial Advertiser*, May 1902) and 'The Three Francescas' (*North American Review*, July 1902). In terms of her later critical writing, meanwhile, which included reflective introductions to new editions of *Ethan Frome* and *The House of Mirth*, Heidi Kunz contends that 'Frustrated throughout her long and prolific career by critics' relative inattention to her artistic priorities, she elucidated her literary values and took her own measure ... contribut[ing] deliberately and significantly to the print conversation about her work in her time.'[6]

In what has become a familiar scenario, Wharton's critical writings are often readily overlooked or summarily dismissed. Millicent Bell concludes, 'Her own contribution to the theory of fiction is slight'; Geoffrey Walton assigns *The Writing of Fiction* to Wharton's 'doldrum period of creative production'; Blake Nevius finds the volume 'an oversimplification of [Henry] James's doctrine', assuring the readers they 'will find nothing original or provocative' as 'she revives the hackneyed discussion of the novel of situation versus the novel of character.' In *Edith Wharton and the Art of Fiction*, Penelope Vita-Finzi describes Wharton's '*attempt* to express a theory of fiction' (my emphasis)—one that 'shows how seriously she regarded fiction as an art', but one that is 'confused and repetitious', inconsistent and contradictory nevertheless.[7] *The Writing of Fiction* disappeared from the critical radar. Dale Bauer's important study, *Edith Wharton's Brave New Politics* (1994), 'a book about the second half of Edith Wharton's career', omits the work.[8] Even the publication of Frederick Wegener's invaluable edition of Wharton's uncollected critical writings in 1996 (paperback 1999), which made readily accessible the author's body of work in this genre for the first time, surprisingly did not appear to prompt a wider revisiting of *The Writing of Fiction* among Wharton scholars or indeed of her work in the genre as a whole. At the time of writing *Edith Wharton and Genre: Beyond Fiction*, the sole edition of *The Writing of Fiction* in print is Simon and Schuster's careless reprint that even omits the epigraph to the volume, a line from the seventeenth-century poet Thomas Traherne's work 'The Vision': 'Order the beauty even of Beauty is'. Thus, the guide is published without its official guide.

All of the author's critical writing merits reconsideration, but *The Writing of Fiction* most of all. By 1925 Wharton was a sixty-three-year-old, internationally-renowned author with a hugely successful track record, decided opinions, and a critic who held strong, but much more flexible than she has been given credit for, views of literary criticism and theory, and of what worked in the writing of fiction, and what did not. As we will see, however, it was the volume of her younger, less experienced male contemporary, Percy Lubbock, that would swiftly come to be regarded as a classic, while Wharton's text was consigned to the sidelines. Like many of the travel texts, her critical writing showcases an unapologetic voice of authority, intellect, knowledge, and professional validation, with the author refusing once again to endorse for her reader perceived short-cuts or dumbing down. Wharton's critical writings can be unfashionable, at the same time as being edgy, even subversive, upending traditional hierarchies of perceived importance. And unlike the travel writing, Wharton sets up and embraces a form of critical writing that at times is decidedly *gendered*. Her work in this field is also very pragmatic, author-friendly, and interconnected in its approach, and much more flexible and open to change than is commonly supposed or as a reader of her private letters might have been led to expect. In no other genre will the writer come under such attack essentially for being a woman seen to be trespassing on a male literary realm. Wharton's gender, career stage, age, class, and image have all worked against her to deny her place as a critical writer of note.

The Writing of Fiction represents Wharton's sole volume in the field, her 'one concerted *attempt* at systematic criticism' according to Wegener (my emphasis),[9] but the author's fascination with the genre can be witnessed as early as Edith Jones' first letters to Anna Bahlmann and the set of mock reviews she wrote to accompany her 'novelette', *Fast and Loose*, her second novel, written as David Olivieri, and completed in January 1867, the month of her fifteenth birthday. These hostile 'reviews', exuberant vignettes parodying the style of contemporary periodicals, are incisive, yet playful and self-deprecative, ensuring that the young author would have the first laugh. Edith Jones' *Nation* determined: 'every character is a failure, the plot a vacuum, the style spiritless, the dialogue vague, the sentiments weak, & the whole thing a fiasco', while *The Saturday Review* could only be 'thankful' it was a 'novelette' and 'no more'.[10] Just as a number of Wharton's earliest published poems underscore her attention to newspaper reports for topical inspiration (see Chap. 2), so the parody of these *Fast and Loose* reviews illuminates the young writer's close familiarity and dexterity with the form and focus of literary reviews of the day. Wharton also hints at reviewers' questioning of the sex of 'David' Olivieri: 'is not…Mr. Olivieri very, very like a sick-sentimental school-girl…?'; and 'a gentleman (?)' which can be read as either a querying of gender or class ('*The Nation*', '*The Saturday Review*', 63, 62). 'This 'fiasco' of a work is linked to an immature femininity ('*The Nation*' 63), while almost sixty years later, 'real' reviewers will take issue with Wharton, the female critical author of *The Writing of Fiction*.

Letters to Bahlmann, meanwhile, evidence an early apprenticeship in the art of critical writing, the governess 'offering a cultivated mind against which Edith could test her literary judgments' (*My Dear Governess* 26), with youthful, engaged critiques of Longfellow, Eliot, Goethe, and Browning, among others. Believable characters, particularly female characters, are a concern of early criticism in both the Bahlmann correspondence and the faux reviews, with saintly, flawless women and the creative short-cut of character 'types' notably critiqued. While Gwendolen in Eliot's newly published *Daniel Deronda* is 'interesting', the fourteen-year old critic writes of Mirah, 'I don't care for your pieces of faultlessness, like the good girls of such extravagant saintliness in Sunday school books—& Mirah is of that type—Like diluted rose-water' (*My Dear Governess* 37). If the 'angelic' Madeline Graham 'be Mr. Olivieri's conception of innocence, we no longer have any difficulty in understanding the motives which prompted Herod to the Massacre of the Innocents', announced the anonymous critic of *Fast and Loose* for *The Saturday Review* (62–63). When it came to *Middlemarch*'s narcissistic Rosamond, Edith Jones expressed 'a sweet faiblesse' for the character, which she supposed denoted 'a sympathetic flaw in [her] own moral structure', while a 'continual desire ... to throttle Mr. Brooke, Mrs. Cadwallader & Cecilia & Sir James only shows how wonderfully life-like they all are' she concluded (*My Dear Governess* 39). Literary criticism was embedded in Edith Jones' letters in-between other news, with reading and critiquing part of the fabric of her everyday life. Correspondence throughout Wharton's lifetime expounded her theories on the art and practice of writing, while the marginal comments and markings in her library collection constitute both the 'form of autobiography', Lee suggests (675), and an extension of her literary criticism. At other times, the author's critical writing would come ensconced in a protagonist's musings, as a passage in a travel guide, or wrapped within a book of design.

Wharton's early professional reviews are confident, thorough, astute, and at times wittily irreverent. On occasion, when she set herself an unenviable task, the resultant review can be heavily plot-driven and descriptive, notably her July 1902 discussion of the 'almost simultaneous production of three plays on the subject of Francesca da Rimini, by play-wrights of three different nationalities' for the *North American Review*.[11] At other times she skilfully uses her reviews as a springboard—with the text in question not left behind *per se*, but integrated into part of a broader discussion, whether of eighteenth-century Italy in the 1905 review of Maurice Hewlett's novel *The Fool Errant* (a matching setting to her own novel *The Valley of Decision* three years earlier), or of critics' inherent failure to respond to a flexibility of poetic form in her 1903 review of Paul's study of Matthew Arnold as referenced in Chap. 2.

Generally overlooked is Wharton's ongoing sharp taking to task of male writers' failures in their portrayals of female protagonists in her critical writings. Her striking accusation in *The Writing of Fiction* that Walter Scott's women are 'Keepsake insipidities' (5)—'conventional and hypocritical when he touched on love and women' (5)—has a precedent stretching back twenty years. In her 1905 review of Hewlett's novel (the same Maurice Hewlett whose volume of verse *Artemision Idylls and Songs* coincides with *Artemis to Actaeon*, as discussed in Chap. 2), Wharton's expert dismantling of his (in)abilities with female characterisations is all the more effective for her spiky wit: 'heroine' Virginia Strozzi 'starts out, for instance, thin to emaciation, and pale to the point of evanescence; but as the novelist warms to his subject (and Mr. Hewlett is nothing if not warm) she grows into the "high-bosomed beauty" with whom his pen habitually consorts' ('Maurice Hewlett's *The Fool Errant* 65). The fact this is viewed as a marked improvement 'from the impersonal phalanx of Mr. Hewlett's earlier leading ladies, of whose carnal charms one has been told in so many more or less similar pages that even these much-emphasised attributes are blurred into a kind of composite portrait' (64) only compounds Hewlett's perceived ineffectuality in this regard. '[O]ne can only assume', concludes Wharton, 'that Mr. Hewlett, bored by the company of a thin girl with no colour, has let his imagination momentarily stray to more congenial society' ('Maurice Hewlett's *The Fool Errant*' 65).

On the other hand, male writers with female protagonists who move beyond 'the caressing hypocrite dear to the novelist of fifty years ago' are highlighted and praised by Wharton the critic.[12] In the same year as her Hewlett review, again for the *Bookman*, the author championed the portrait of Cissy Eccleston in Howard Sturgis' novel *Belchamber* as 'perhaps the most brilliant study in the book' (309)—a 'callous', devious, vindictive woman who causes misery with 'savage indifference' ('Mr. Sturgis's *Belchamber*' 309). Wharton would establish herself as a masterly creator of flawed, three-dimensional women, and at times the reviews offered the opportunity to insist on their representation, not the 'Keepsake insipidities' of yesteryear—the description here of Cissy as 'a bold huntress who…lands her prey' ('Mr. Sturgis's *Belchamber*' 309), namely a husband, decidedly reminiscent of Lily Bart 'tranquilly studying her prey [Percy Gryce] through downcast lashes as she organised her method of attack' on the train to Bellomont (*HM* 26). (The serialisation of *The House of Mirth* was running in *Scribner's Magazine* at the time of this review). In turn, Wharton's defence of Sturgis' 'heroine's reckless indifference to consequences' (309) and 'an extreme expression of a selfish nature's unwillingness to pay for what it has got' ('Mr. Sturgis's *Belchamber*' 309) anticipates the ruthless drive of Undine Spragg eight years down the creative line. With her critical attention to, and implicit insistence that others pay attention to, female protagonists as well as male, Wharton was setting her own terms for what mattered in a literature review and in narrative representation—and at times they were terms by which male authors in her critical writings were very conspicuously seen to fail.

In May 1902 Wharton reviewed for the *Bookman* a critical study of George Eliot by Victorian scholar (and father of Virginia Woolf) Leslie Stephen. Part of the 'English Men of Letters' series, Stephen's study was its first of a woman. Challenging the 'principal charge' and prejudice against Eliot that 'she was to [sic] "scientific," that she sterilised her imagination and deformed her style by the study of biology and metaphysics' ('George Eliot' 247), Wharton notes in her review the similar fascinations of Goethe, Tennyson, and Milton with 'the investigation of science' and asks outright the arresting question, 'Is it because these were men, while George Eliot was a woman, that she is reproved for venturing on ground they did not fear to tread?' (248). As a novelist, Wharton will brilliantly underscore the double standard that judges the lives and reputations of men and women, and here—as a female critic (with her own interdisciplinary interests in metaphysics)—she places that exposure of the double standard at the heart of her review of a male writer's study of a female author, adding 'Dr. Johnson is known to have pronounced portrait-painting "indelicate in a female"; and indications are not wanting that the woman who ventures on scientific studies still does so at the risk of such an epithet' ('George Eliot' 248). Not for the last time, Wharton's critical writing is gendered and inherently feminist (however much she might have hated such a term).

Wharton was of course by no means a lone female critic in the late nineteenth and early twentieth centuries—though by the time of *The Writing of Fiction* there were few of her stature. Writers active in this field included Vernon Lee, Virginia Woolf (discussed below), Willa Cather, Dorothy Richardson, Rebecca West and many others. Cather's short article 'The Novel Démeublé' published in the *New Republic* in April 1922 made a strikingly similar case to Wharton's in *The Writing of Fiction* about the importance of selection in a writer's skill set, while in '[Why] Are There No Great Women Critics?' Susan Sniader Lanser and Evelyn Torton Beck point out that many of Lee's theories in her 1895 essay 'On Literary Construction' and elsewhere became 'mainstays of twentieth-century criticism'.[13] Lanser and Beck conclude, however, that 'the status of the woman critic in the literary world' is to be 'ignored, undervalued, or dismissed if at all possible, especially if she challenges the status quo' (85), with the female critical tradition deeply 'buried and obscured' (81). In the four decades since Lanser and Beck's assessment, more female critical voices have been restored, but Wharton has to a large extent been excluded from this process—and, as Wegener astutely points out, Wharton does not feature in their essay ('"Enthusiasm Guided by Acumen"' 46). Yet Wegener, the scholarly powerhouse behind the making of the critical writings outside *The Writing of Fiction* visible with his edition, suggests that the author 'evidently thought very little of her own efforts in critical writing' and that '[u]ltimately, no aspect of her own work mattered less to Wharton, it appears, than her criticism', describing *The Writing of Fiction* as 'a volume itself somewhat cobbled together' ('"Enthusiasm Guided by Acumen"' 15).

It has been suggested that Wharton seriously resisted putting herself forward as a professional critic. Wegener writes of 'the diffidence and self-distrust that continually bedeviled her attempts to exercise her critical faculties' ('The Difficult Writing' 60–61), of an author 'assailed by anxieties and constraints' ('The Difficult Writing' 70), 'the *phobias* that had kept Wharton inactive as a critic for so much of her career [my emphasis]' ('The Difficult Writing' 70), while the introduction to his critical edition notes Wharton's 'painful and lingering doubts about her own abilities in that mode', the writer 'struggling … so doggedly to express herself as a critic', 'the very area in which Wharton's struggles as a writer are especially pronounced and poignant' ('"Enthusiasm Guided by Acumen"' 6, 46, 43). Wegener 'senses…that she was afflicted by a … pervasive and profoundly inhibiting sense of unworthiness along these lines' ('"Enthusiasm Guided by Acumen"' 5), reaching the conclusion that *The Writing of Fiction* represents 'a moving testament to the determination with which Wharton, *even as she entered her sixties*, gamely subdued a host of doubts and uncertainties that would have defeated a fainter spirit [my emphasis]' ('The Difficult Writing' 77). On the contrary, I would suggest we can see Wharton had a very self-confident voice as a critic from the early 1900s and knew the 'game' of criticism even as an adolescent. And a writer entering their sixties is surely *exactly* the moment when we might expect a major, established author really to weigh in with their views. Certainly Wharton made dramatic claims in correspondence with friends, most notably to William Crary Brownell in October 1924: 'The truth is, my irrepressible desire to write critical articles is equalled only by my cowardice & incapacity when I sit down to the task. Each time I swear, Never again!'; '"Fiction" II & III only half done, & more terrifying to me than any novel I ever undertook'; 'I shall…tremble like an aspen when you read "Fiction I"' (cited 'The Difficult Writing' 70). Yet on the one hand the bar was set extraordinarily high in Wharton's estimation here—she opened her tribute to Brownell shortly after his death by describing him in *Scribner's Magazine* as '[t]he most discerning literary critic of our day',[14] and on the other Wharton's letters so often play to her audience. As we have seen, she would use a similar line with Brownell over her poetry, expressing uncertainty that she had 'ever reached the "poetry line"'

(*Letters* 75), and at times she combined self-deprecation and subservience, even exaggerated, affected prostration, along with a sense of playfulness. And the author could be entirely disingenuous in that role. Take her 'Talk to American Soldiers' in the spring of 1918. Having been asked to 'talk about France', the writer opens with a series of ingratiating comments. 'I never expected to speak in public. I consider it a man's job and not a woman's', she demurs, appealing to her audience: 'you must make allowances for my timidity, and encourage me by laughing at all my jokes'.[15] Self-deprecation and ingratiation cast aside, Wharton then launches into a highly eloquent, rousing defence of France. At times Wharton would fall her own victim of playing to an image or to expectations: the grande dame; amateur lady critic; female disciple of her men of letters friends, whether Brownell, Percy Lubbock, Gaillard Lapsley, or Henry James who had died in 1916. Yet this was a consummately professional writer with a hugely successful career, who by the 1920s also found that career being questioned as never before. By 1925, she wanted her thoughts on the writing of fiction on public record. And Wharton went one step further than many female contemporaries and immediate predecessors. Not content with individual essays, she presented a *volume* of critical writings, a further act of professional validation.

One of the pervasive myths surrounding *The Writing of Fiction* remains that it is wholly, fiercely, even vehemently, anti-modernist. The text in this respect has been tainted by association with some of Wharton's late critical writings which targeted—and indeed named—a number of 'offending' modernist writers. In her April 1934 essay, 'Permanent Values in Fiction', published in the *Saturday Review of Literature*, Wharton carefully directed her aim, arguing that to an older generation the novel is 'a work of fiction containing a good story about well-drawn characters' but to 'a generation nurtured on Mr. Joyce and Mrs. Woolf such a definition would seem not only pitifully simple, but far from comprehensive.'[16] Fashions notwithstanding, Wharton believed throughout her career that character creation was the lifeblood of fiction and the results of that thinking are clear: an oeuvre with a dazzling array of characters unsurpassed in modern literature. She cites D. H. Lawrence as one of the modern writers whose characters are often 'no more differentiated than a set of megaphones, through all of which the same voice interminably reiterates the same ideas' ('Permanent Values in Fiction' 603). Wharton bewails in this essay 'a cultured mediocrity' (604), 'the dissemination of pseudo-culture' (604), 'current literary contagions' (604), while suggesting a 'long course of cinema obviousnesses and of tabloid culture has rendered the majority of readers insensible to allusiveness and to irony' (604). Four months earlier, in 'Tendencies in Modern Fiction', also published in *Saturday Review of Literature*, the writer brusquely surmised that 'so far as the new novelists may be said to have any theory of their art, it seems to be that every new creation can issue only from the annihilation of what preceded it'; 'the trend of the new fiction, not only in America and England, but on the continent, is chiefly toward the amorphous and the agglutinative.'[17] In her more interesting, layered 1927 essay for the *Yale Review*, 'The Great American Novel'—notably short on American novels on the whole (though along with the discussion of Sinclair Lewis, Wharton hails his predecessors Robert Grant's *Unleavened Bread*, the heavy-hitting David Graham Phillips' *Susan Lenox: Her Fall and Rise* and Frank Norris' *McTeague* as 'not only "great American novels," but great novels'—which is rather her point)—the author starkly suggests nevertheless that American culture offers 'so meagre a material to the imagination' and a 'safe, shallow, and shadowless world'.[18]

The Writing of Fiction is not a mould of any set formula but offers instead a less rigid presentation than generally remembered, a welcome antidote to those crystallised images of Wharton as the relic, set in her ways. 'Order the beauty even of Beauty is' swiftly gives way to language imbued with a pervasive tenor of flexibility and possibility, a tenor advertised to readers in the opening line: 'To treat of the practice of fiction is to deal with the newest, most fluid and least formulated of the arts' (*WF* 3) (though of course the absence of film here among those newest arts is telling), while fiction itself is described as still 'an art in the making, fluent and dirigible, and combining a past full enough for the deduction of certain general principles with a future rich in untried possibilities' (*WF* 8). '[I]n the glorious brain of Balzac', writes Wharton, 'sprang that strange chameleon-creature, the modern novel, which changes its shape and colour with every subject on which it rests' (*WF* 61). The text memorably warns against excessive prescription: 'General rules in art are useful chiefly as a lamp in a mine, or a hand-rail down a black stairway; they are necessary for the sake of the guidance they give, but it is a mistake, once they are formulated, to be too much in awe of them' (*WF* 42). In its openness and flexibility, *The Writing of Fiction* pushes critical writing beyond prescriptive boundaries, and that flexibility is essential for Wharton's artistic vision in which 'genius' and 'inspiration' are the *sine qua non*, but insufficient on their own to make art: 'To its making go patience, meditation, concentration, all the quiet habits of mind now so little practised, so seldom inculcated; and to these must be added the final imponderable, genius, without which the rest is useless, and which, conversely, would be unusable without the rest' (*WF* 98).

Scholars have found Wharton's mix problematic when it comes to 'her theorizing on the art of fiction'. Vita-Finzi, for example, suggests that Wharton's 'intellectual wish for rules and formulae to guide the writer could not override her intuitive knowledge of an inexplicable, subjective quality coming from an unknowable source within the individual artist', placing her 'between the two stools of dogmatic assertion and vague speculation' in her theory.[19] Wegener, meanwhile, 'senses Wharton hovering indecisively…in trying to settle upon a primary originating agent of both imaginative and critical labor' between the two candidates of 'rigorous, hard-nosed technical schema' and 'the ancient mystique of "inspiration"' ('"Enthusiasm Guided by Acumen"' 30). As Jennifer Haytock recognises, 'Something about art, she found, would not submit itself entirely to rules' (164). And *The Writing of Fiction* does not disguise that; it recognises, highlights, even embraces it. Wharton produces a user-friendly handbook that acknowledges and validates the space, the mystery, the licence to be individual. At the same time, taking its place as one of Wharton's most interdisciplinary texts, *The Writing of Fiction* also works against undue reverence, peppered as it is with references reaching out to other pragmatic creative disciplines, practitioners and forms: musicians, actresses, cooks, dressmakers, even a chocolatier. This is also a practical text, promoting craft, the emphasis on the active, on communication: '*Telling* A Short Story', '*Constructing* A Novel' (my emphasis) and the volume's very title. '[H]omely analogies confirm the lesson', suggests the writer: 'the seemingly simplest sauces are those that have been most cunningly combined and then most completely blent, the simplest-looking dresses those that require most study to design' (*WF* 53–54). Wharton recounts the story of the French confectioner in New York who explains that his chocolate is not equal to that made in Paris because it cannot be worked over as many times as the French confectioner's, on account of the expense (*WF* 53). In an undated letter to Morton Fullerton Wharton linked the last analogy explicitly to the writing of prose: 'prose, like chocolate, must be "worked" *twelve times* to reach a proper consistency' (cited by Haytock 163).

An explicit address to modernism in *The Writing of Fiction* is largely confined to its bookends: part of the general discussion of the opening chapter, while the volume closes with the particular, an examination of

Proust in chapter five. Wharton carefully assigns 'modern' a 300-plus-year history, tracing the origins of modern fiction to the seventeenth century when 'the "action" of the novel was transferred from the street to the soul' (*WF* 3). And, tellingly, the first writer referenced in *The Writing of Fiction* is a woman. Wharton, seen at times to be hostile or at best ambivalent to women writers and scholars, credits a female writer as 'probably' the first to make that epoch-defining step of transferring action from street to soul—seventeenth-century author Madame de La Fayette (*WF* 3). Later writers join an illustrious list—Abbé Prévost (Wharton, as we have seen in Chap. 3, would adapt his novel, *Manon Lescaut*, into a play), Denis Diderot, Henry Fielding, Tobias Smollett, Samuel Richardson, Walter Scott, Goethe, with 'modern fiction… differentiated by the great dividing geniuses of Balzac and Stendhal' (*WF* 4–5). In such company Wharton undercuts any idea of modern literature as a twentieth, even nineteenth-century concept, closely interweaving it instead into a three-century-old tapestry of which Raymond de Chelles in *The Custom of the Country* might have been proud. In turn, she then moves to posit a different reading of modernism, notably challenging its claims to originality, disputing, for example, the newness of the stream of consciousness technique. Wharton reads it instead as a re-emergence of *tranche de vie*, 'the old trick of the early French "realists"' (*WF* 10): '…the slice of life… has lately reappeared, marked by certain unimportant differences, and relabelled the stream of consciousness; and, curiously enough, without its new exponents' appearing aware that they are not also its originators' (*WF* 11). In the final chapter devoted to Proust, Wharton is herself innovative by virtue of being one the earliest American admirers of Proust—though she tellingly reads him as a 'renovator', not an innovator: 'his strength is the strength of tradition' (*WF* 154). The author states her case that 'the greatest novelists' have 'never been deluded by the idea that the subconscious … could in itself furnish the materials for their art'; they 'have made use of the stammerings and murmurings of the half-conscious mind whenever—but only when—such a state of mental flux fitted into the whole picture of the person portrayed' (*WF* 12–13). (In February 1922 Wharton asked Berenson that Mary should not 'befuddle' her young friend Philomène de Lévis-Mirepoix 'with Freudianism & all its jargon': 'She'd take to it like a duck to—sewerage. And what she wants is to develop the *conscious*, & not grub after the sub-conscious. She wants to be taught first to see, to attend, to reflect' [*Letters* 451]).

Perhaps too easily forgotten is that many of the texts we now think of as cornerstone works of modernism had still to be published as Wharton worked on *The Writing of Fiction*. Indeed a number of these texts emerged at the same time as the volume, in a year of extraordinary literary cultural production. The year 1925 saw the release of Fitzgerald's *The Great Gatsby*, Stein's *The Making of Americans*, Hemingway's *In Our Time*, Loos' *Gentlemen Prefer Blondes*, as well as Dreiser's *An American Tragedy*, Kafka's *The Trial*, Cather's *The Professor's House*, Locke's anthology *The New Negro: An Interpretation*, her own *The Mother's Recompense*, and Woolf's *Mrs Dalloway* with which Wharton's work had been unfavourably compared. It was also the year in which *The New Yorker* was established. Not even Edith Wharton can be expected to account for what did not exist.

Instead, *The Writing of Fiction* argues more generally against short-cuts (always Wharton's *bête noir*) in art, against ignorance, fear, perceived gimmicks. In many ways, this is all part of Wharton's creative connectedness, her acute sense of place, of cultural indebtedness, of what has gone before. She argues unapologetically for selection ('in fiction, as in every other art...any theory must begin by assuming the need of selection' [*WF* 8])—and indeed the volume illuminates Wharton as an avowed minimalist: in a short story, 'the real achievement...is to suggest illimitable air within a narrow space' (*WF* 55); a narrator's ability to '"situate" his tale in an opening passage...shall be a clue to all the detail eliminated' (*WF* 53); 'To choose between all this material is the first step toward coherent expression' (*WF* 9). The writer with the reputation for detail and the intricacies of interior design in her description of domestic space advocates for a few, well-chosen strokes, reminding us that the most powerful resonances of Wharton's work often lie in the gaps, the silence, what remains unsaid. If this in itself seems worthy of Ernest Hemingway, many other stand-out quotes from *The Writing of Fiction* would find a place in the toolbox of the boldest, new modernist writers about to break through in 1925. Wharton suggests, for example, 'that the same experience never happens to any two people' (*WF* 86–87); she acknowledges '[i]n a sense classification is always arbitrary and belittling' (69); she values means of economy (55–56) (very different from short-cuts); as in *Italian Backgrounds*, she opens up parentheses (119); she argues against 'the indolent habit' of decorating the surface of a subject (56). Certainly she proposes 'types' of novels (manners, character or psychology, adventure) but these then stretch to 'subdivisions' (*WF* 66), before the category-defying take pride of place: 'in the zone of the unclassifiable float such enchanting hybrids' (*WF* 67) (and the volume subverts the traditional hierarchy of literary discourse by placing the chapter on the short story ahead of that on the novel). Wharton as a critic shows no fear for the spaces, the indefinable, that which is in-between.

The Writing of Fiction certainly advocates for an overarching form, but even here Wharton's definition, 'the order, in time and importance, in which the incidents of the narrative are grouped' (81), is an expansive one pushing past conventional parameters, and indeed eleven years earlier in her essay 'The Criticism of Fiction' for the *Times Literary Supplement* she challenged 'the oddly limited senses in which the word is generally used by English-speaking critics; that is, either as an antithesis to subject or as something that subject puts on like an outer garment.'[20] 'True originality', writes Wharton, 'consists not in a new manner but in a new vision' (*WF* 18). For this author, the 'distrust of technique and the fear of being unoriginal' are dangerous precedents, seen to lead to 'pure anarchy in fiction', a situation where 'in certain schools formlessness is…regarded as the first condition of form' (*WF* 14). Yet the same writer also praises Balzac and Stendhal for being 'the first to seem continuously aware that the bounds of a personality are not reproducible by a sharp black line, but that each of us flows imperceptibly into adjacent people and things' (*WF* 7). This is not a 'confused' and 'repetitious' attempt to express a theory of fiction, but a more balanced thesis than detractors have claimed, Wharton avowedly reading practices of the 'now' within three centuries of literary and historical context, with young contemporaries one part of a much bigger picture, not its whole. Collectively Wharton's theories may not have been considered fashionable—indeed she had major issues with what she perceived as fashionable theories—but un-fashionability does not automatically invalidate her views or prove that her convictions about the writing of fiction illuminate 'regressive social and political views'.[21] In her chapter on Marcel Proust, she addresses this directly: 'Fashions in the arts come and go, and it is of little interest to try to analyze the work of any artist who does not give one the sense of being in some sort above them' (*WF* 156).

The warnings about perceived literary short-cuts and fashions expressed in the theory of *The Writing of Fiction* would later manifest and personalise themselves in the plots of Wharton's Vance Weston novels, *Hudson River Bracketed* (1929) and *The Gods Arrive* (1932). As early as 1913, Wharton had begun planning an ambitious novel (seven books, forty-two to forty-five chapters) to be called *Literature*, exploring the making of a writer, Dick Thaxter, from childhood through the challenges of false starts and false muses, literary experiments, and the conflicting demands of commercial and literary success. (In an early notebook entry, the title of one of Dick's books is listed as 'Vision', again recalling the work by Traherne which showcases Wharton's motto.) *Literature* was a project derailed by the onset of the First World War, but one for which she continued to cherish ambitions into the 1920s, with many of its ideas eventually re-imagined for her portrait of the artist in *Hudson River Bracketed* and *The Gods Arrive*, carefully transposed to a postwar setting. A notable misdirection in the character Vance's literary journey will be *Colossus*, perceived as being too heavily influenced by 'fashionable', 'modern' trends: 'much too long, nothing particular happened in it, and few people even pretended to know what it was about.'[22] A potential parody of *Ulysses*, '"Colossus" was not his own book, brain of his brain, flesh of his flesh, as it had seemed while he was at work on it, but a kind of hybrid monster made out of the crossings of his own imaginings with those imposed on him by the literary fashions and influences of the day' (*GA* 393). Hybrids and chameleons for Wharton have the potential to be glorious and enchanting, as described in *The Writing of Fiction*, but also monstrous if they involve what she perceives as a synthetic grafting of fashion for fashion's sake. Wharton tellingly does not advocate censorship. She regrets both the 'tidal wave of prudery' (*WF* 62) that hampered the nineteenth-century British novelist, and the contemporary, perceived 'opposite excess of dirt-for-dirt's sake' in the '"now-that-it-can-be-told school"' (*WF* 65). The latter she sees as an 'inevitable' reaction and believes the 'balance will right itself with the habit of freedom' (*WF* 66).

While most 1920s reviewers of *The Writing of Fiction* offered a mix of courtesy and condescension there were two remarkably effusive reviews (among those missing from the usually invaluable volume, *Edith Wharton: The Contemporary Reviews*). One, 'An Artist on Her Art', was penned by writer Zona Gale, recipient of the Pulitzer Prize for drama, the same year Wharton won for fiction—another first for a woman; the second was a three-part review in *The New York Herald Tribune* of the serialised articles by an anonymous reviewer, whom Wharton would, via an enquiry to Charles Scribner, identify as the art critic Royal Cortissoz (see *Letters* 486).[23] In their effusiveness, however, both reviews ultimately succeeded best in setting Wharton apart, severing her from the present. In his expansive appraisal, Cortissoz presented his reader with an invitation to join the initiated elite: 'Mrs. Wharton's reflections urgently commend themselves to those who take their fiction seriously, asking of it more than passing entertainment' ('The Secrets of Fiction'). His review went far beyond an exposition of the work in question, Cortissoz seizing the opportunity to validate and reinforce a perceived shared artistic creed. Wharton may have described both reviews as 'wonderful' in private correspondence[24]—she was after all portrayed as courageous, authentic, luminous and wise, with the reviews in stark contrast to the condescensions noted below—but the tone of sneering elitism expressed by Cortissoz was more his invention than *The Writing of Fiction*'s. 'With proud loyalty to the high principle of a great art she makes such a statement as the uneasy little so-called "liberals" could not even understand', writes Cortissoz in 'The Art of Fiction', while in 'The Secrets of Fiction' he takes the liberty of '[t]ransposing' Wharton's 'polite argument into blunter terms' to 'say that what a good deal of contemporary fiction needs is more brain-stuff.' While her very late critical writings were undoubtedly more acerbic, the streak of venom that marked some of Wharton's private correspondence in her assessment of younger contemporaries did not transfer wholesale to the critical writings in 1925.

Gale's review, meanwhile, one of the few by a woman, came close at points to hagiography, but more interesting was her statement that '[t]he writing of fiction here means the writing of fiction as it has been written in its best examples in the past; the writing of fiction, moreover, in France and in England, or by Tolstoy, Dostoievsky or Goethe.' In a rare criticism, Gale saw Wharton's vision as insufficiently modern and, mirroring Virginia Woolf's review, insufficiently *American*: 'mentioning nobody now living save, fleetly, Hardy and Mr. Kipling; and nobody in America, save Hawthorne, Poe and Henry James (and once "The Emperor Jones"); one's desire for more is yet frankly avid' ('An Artist on Her Art'). In her wish that Wharton had drawn examples 'from to-day as well as from yesterday', Gale seems to overlook the fact that one of the five chapters is devoted to Proust, one of the most influential writers of the early twentieth century who had died only three years previously ('An Artist on Her Art'). A critical volume to which Gale had contributed three years before the appearance of *The Writing of Fiction* unexpectedly illuminates the possibilities, the openness, and indeed the progressive nature of Wharton's vision. *The Novel of Tomorrow And The Scope of Fiction*, published in 1922, comprised a series of articles that had first appeared in April of that year in a supplement to *The New Republic*. (Cather's 'The Novel Démeublé' and

Theodore Dreiser's 'The Scope of Fiction' appeared in *The New Republic*, but were not included in the volume.[25]) The volume's author line told it all: 'The Novel of Tomorrow And the Scope of Fiction By Twelve *American* Novelists [my emphasis]'. The novel of tomorrow, it seems, was certainly American, its evaluator white and primarily male (nine of the volume's twelve contributors were men). The American novel, determined Gale, requires an 'organic beauty', currently lacking.[26]

Proust notwithstanding, Gale is correct that twentieth-century figures are barely name-checked in Wharton's volume, and, other than allusions to Henry James, notably his Wharton-termed 'entangled prefaces' to the New York edition of his works (*WF* 45), American writers of any time period are rarely referenced at all: in passing, her predecessors Poe, Hawthorne, and Melville. In direct opposition to Woolf's complaint that some American writers essentially were insufficiently 'American' in their work, Wharton's 1927 essay, 'The Great American Novel', argued against the reductive expectation that 'really to deserve the epithet "American"', the 'novelist's scene must be laid in the United States, and his story deal exclusively with citizens of those States' and that 'it must tell of persons so limited in education and opportunity that they live cut off from all the varied sources of culture which used to be considered the common heritage of English-speaking people' ('The Great American Novel' 647). Such requirements would have ruled most of Wharton's own work out of contention. The author proposes instead in the essay's closing paragraph a widening of horizons, that the 'greatest American novel' 'will probably turn out to be very different….Its scene may be laid in an American small town or in a European capital; it may deal with the present or the past, with great events or trivial happenings; but in the latter case it will certainly contrive to relate them to something greater than themselves' ('The Great American Novel' 656). Wharton counters that when such a novel comes 'there is every chance that it will catch us all napping, that the first year's sales will be disappointingly small, and that even those indefatigable mythomaniacs, the writers for the jackets, may for once not be ready with their superlatives' ('The Great American Novel' 656). Expect the unexpected. Once again, while they have been customarily read as fixed and inflexible, cut to fit the cloth of their author's imperious grande dame image, Wharton's critical writings can often be seen to open up possibilities rather than close them down, and here we see that stance against small thinking, against nationalism, provincialism and standardisation. By allowing for individuality, by embracing difference, by not enforcing a rigid rule book, *The Writing of Fiction* implicitly offers up a less elitist vision of the artist and it is one that never suggests men only may apply.

A number of reviewers expressed uncertainty over the intended audience for the book: namely whether it was addressed to reader, critic, student or novelist. '[T]he doubt remains—for whom precisely is such a critical *sketch* as this designed? [my emphasis]' asked the eager-to-pinpoint, normally all-embracing, interdisciplinary British publication, *The Saturday Review of Politics, Literature, Science and Art*.[27] The *Times Literary Supplement* was clear about the choice, if uncertain of its wisdom: 'Mr. Percy Lubbock's book, *The Craft of Fiction*, was addressed rather to the reader and the critic of fiction than to the novelist. Mrs. Wharton's is addressed rather to the novelist than to the reader.'[28] Lubbock's focus had been intentionally 'modest':

> A few familiar novels, possibly a dozen, by still fewer writers ... And I shall consider them, too with no idea of criticizing all their aspects, or even more than one...And as for the few novels that I shall speak of, they will be such as appear to illustrate most plainly the various elements of the craft...The beginning of criticism is to read aright, in other words to get into touch with the book as nearly as may be.[29]

Wharton's volume, by contrast, is again distinctive in that it is often addressed primarily to the writer rather than the armchair reader. Its title is the writing of fiction, after all, not the reading or critiquing. She describes the volume as 'the quest [very different from 'attempt'] for an intelligible working theory' (*WF* 118) on the writing of fiction and it is her most user-friendly text, offering clear and sound advice without reducing good writing to an intransigent formula. Wharton, who in many ways is an author being sidelined or written out as part of that Age of Vulnerability, is claiming her writer's place: she's one of them, she's part of a rich tradition stretching back for centuries. And as a writer who is being increasingly critiqued for inflexibility she is almost perversely coming under question for the very malleability of her critical writing.

The Writing of Fiction and a number of Wharton's critical essays display a nuanced sensitivity to the conflicting pressures facing writers and debilitating market conditions that require both work produced at speed and more of the same work: 'the novelist of the present day is in danger of being caught in a vicious circle, for the insatiable demand for quick production tends to keep him in a state of perpetual immaturity' (*WF* 17–18);

'This habit of the reader of wanting each author to give only what he has given before...is one of the most insidious temptations to the young artist to go on doing what he already knows how to do, and knows he will be praised for doing' (*WF* 115); critics display 'their eagerness to stake out each novelist's territory, and to confine him to it for life' (*WF* 115). *The Writing of Fiction* represents Wharton's fiercest attack on the marketplace (on which she was dependent) since *The Custom of the Country*. And as Wharton does so masterfully in her fiction she presents that attack in the language of the market, but re-appropriates its terms: 'economy', 'expenditure', 'expense' (*WF* 56–57). '[T]rue expenditure' is 'devoting time, meditation and patient labour to the process of extraction and representation', while expense is 'expense of time, of patience, of study, of thought, of letting hundreds of stray experiences accumulate and group themselves' (*WF* 57). Again there are no short-cuts. Wharton is on the writer's side, and in this regard much of her published critical writing incorporates a critique of critics and marketplace forces seen to place obstacles in the writer's path to artistic maturity and permanence.

While Wharton was broadly seen to be contributing to a burgeoning critical tradition, with contemporary reviewers referencing critical writing by William Dean Howells, Henry James, Robert Louis Stevenson, Émile Zola, Percy Lubbock, Herbert Spencer, among others, her contribution was often viewed as thin, derivative, or out of step. Most often, *The Writing of Fiction* was held up for comparison with the author's (then) friend Lubbock's *The Craft of Fiction*, published four years earlier, and Wharton's volume found wanting. *The Craft of Fiction*, enthusiastically and generously promoted by Wharton, was seen as the standard bearer which the female critic could not quite match. For J. B. Priestley, Wharton offered 'scattered notes instead of a closely-woven argument (like that of Mr. Lubbock)', a thesis he reiterates: 'The fact that her study is slight and scrappy—a bundle of notes rather than a closely-woven argument—makes it disappointing, and we cannot accept it as a companion volume to Mr. Lubbock's *Craft of Fiction*.'[30] Indeed, the language of diminution permeates the contemporary reviews: 'this little volume', 'all-too short treatise', her 'little book', her 'little study',[31] alongside Priestley's judgement of 'rather slight', 'rather scrappy', subsequently downgraded to 'slight and scrappy' ('The Novelist's Art' 386). The *Times Literary Supplement* opened its review of *The Writing of Fiction* not with Wharton's work, but with reference to 'Mr. Percy Lubbock's book, *The Craft of Fiction*...' before suggesting 'it is amusing to compare what she says of particular novelists with what Mr. Percy Lubbock says of them' (*TLS* 388). Literary history seemed to be repeating itself. While early reviews of Wharton's work had held her writing up for comparison with Henry James, here was a subsequent generation of reviewers holding her work up for unfavourable comparison with James' 'disciple' Lubbock. In *Revue Anglo-Américaine*, twenty-four-year-old Henri Peyre, still to become internationally renowned, was more open to a different approach, though even so not without a whiff of comparative condescension: 'Il ne faut pas chercher ici d'étude détaillée de tel ou tel roman russe, français, ou anglais, de ces études pénétrantes et fouillées qui faisaient la valeur de l'ouvrage de Percy Lubbock sur *The Craft of Fiction*—mais on y trouvera en revanche un certain nombre de remarques fines, inspirées par une intelligence claire et un goût sûr et expérimenté.'[32] Even the approbation of the *New Statesman* was unmistakably gendered: 'These essays are well thought out and expressed with (if the adjective be not offensive in this connection) masculine brevity and clearness.'[33] In a pivoting masculinist and imperialist analogy, Priestley described the criticism of fiction as 'still a gigantic virgin continent', casting James and Lubbock among the explorers setting out for this 'unknown territory' or group of 'pioneers' clearing away some of the undergrowth. James in his critical prefaces 'made camps and trails right across the continent', before Lubbock, with *The Craft of Fiction*, 'succeeded in linking up all these camps with a light railway'. Wharton, meanwhile, only brought up the rear, taking a 'trip on this railway' and occasionally making 'not unladylike excursions into the surrounding jungle' ('The Novelist's Art' 386). Mrs Wharton was the lady explorer in a still primitive, male realm. It was an unknown province penetrated by men—in this case two men who happened to have been Wharton's friends.

The male 'pioneers' James and Lubbock were important members of the author's inner circle, with Wharton the only woman at its core. In her memoir, she would reminisce over the group as 'our little knot of friends' (*BG* 255), the 'inner group' (231), 'my intimate friends' (296), a combination of famous and now forgotten names, including James, Lubbock, Howard Sturgis, Walter Berry, Gaillard Lapsley, John Hugh Smith, and Robert Norton. It was a circle that survived the death of James in 1916, though a decade later Wharton and Lubbock had an irreparable falling-out over his marriage to Sybil Cutting, the woman Wharton accused of 'annexing' her friends. Susan Goodman recognises that '[t]he men of the inner circle praised, coddled, and loved Wharton, but they ultimately believed in and prided themselves on the supremacy of their own sex.'[34] Lee, meanwhile, suggests that though it was 'the only family where Wharton felt secure' (244), 'this group of friends surrounding James was a snobbish group of minor talents, imitating the Master's manner without his genius' (244). 'Their attitudes', continues Lee, 'would affect Wharton's posthumous reputation, which was fixed by them, for many decades, as the "piece of work" they all enjoyed admiring and resenting, the Master's domineering friend and his inferior' (244–45).

If Wharton's reputation ultimately suffered from her association with the inner circle, Lubbock certainly profited from his. He was enthusiastically endorsed and promoted by both Wharton and James. Wharton recalled James describing Lubbock as 'the only *man of letters* in England' (*Letters* 276), while Wharton campaigned in 1916 for Lubbock to edit James' letters, praising his 'extraordinary literary sense and his experience in biographical work' (*Letters* 378), deeming him 'the one person fitted for this very delicate task' (*Letters* 376). Described as 'an ardent disciple of Henry James' by Lewis and Lewis (*Letters* 175, fn2) and as James' acolyte by Goodman (16), Lubbock (1879–1966) when he met Wharton in 1906 was just starting out, beginning his appointment as the librarian of the Samuel Pepys Collection at Magdalene College, Cambridge, while Wharton was already a writer of international renown. 1906 saw the publication of Lubbock's first book, *Elizabeth Barrett Browning in Her Letters*. Best remembered for *The Craft of Fiction* (Wharton would send a copy of her friend's 1921 book to Sinclair Lewis, describing it as 'full of interesting and suggestive things for people of our trade' [*Letters* 449]) and the two-volume edition of James' letters, published in 1920, Lubbock would also edit the diary of A. C. Benson, write two novels and memoirs. Goodman records that the early relationship between Wharton and Lubbock 'cast him as the courtly admirer of the "dear & great & dear lady," who always "instantly understood" and "clarified and made all large & fine & beautiful"' and that he 'at one time found Wharton's criticism the only standard by which his work deserved to be judged'.[35] By 1925, the balance had shifted. A November 1925 letter from Lubbock (still to 'Dearest Edith' from 'Your affcte PL'), found in the copy of *The Writing of Fiction* in Wharton's library, and written shortly after they had exchanged gifts of Wharton's volume of critical writing and Lubbock's novel, *The Region Cloud* published the same year, is revealing. Though it offered an enthusiastic response to Wharton's volume of critical writing, the language simultaneously established the idea of transgression, the notion that generic territories had been crossed on both sides, validating Lubbock as the critic and Wharton as the novelist:

> Our parts seem to have got mixed—I sending you fiction, you sending me directions for writing it!—well, it is very clear to me, fresh from your book this morning, that my pen in your hand is a good deal sharper than yours in mine—I do like this book—especially the first part—so lucid & incisive—all that I miss in the later chapters is simply more—more expansion, and more illustration (such an easy demand, I know—& such a troublesome one—it's so difficult to find the illustration that exactly fits)—& after all it is just your brevity & clarity that may pierce the young novelists & shake them with wholesome qualms—it will do them much good. As for me, I shall be careful how I poach again.[36]

Private comments were one matter; public record was another, and *The Craft of Fiction* made no reference to Wharton or her work. By 1921 Lubbock was seen to have been validated by his work in the field, not least the two-volume edition of James' letters, and the authority of his subject, two volumes which—though selective and protective—had been greeted with almost universal acclaim and became the standard bearer edition for several decades. Wharton's *The Writing of Fiction*, by contrast, was not afforded that badge of legitimacy. *The Craft of Fiction*, by a man, was swiftly regarded as a classic; *The Writing of Fiction* was swiftly overlooked, while the 'critical reception of her treatise on fiction writing continued to deny her the status of a literary professional and, additionally, refused to accord her that of a literary-critical professional.'[37] Wharton, who did so little to advocate openly for the advancement of women, was staking a claim to a literary realm still largely perceived as a male domain, not via an individual article or opinion piece, but through a volume of criticism that unabashedly advertised itself as such. Her prizes, acclaim, literary pedigree and commercial success would not guarantee a fair hearing—and the early indications were that she would not get it.

There is no evidence that *The Writing of Fiction* was among Virginia Woolf's prolific reading, but four years later as she awaited publication of her own 'treatise', *A Room of One's Own*, her diary musings anticipated a critical response echoing a number of features that surfaced in the reception of Wharton's earlier text:

> I will here sum up my impressions before publishing a Room of One's Own....I forecast, then, that I shall get no criticism, except of the evasive

jocular kind, from Lytton, Roger & Morgan; that the press will be kind & talk of its charm, & sprightliness; ... I am afraid it will not be taken seriously. Mrs Woolf is so accomplished a writer that all she says makes easy reading ... this very feminine logic...[38]

Woolf's suspicions proved right on a number of levels. In 'Queen of the Highbrows', a review in the *London Evening Standard*, Arnold Bennett wrote that Woolf in *A Room of One's Own* was 'merely the victim of her extraordinary gift of fancy (not imagination)'. The *Times Literary Supplement* review was favourable, but condescending in its labelling of the text as 'a delightfully peripatetic essay'. Rebecca West, meanwhile, judged Woolf's study 'an uncompromising piece of feminist propaganda: I think the ablest yet written'.[39] Wharton's volume stands as a concrete pre-validation of many of the central tenets of Woolf's 1929 *A Room of One's Own*. Wharton had money, she had many comfortable rooms of her own, but *The Writing of Fiction* was still denied legitimacy, and Wharton was perceived to be as much of a trespasser as Woolf's narrator crossing an Oxbridge college lawn.

The Writing of Fiction was dedicated to Gaillard Lapsley, an important figure both in Wharton's mature years and her immediate posthumous critical reception. Born in New York in 1871, he graduated from Harvard in 1893, became an expert on medieval constitutional history and was elected a Fellow of Trinity College Cambridge University in 1904 where he remained until 1937, when ill-health and the threat of war prompted his return to the United States where he died in 1949.[40] Wharton and Lapsley first met in 1904 and were friends for over thirty years. His significance is often downplayed in Wharton scholarship, Lapsley homogenised simply as one of the author's male coterie, one of the so-called 'male wives'. Yet it was Lapsley who was selected not only as friend and advisor, but as editor and literary executor for Wharton, and in those later roles he left a lasting critical imprint. Wharton bequeathed him responsibility for all of her 'manuscripts, literary correspondence and documents, with the request that he shall take care of the publication, sale, preservation or destruction of all such documents and manuscripts', calling if necessary on Kenneth Clark for help (cited Lee 754). Lapsley handled Wharton's papers; he sold the letters and manuscripts to Yale University in 1938, stipulating an embargo on the publication of anything of a biographical nature for thirty years. He was instrumental in the publication by Appleton-Century in 1939 of *Eternal Passion in English Poetry*, the anthology of love poems selected by Wharton and Robert Norton, 'with the collaboration of

Gaillard Lapsley', a volume for which Wharton had prepared a brief preface, as discussed in Chap. 2. Lapsley produced from Wharton's typescripts the edition of her final, unfinished novel, *The Buccaneers*, published posthumously in 1938. His preface and afterword to the novel explicated a range of dilemmas faced in the process, with, in his words, publication of an incomplete manuscript raising 'critical and literary questions of considerable interest' (*B* v) as he prepared the 'torso' (*B* 361) of a volume for public scrutiny, examining Wharton's working practices, manuscript variants, and writing processes. He would also appoint Percy Lubbock as Wharton's first official (and controversial) biographer. In his preface to *Portrait of Edith Wharton*, taking the form of a letter written to Lapsley in September 1944, Lubbock described the discussions the two men had held regarding the 'kind of book' he should write (v). They had agreed: '[c]ertainly not a formal biography…; her own *Backward Glance*, informal as it is, seemed biography enough.' Instead it was to be 'a portrait, a likeness of her as her friends knew her and she lives in their memory' (*Portrait* v). In the preface, Wharton would be objectified, treated as a case study, the two men determining the terms on which the female subject would be conveyed.

Intriguingly, Lapsley also made preparations after Wharton's death for his own proposed edition of her uncollected critical writings. Papers in Lapsley's archive at Trinity College Library, Cambridge University related to this project include sheets of handwritten pencilled commentary on a selection of Wharton's essays, correspondence with editors concerning the reprinting of essays, copies of essays, drafts of 'A Further Glance' (a memoir referenced in Chaps. 3 and 7), and sixty-two pages of work on his introductory essay. The project was never completed. While the notes and draft are undated, of the fifteen letters regarding permission for Lapsley to copy and use works by Wharton first published elsewhere, four are dated between September and December 1939, the remaining eleven between January and May 1943. The letter from John L. B. Williams at Appleton-Century agreeing to Lapsley's plan for the introduction to the volume is dated 9 February 1943. The edited volume was to be called 'The Service of Letters: A Collection of Edith Wharton's Literary, Critical and Biographical Studies', a reference both to Wharton's Gold Medal for Literature of the National Institute of Arts and Letters (given in recognition of her 'services to Letters'), and the 1936 foreword to the dramatisation of *Ethan Frome*, where Wharton again describes herself as 'a faithful servant of English letters'.[41]

The archive suggests that Lapsley's project would have offered a mixed bequest. On the one hand, the very nature of his project admirably underscores a rare, early acknowledgment of the value of Wharton's critical writings as a body of work at a point when few people even recognised, let alone rated her work in this field. At the same time, draft ideas for his introduction illuminate a highly restricted view of the author and her critical writing—the outline approach of this ultimately unfulfilled endeavour mirroring in many ways the wider history of critical reception of Wharton's work in this genre. The notes reinforce the notion of Wharton as an idiosyncratic autodidact, with a hard-won, but patchy acquisition of knowledge. Wharton is again seen as inflexible and out of touch. Transcribing sections of the chapter, 'Constructing a Novel' from *The Writing of Fiction* to support his assertion, Lapsley presents Wharton as a critic whose discussion fails not only to look at the other side of an argument but even to acknowledge there *is* another side—a stark assessment that overlooks the deep engagement of a writer, who, as scholars such as Jennifer Haytock have highlighted, also read and appreciated Conrad, Yeats, Gide, Huxley, Colette, Rilke and Cocteau, among many others.[42] Lapsley's plans offer a heavy biographical emphasis: designs for the introduction subdivided by biographical headings, alongside biographical speculation, even comments on Wharton's dress sense. In their provisional status, the notes collectively suggest an uneasy equation: on the one hand Wharton's uncollected literary and critical writings were evidently perceived as meriting a volume; on the other it was to be a volume largely legitimised only by biographical exposition, with preparations outlining a restricted frame of reference, and the reinforcement of a number of prejudices that lingered around the scholarship of Wharton's life for many decades and that continue to linger around perceptions of her critical writings. The pencilled handwriting of the archival notes is now fading, a telling, physical indicator of the slow process of erosion of the images of Wharton, and her work perpetuated in them.

'Hospitable to New Ideas' ran the climactic heading of Wharton's *New York Herald* interview in November 1936. This was headline news. Noting that Wharton had 'written forty books, each contributing to or consolidating her position as America's foremost woman novelist', the interviewer Loren Carroll reported: 'Mrs. Wharton is hospitable to new ideas and methods in fiction but she believes the fundamental purpose of the novel is and always has been—the creation of character. When modern American novelists…achieve living characters they have nothing to fear from comparison with the past. But many "radical" novelists, she thinks, are only deceiving themselves' ('Edith Wharton in Profile'). Wharton's critical writings, sustained and substantive, are often unfashionable, difficult to categorise, unable to fit to a set mould. And at times they are subversive: Wharton the woman in a male critical realm forging her own path. While still conceived as elitist, her work in this field, notably *The Writing of Fiction*, often opens up possibilities, argues against narrow thinking, against standardisation, sets a different range of priorities. By allowing for individuality, by embracing difference, by not enforcing a rigid rule book, *The Writing of Fiction* implicitly offers up a less elitist vision of the artist and it is one that never suggests men only. Wharton legitimises individual space for artists to be flexible, malleable, create their own work. And the immediate audience is often the practicing writer not the armchair reader, distinctive from other critical texts. Wharton sees herself and any writer as part of a tradition stretching back centuries, part of an interconnectedness. And the conversation continues: *The Writing of Fiction*, like a modernist text, is open-ended and rejects any conclusive summing up or closing down. And Wharton will never make it easy for us. The same 'Hospitable to New Ideas' interview draws to a close by quoting Wharton making an unblinking bigoted statement: 'In general, I don't believe that women have the same stamina as men for arduous intellectual labor. Writing is hard work' ('Edith Wharton in Profile'). Still, at its best, Wharton's critical writing is not rule-bound or formulaic—it skirts and crosses thresholds, and any reader of Wharton knows thresholds can bring danger if one goes beyond, but they can also open up realms of individual possibilities. *The Writing of Fiction* showcases an unwavering voice of authority, intellect, knowledge and professional validation, with its author refusing once again to endorse what she perceived as short-cuts or dumbing down. And that same author had to watch as the volume of her younger, less experienced male contemporary swiftly came to be regarded as a classic, while her own text was diminished. In evaluating her work in this genre, Wharton's gender, at times career stage, age, class and image have persistently worked against her. Her critical vision is open and flexible, not incoherent or inchoate. And when it came to *The Writing of Fiction*, at the very moment Wharton was seeing herself sidelined, preparations made for her to be written out, she picked up her pen and wrote herself and her ideas back in.

Notes

1. Edith Wharton, 'George Eliot' [review of Leslie Stephen's *George Eliot*], *The Bookman: A Literary Journal*, XV (May 1902), 247–51; 248: https://babel.hathitrust.org/cgi/pt?id=njp.32101077276895&view=1up&seq=255. Subsequent references to this work are included in the text.
2. Address cited in Clare Colquitt, Susan Goodman and Candace Waid, 'Introduction', in Colquitt, Goodman, Waid (eds.), *A Forward Glance: New Essays on Edith Wharton* (Newark: University of Delaware Press, 1999), 13.
3. Gerald Bullett, *Saturday Review* [London], 139 (May 1925), cited in Benstock, 385.
4. Letter from Wharton to Zona Gale, 22 October 1922, cited in Elsa Nettels, 'Edith Wharton's Correspondence with Zona Gale: "An Elder's Warm Admiration and Interest"', *Resources for American Literary Study*, 24:2 (1998), 207–34; 217. Subsequent references to this article are included in the text.
5. Wharton's initial proposal for two articles on 'the Art of Fiction', a suggestion on which her jilted publishing house Scribner's eagerly seized, became three, then four (these articles first published in *Scribner's Magazine* from December 1924 to October 1925), accompanied by the addition of the final chapter on Proust (appearing originally in *The Yale Review*).
6. Heidi Kunz, 'Contemporary Reviews, 1877–1938', in Rattray (ed.), *Edith Wharton in Context*, 73–82; 73.
7. See: Bell, 289–90; Geoffrey Walton, *Edith Wharton A Critical Interpretation* (Fairleigh Dickinson, 1970), 161–62; Blake Nevius, *Edith Wharton* (Berkeley: University of California Press, 1953), 31, 27, 130; Penelope Vita-Finzi, *Edith Wharton and the Art of Fiction* (London: Pinter, 1990), 46. Subsequent references to the works by Nevius and Vita-Finzi are included in the text.
8. Dale Bauer, *Edith Wharton's Brave New Politics* (University of Wisconsin Press, 1994), xi.
9. Frederick Wegener, 'Edith Wharton and the Difficult Writing of "The Writing of Fiction"', *Modern Language Studies*, 25:2 (Spring 1995), 60–79; 68. Subsequent references to this work are included in the text.
10. 'From The Nation' and '"Fast and Loose—A Novelette" by David Olivieri', *The Saturday Review*, in Rattray (ed.), *The Unpublished Writings of Edith Wharton*, Vol. 2, 63, 62. Subsequent references to these works are included in the text.

11. Edith Wharton, 'The Three Francescas', *The North American Review*, 175:548 (July 1902), 17–30; 17: https://www.jstor.org/stable/25119269.
12. Edith Wharton, 'Mr. Sturgis's *Belchamber*', *The Bookman: A Literary Journal*, XXI (May 1905), 307–10; 309: https://babel.hathitrust.org/cgi/pt?id=njp.32101077276952&view=1up&seq=319. Subsequent references to this work are included in the text.
13. Susan Sniader Lanser and Evelyn Torton Beck, '[Why] Are There No Great Women Critics? And What Difference Does It Make?', in Julia A. Sherman and Beck (eds.), *The Prism of Sex: Essays in the Sociology of Knowledge* (University of Wisconsin Press, 1979), 79–91; 83. Subsequent references to this work are included in the text.
14. Edith Wharton, 'William C. Brownell', *Scribner's Magazine*, 84 (November 1928), 596–602; 596.
15. 'Talk to American Soldiers', Typescript, Edith Wharton Collection, Yale Collection of American Literature, Beinecke Rare Book, and Manuscript Library, Yale University. Box 19, folder 612.
16. Edith Wharton, 'Permanent Values in Fiction', *Saturday Review of Literature*, X: 38 (7 April 1934), 603–4; 603. Subsequent references to this work are included in the text.
17. Edith Wharton, 'Tendencies in Modern Fiction', *Saturday Review of Literature* X: 28 (27 January 1934), 433–34.
18. Edith Wharton, 'The Great American Novel', *Yale Review* (July 1927), 646–56; 648, 650, 651. Subsequent references to this work are included in the text.
19. Vita-Finzi, 2, cited by Jennifer Haytock, *Edith Wharton and the Conversations of Literary Modernism* (New York: Palgrave, 2008), 165. Subsequent references to this work are included in the text.
20. Edith Wharton, 'The Criticism of Fiction', *Times Literary Supplement*, 14 May 1914, 229–30, The Times Literary Supplement Historical Archive. Subsequent references to this work are included in the text.
21. Wegener suggests, for example, 'Wharton's regressive social and political views—now more and more regretfully acknowledged, but still denied any vital connection to her imaginative work—are closely intertwined with her convictions about the writing of fiction and the making of art.' See Frederick Wegener, 'Form, "Selection," and Ideology in Edith Wharton's Antimodernist Aesthetic', in Colquitt, Goodman, Waid (eds.), *A Forward Glance: New Essays on Edith Wharton*, 116–38; 134.
22. Edith Wharton, *The Gods Arrive* (London: Virago, 1987), 355. Subsequent references to this work are included in the text (*GA*).
23. Zona Gale, 'An Artist on Her Art', *New York Herald Tribune*, 31 January 1926, ProQuest Historical Newspapers: New York Tribune/Herald

Tribune, E5; [Royal Cortissoz], 'The Secrets of Fiction', 'An Artist on an Art', 'The Art of Fiction', *New York Herald Tribune*, 7 December 1924, 19 April 1925, 31 May 1925, ProQuest Historical Newspapers: New York Tribune/Herald Tribune. Subsequent references to these works are included in the text.

24. See letter from Wharton to Mary Cadwalader Jones, 12 June 1925 ('I have just had a perfectly wonderful review of my last "Fiction" article in the N. Y. Herald. Who *can* have written it? I can't believe my eyes. It's educated & intelligent!' [*Letters* 485]), and a letter from Wharton to Gale on 5 March 1926 about her 'wonderful review' of *The Writing of Fiction*: 'Why, you've read my book! You've thought about it! You've re-thought it, actually, in your own mind!' (letter printed in Nettels [223]).

25. In a note prefacing the volume, published for the benefit of the Authors' League Fund for writers in distress, the editors of *The New Republic* recorded their 'regret' that 'previous arrangements on their part prevent the inclusion of Willa S. Cather's "The Novel Démeublé" and Theodore Dreiser's "The Scope of Fiction"'. *The Novel of Tomorrow and The Scope of Fiction* 'by Twelve American Novelists' (Indianapolis: Bobbs Merrill Company Publishers, 1922).

26. Gale, 'The Novel of Tomorrow', in *The Novel of Tomorrow and The Scope of Fiction*, 65–74; 65.

27. 'The Art of Fiction', *The Saturday Review of Politics, Literature, Science and Art*, 141 (16 January 1926), 65–66.

28. 'The Writing of Fiction', *Times Literary Supplement*, 17 December 1925, 878, reprinted in *Edith Wharton: The Contemporary Reviews*, 388–90; 388. Subsequent references to this review are included in the text.

29. Percy Lubbock, *The Craft of Fiction* (London: Jonathan Cape, 1954), 12–13.

30. J. B. Priestley, 'The Novelist's Art', *Spectator*, 135 (5 December 1925), 1047, reprinted in *Edith Wharton: The Contemporary Reviews*, 386–88. Subsequent references to this review are included in the text.

31. Brander Matthews, 'A Story-Teller on the Art of Story-Telling', *Literary Digest International Book Review*, 3 (October 1925), 731–32; 'This Week's Books', *Spectator*, 135 (7 November 1925), 836; Lloyd Morris, 'Mrs. Wharton Discusses the Art of Fiction', *New York Times Book Review*, 15 November 1925, reprinted in *Edith Wharton: The Contemporary Reviews*, 379–93.

32. Henri Peyre, 'Edith Wharton: The Writing of Fiction', *Revue Anglo-Américaine*, 3 (April 1926), 366–68; 368.

33. '"The Writing of Fiction"', *New Statesman*, 26 (12 December 1925), supplement, xxii, xxiv, reprinted in *Edith Wharton The Contemporary Reviews*, 388.

34. Susan Goodman, *Edith Wharton's Inner Circle* (Austin: University of Texas Press, 2011), 84. Subsequent references to this work are included in the text.
35. See Goodman, 128 (fn 46), 80. Goodman cites the letter of Lubbock to Wharton, 7 January 1913 (Beinecke).
36. Cited Ramsden 140, n.256. (In the original letter, housed at the Mount, Lubbock underlines two words for emphasis: 'I do like this book—especially the first part—so lucid & incisive'). Heartfelt thanks to Nynke Dorhout, Librarian at the Mount.
37. Lyn Bennett, 'Presence and Professionalism: The Critical Reception of Edith Wharton', in Gary Totten (ed.), *Memorial Boxes and Guarded Interiors: Edith Wharton and Material Culture* (Tuscaloosa: University of Alabama Press, 2007), 19–43; 36.
38. Virginia Woolf, *The Diary of Virginia Woolf*, ed. Anne Olivier Bell, Vol. III (1925–1930) (San Diego: Harcourt Brace Jovanovich, Inc., 1980), 262. My thanks to Bryony Randall for this reference.
39. See Robin Majumdar and Allen McLaurin (eds.), *Virginia Woolf: The Critical Heritage* (London: Routledge, 2014), 250–60, and Virginia Woolf, *A Room of One's Own* and *Three Guineas,* ed. Anna Snaith (Oxford World Classics, 2015), 259.
40. A brass, memorial plaque in the ante-chapel at Trinity College describes Lapsley (in Latin) as '[a]n American citizen ... [who] loved the British way of life.'
41. See Wegener, '"Enthusiasm Guided by Acumen"', 42.
42. For discussions of Wharton's engagement with, and responses to, modernism, see Haytock, *Edith Wharton and the Conversations of Literary Modernism,* and Haytock, 'Modernism', in Rattray (ed.), *Edith Wharton in Context,* 364–73.

CHAPTER 7

Life Writings

I began a few months ago to write my memoirs (like everybody else old enough, or young enough, to hold a pen). At first I was bored & bewildered, but gradually I got the hang of it, & now I am warming both hands at my dear old memories.[1]

The 1930s were boom years for autobiography. Virginia Woolf observed in 1940, 'No other decade can have produced so much autobiography as the ten years between 1930 and 1939.'[2] In his pithy summary of 1930s literature in November 1939, Malcolm Cowley concluded the decade would be recognised as 'lean years for poetry, with no major figures appearing', 'middling rich years for the novel', 'lively years for criticism', but 'decidedly rich years for autobiography'.[3] Subsequent critics have confirmed culturally reflective conditions that proved ripe for the production of autobiography. Janet Montefiore notes that 'much of the writing of and about the 1930s is a self-conscious literature of personal memory' (Montefiore 2); David Lodge suggests '[t]hirties writing tended to model itself on historical kinds of discourse—the autobiography, the eye-witness account, the travel log'[4]; Peter Conn illuminates in his study of the American 1930s 'one of the main subjects to which the decade's writers turned again and again: the past'.[5] In Europe especially, the memory of the Great War was 'an unforgotten shadow' (Montefiore 2) in much of the decade's writing, while in America the convulsions and aftershocks of the Great Depression prompted an intense reflection on the nation's identity.

In an insightful summary, Conn foregrounds an influential tally of the decade's autobiographical titles, including Wharton's own *A Backward Glance* (1934), Gertrude Stein's *Autobiography of Alice B. Toklas* (1933), 'a self-portrait written from the assumed point of view of her companion', Harriet Monroe's *A Poet's Life* (1938), Theodore Dreiser's *Dawn* (1931), Langston Hughes' *The Big Sea* (1940), Nora Waln's *The House of Exile* (1933), Emma Goldman's *Living My Life* (1931), Lincoln Steffens' *The Autobiography of Lincoln Steffens* (1931), Frank Lloyd Wright's *An Autobiography* (1932), a number of Native American autobiographies, among them *Black Elk Speaks* (1932), and the bestselling, Book-of-the-Month Club autobiography of the 1930s, the now largely forgotten *An American Doctor's Odyssey* (1936) by Victor Heiser (see Conn 135–53).

With *A Backward Glance*, published as a volume in April 1934, Wharton tapped into the decade's fascination with autobiography, though she had been preparing the way for such a project for many years. The author had embarked on at least one earlier version of a memoir, while prefacing entries in her copy-book 'Quaderno dello Studente' with an alluring calling card, dated 1927: 'If I ever have a biographer, it is in these notes that he will find the gist of me' ('QS' 208). Having received a magazine request for a series of articles on her 'recollections of New York Society', noting with her customary business acumen 'at $2.500 an article', Wharton informed Appleton editor Rutger Jewett in February 1923 that the magazine's proposal had reminded her of a plan that had been 'vaguely floating through [her] mind for some time', namely the writing of her 'early memories', which would interweave recollections of her childhood and the beginnings of her literary life (*Letters* 465). As the writer sketched her ideas to Jewett, 'Life and I'—a memoir devoted to her formative years, but one that would ultimately remain incomplete, and unpublished until many decades after her death—may well have been underway or, indeed, its extant chapters written. In 1919 Wharton had been working on the New York of her childhood for the setting of *The Age of Innocence*, published the following year, while she had returned to period scenes—from the 1840s through the 1870s—for what would become the *Old New York* quartet. The epic war casualty *Literature*, in which pivotal episodes portray the childhood of the young writer protagonist, retained a place on the literary agenda, its wider narrative dilemmas unresolved.[6] Ultimately Wharton would write several versions of her childhood. In addition to 'Life and I', *A Backward Glance* included her early years, a topic to which she returned in 'A Further Glance' (published posthumously in *Harper's*

Magazine as 'A Little Girl's New York'), while 'Adventures with Books'—a phrase she used in *A Backward Glance* and as titles for two swiftly abandoned reminiscences (one a single side, the other four)—also prepared to look back, encompassing topics such as childhood reading, 'the high regard in which letters are held in France', and the importance of her father's library.[7]

Wharton claimed a clear reasoning for thinking about the writing of her 'early memories': 'One of my objects in doing this would be to avoid having it inaccurately done by some one else after my death, should it turn out that my books survive me long enough to make it worth while to write my biography' (*Letters* 465). While Wharton courted publicity for her books, and indeed habitually hassled her publishers over what she regarded as insufficient advertising for them, she was highly wary of other types of personal publicity—and with good reason. This, after all, was a writer who had been publicly shamed as a young woman over the ending of her first engagement, the weekly periodical *Town Topics: The Journal of Society* reporting in October 1882 that 'the only reason for the breaking of the engagement hitherto existing between Harry Stevens and Miss Edith Jones is an alleged preponderance of intellectuality on the part of the intended bride.' 'Miss Jones', the report noted, 'is an ambitious authoress, and it is said that, in the eyes of Mr. Stevens, ambition is a grievous fault' (cited Benstock 46). Intellect, authorship, ambition: the triple whammy implied as ample reason for the young woman to lose her man. Years later, as noted in Chap. 3, Wharton's theatre work again made her the subject of gossip in national newspapers and theatre columns—reported arguments with the actress (Campbell), heated 'rows' with a fellow playwright (Fitch), disagreements with the producer (Frohman)—while Melanie Dawson reminds us that public criticism of Wharton's 'supposedly unfeminine intellectualism' resurfaced when she sought a divorce in 1913.[8]

Indeed, we have underestimated at times the extent to which Wharton's life choices and behaviour came under very public (and often sexist) scrutiny from an early age. Charting the long and imaginative course of *Town Topics'* coverage of Wharton, for example, is illuminating. In June 1887 it commented on the misfortunes to have befallen the house of one of Newport's denizens, Mrs Paran Stevens, notably the death of her son Harry: 'Mr. Stevens was at one time engaged to Miss Edith Jones, who is now Mrs. Edward Wharton, and he keenly felt the breaking of this engagement.'[9] There were numerous unspoken layers wrapped into such a statement: the young woman by contrast evidently had not keenly felt the break-up; now married, she had left in her wake a sensitive, blameless man—so sensitive perhaps, the phrasing implied, to have made the breaking of the engagement a factor in his early demise. (The *New York Times* reported the cause of Harry Stevens' death in July 1885 as stomach cancer 'brought about by too violent exercise at athletics'.[10]) The account gave *Town Topics* a convenient segue into a judgemental commentary on Wharton's personal attributes, talents, and her second—and seemingly second-rate—choice of husband: 'Mrs. Wharton spends her summers at Newport, and is there now, having taken a cottage. Although not by any means a beauty, she has a well-bred air, and adds to it what the French describe as *chic*. She was always considered rather a clever girl, although a trifle given to affectations. This latter fact may account for her final choice of a husband' ('Saunterings', *Town Topics*, 23 June 1887). The journal reiterated its theme the following summer: 'Another arrival at Newport is that of Mr. Edward Wharton of Boston. Mr. Wharton may be recalled as the husband of Miss Jones who would have become Mrs. Harry Stevens if Providence had not ordered it otherwise.'[11]

Later years were accompanied by speculation about the Whartons' travel and living arrangements: 'When Mrs. Edith Wharton, the novelist, went abroad there were many reports as to why her husband, Edward R. Wharton, was left behind'[12]; 'Edward R. Wharton has finally gone abroad to join Mrs. Wharton, who has been over in Italy for a year, storing away "color" for her future work and enjoying the companionship of close friends.'[13] Again, it was the woman's behaviour that was under critical scrutiny: 'Since she has been abroad the author has entirely cut off correspondence with some of her Lenox friends and little has been known of her...' (*Town Topics*, 30 September 1909). There was, in turn, contradictory speculation about Wharton's reasons for both building and selling the Mount. In one report the couple had built the property after being 'fêted by the rich in their country homes, and catching the spirit'.[14] The decision to sell-up by contrast was attributed to a 'social blight' following the publication of *The House of Mirth*. With 'its intimate portraits of persons in society', 'Lenox residents damned the book first, last and all the time, and cried aloud against such profanation by the unmirthful novel. ... Fewer and fewer became the cards left at The Mount and finally the Whartons quit the game and went abroad' (*Town Topics*, 31 August 1911). *Edith* Wharton's behaviour, however, was even seen to threaten the sale: 'Mrs. Edith Wharton has availed herself of woman's constitutional prerogative ... The high intellectual temperament of the literary lady is said to have ended negotiations.'[15] Yet by May 1912, *Town Topics* had determined that '[t]he vivacious historian of Lily Bart sold the place, not because she liked it not, it is averred, but because the neighbors were so "damned inquisitive."'[16]

Town Topics delighted in probing the nature (read scandalous potential) of Wharton's friendship with Walter Berry. In August 1911, the journal reported 'Edith Wharton and Walter Berry are the most devoted of friends. She has sketched him in more than one of her novels and the hero of "The House of Mirth" is said to be an accurate picture of him.'[17] By the summer of 1913, gossip was rife:

> RIGHT or wrong, all Edith Wharton's friends believe she will get a divorce to marry Walter Berry. Mr. Wharton is in this country to stay, his family say, and will neither deny nor affirm that he and his wife are separated, while Edith and Walter are in Paris and as constantly together as ever. A tender and intimate friendship has existed between this brilliant author and Walter Berry for many, many years. She has worked him into more than one of her books, and he has never married because of love for her. Without his sympathy and inspiration her work is said to be colorless; so what more natural, since it is many moons since she began to disagree with her husband, than that Walter should take his place?[18]

By September 1913, the 'affair' remained unresolved: 'Walter... is devoted heart and soul to Edith Wharton and is ever at her beck and call. No one of their friends seems to know how this affair between Edith and Walter is going to end. The Whartons are not yet divorced, but everybody thinks they will be and everyone believes that Edith will become Mrs. Walter Berry when they are. It is most amusing.'[19] Wharton was presented as the demanding, yet dependent famous author, much of whose success could be attributed to a devoted, selfless male muse.

Whatever the skewed public scrutiny, by the postwar years the question of a legacy image was of increasing concern to Wharton. In May 1924, she mused: 'When I get glimpses, in books & reviews, of the things people are going to assert about me after I am dead, I feel I must have the courage & perseverance, some day, to forestall them'—an entry written in the same copy book in which the author advertised herself to potential biographers ('QS' 211). In November 1927, Wharton would even assemble a packet of documents labelled 'For My Biographer' (cited Lewis xi). Lewis interprets it innocently as a sign of 'an uncommonly cooperative' subject (xi)—but it was also the act of a writer concerned to influence the biographer's path. As Susan Goodman succinctly phrases it, 'she tried her best to guide—if not ghostwrite—the various ways her story could be told.'[20] In *A Backward Glance* Wharton would steal a march and self-consciously stake her claim to ownership of the terrain, and its uses, in her choice of opening title: 'A FIRST WORD' (vii).

Wharton was keen to capitalise on the popularity of autobiography in the 1930s, though her placement choices again illuminated a concern for both financial rewards and esteem. In April 1933, *The Atlantic Monthly*, the prestigious journal that more than half a century earlier had published poems by Edith Jones, featured work that would appear as 'The Secret Garden' chapter of *A Backward Glance*, albeit run in the journal under a somewhat sensational, even titillating title 'Confessions of a Novelist'. Indicative of the interest in material of this nature, *The Atlantic Monthly* would that year also run excerpts from Stein's *The Autobiography of Alice B. Toklas* over several months, and Woolf's fictional biography of Elizabeth Barrett Browning's dog, *Flush*, among others.[21] The lucrative serialisation of *A Backward Glance*, though, ran in the *Ladies' Home Journal*, and it was one with which Wharton was deeply unhappy. She would warn friends against reading 'the wretchedly abridged & garbled version of [the] reminiscences' cut into segments by the 'untutored tooth of some office underling'.[22] In October 1933, Wharton wrote to Daisy Chanler: 'It makes me sick to think of any of my friends reading these choppy fragments of my reminiscences in the Ladies' H.J.[sic] They give no idea of the book, & I wish you'd tell everyone to wait & read that' (*Letters* 571). When the magazine's editor, Loring Schuler proposed (during the Depression) cutting the manuscript by 40,000 words and reducing the fee from $25,000 to $20,000, Wharton dashed off a cable to Jewett: 'Absolutely decline reducing price and will sue him unless agreement kept' (cited *Letters* 560). Often overlooked in the author's threat was her counter-proposition with '[t]he only change' she could agree to, namely that 'everything about Henry James' should be in the portion rejected by the journal. Wharton clearly regarded the James' portrait as sellable (and indeed many reviews highlighted this chapter), continuing: 'This might enable me to place elsewhere this study of Henry James which "Life and Letters" is already anxious to get' (*Letters* 560).[23] Wharton got her money.

The six-part monthly serialisation of *A Backward Glance* ran in the *Ladies' Home Journal* from October 1933, very substantially abridged. Schuler had been forthright in an exchange with Jewett when he read an early submission, deeming 'parts of the story' 'delightful', but 'a far larger part ... so "snooty" and consciously intellectual that it would be over the heads of a tremendous portion of a popular audience'.[24] Wharton's original paragraphs were brusquely filleted by magazine staff into very short units, with explanatory headings added to ease the reader's path ('Learning about Life From Foxy', 'When America Was Young', 'Life at Newport', 'On the Riviera', 'Friendship and Travels', 'Architects and Architecture'). French phrases were excised, social connections explained, and many scenes in Europe condensed or omitted. Mary Chenoweth Stratton notes that the last two chapters of the book were 'slashed' in the serialisation, with nineteen of the twenty-four pages of 'The War' chapter 'thrown out' and sixteen pages cut from the final nineteen-page chapter (88–89). The *Ladies' Home Journal* staff implicitly advertised the memoir as an *American* text with its banner image of Fifth Avenue headlining the first installment, while an advertisement for Telechron clocks spoke to, and assured, its Depression era readership, 'Better Times Are Here and here's Better Time!': 'The New Deal has pushed some prices up already—may increase others later. *Buy now*.'[25] Unsurprisingly, Wharton's references to 'editorial timidity' and magazine censorship 'disappeared', while the serialisation included most of the James' chapter 'just as she had written it but removed her criticism of his late novels' (Stratton 88).

The magazine's filleted approach, however, did help to highlight Wharton's writings in parts, even in the absence of 'The Secret Garden' chapter. 'Beginning the Recollections of a Great Literary Career' ran the capitalised heading to the opening instalment. November's issue referenced the writing of *The Decoration of Houses*, *The Greater Inclination*, *The Touchstone*, *Crucial Instances*, *The Valley of Decision*, *Italian Villas and their Gardens*, and *Italian Backgrounds* (from chapters five and six of the published volume), while part three in December, complete with image of Father Christmas bearing gifts, drew attention to *Ethan Frome*, *Summer*, the dramatisation of *The House of Mirth* and *The Joy of Living*. Illustrations accompanying the serialised text included portraits of Wharton at various life stages, pictures of her ancestors, images of the Mount, and the Metropolitan Opera House. The advertisements, meanwhile, told their own story. Readers' attention was called to Jenny Wren's ready-mixed flour ('Easy, economical, a pleasure to use... praised by hundreds of thousands of housewives who demand the best!'), sun-maid raisins ('foods that would otherwise be plain become delicious treats'), and Nazareth children's underwear ('Always good value', 'popularly priced'). An advertisement for Colman's mustard under the column heading of 'A YOUNG WIFE'S DIARY' featured a smiling young woman presenting a turkey for Thanksgiving dinner: 'I was a bit worried about cooking my first turkey. But I needn't have been—not with Colman's Mustard in the dressing! Dad and Jim both said I cook like a regular chef.' A picture of a mother and daughter heralded '*Beauty ... from teens to forties*', the Barbara Gould system of home treatments making 'proper care of the complexion extremely simple and most surprisingly economical'. 'You too', assured the advertisers, 'may enjoy lasting loveliness and the greater happiness that goes with it': 'THE LOVELY PICTURE of mother and daughter is convincing evidence of the fact that beauty no longer depends on age.'[26] The advertisements spoke to young womanhood, wifehood, and motherhood. With a delicious irony, the same magazine that rendered a woman beyond her forties invalid and invisible paid its seventy-one-year-old female contributor an unprecedented fee. Wharton was still breaking the mould.

The author expressed certainty that *A Backward Glance* would have 'a very large sale' (*Letters* 559), but while first-year sales of the volume totalled over 10,000 copies, interest swiftly dwindled, with only 505 copies purchased the following year (cited Stratton 109–10). Wharton, predictably, turned her fire on her publishers. Some of the writer's spikiest business correspondence relates to *A Backward Glance*, notably exchanges with Jewett's replacement at Appleton, John Williams, in which Wharton made vociferous complaints about a perceived 'lack of advertising' for the work: 'I have looked with curiosity ... for the smallest advertisement of my book—but in vain!' Authors 'can only change their publishers. I may as well tell you frankly that I intend to do this for the simple reason that I cannot afford to neglect any chance of selling my books. ... I feel that I ought to have an equal chance with other authors, and I am far from getting it' (see *Letters* 578–80).

When it came to *A Backward Glance* in 1934, Wharton explained to her readers that she would not be addressing there 'any general theory of technique' as she had 'to the best of [her] ability, analyzed this process' (199) in her 1925 volume *The Writing of Fiction* (see Chap. 6). Instead, in the chapter 'The Secret Garden', she proposed she would deal 'simply with the question of how some of my own novels happened to me' (*BG* 199–200). She could not resist the occasional well-timed hook aimed at her critics, however—among them 'the modern critic requires every novelist to treat the same kind of subject, and relegates to insignificance the author who declines to confirm. ...There could be no greater critical ineptitude than to judge a novel according to *what it ought to have been about*' (*BG* 206). Despite her robust defence nine years earlier in *The Writing of Fiction*, increasing numbers of critics were viewing both Wharton and her writing of the 1920s and 1930s as anachronistic. For many decades, even as Wharton's star was posthumously reinstated, such a judgement on the later writings stood largely unchallenged. *This* 'Mrs. Wharton' was presented as a guest who had not known when it was time to leave. Wharton continued to have good reason to take her critics to task. As Robert A. Martin and Linda Wagner-Martin astutely observe: 'who among the American writers in Paris was more "contemporary" than Wharton? *The Gods Arrive* features Halo Tarrant's out-of-wedlock pregnancy, *A Mother's Recompense* has a run-away mother looking for complete sexual satisfaction, and *The Children* deals, discretely, with the theme that Nabokov was to make a fortune from years later in *Lolita*.'[27] Work-in-progress included *The Buccaneers*, the nineteenth-century period setting of which has fostered benign readings of narrative 'serenity' and an 'air of fairy-tale enchantment' (Lewis 524). As Lee keenly observes, however, 'under its frothy surface is a harsh exposure of society marriage as a form of prostitution and gambling, mothers trading their daughters, sex as a threat and a bargain, marital sadism and neglect, and several kinds of prejudice and racism' (726). Notably, the synopsis for the unfinished novel indicates in explicit, unambiguous terms that the 'great-souled' 'adventuress' (*B* 357) Laura Testvalley—one of the author's most memorable later female protagonists—will pay a heavy price for facilitating the happiness of her former charge Nan St. George, going 'back alone to old age and poverty' (*B* 359). The septuagenarian Wharton, whatever her critics might have argued to the contrary, had not lost her edge.

Wharton, however, also had other, less obvious weapons at her disposal to counter her critics. While *A Backward Glance* was in progress, she was producing some of the finest short stories of her career. When Louis Auchincloss lists the work on which he believes Wharton's 'ultimate reputation in American letters' will rest, each of the stories selected— 'Pomegranate Seed', 'Roman Fever', and 'After Holbein'—notably dates from the author's final decade. (Still Auchincloss appears to find no anomaly between that choice and his convictions regarding 'the failing energy', 'the drop in quality', and the 'lapse of style and taste' of much of Wharton's later work,[28] symptomatic of the fact that a recognition of the calibre of her thirties' stories generally failed to translate into a wider appreciation of the author's late career.) At times foreshadowing the development of

Laura Testvalley, the cast lists of Wharton's late short story collections are revealing, with many individual stories featuring women, generally of a certain age, who are not at all as they seem. In 'Confession' the innocuous Kate Ingram is unmasked as the infamous Kate Spain who was sensationally tried for the murder of her father; in 'Her Son', Catherine Glenn, the very pillar of dull respectability, sets off in search of her illegitimate child abandoned almost thirty years previously while the adoptive, devoted 'parent' metamorphoses into a cruel, manipulative mercenary, the lover of her 'son'. In 'Diagnosis', Eleanor Welwood, long-time mistress of Paul Dorrance, finally secures a marriage certificate by concealing the fact that he is not terminally ill as supposed; in 'The Day of the Funeral' a docile, unvalued wife astounds her husband by displaying such unexpected springs of passion to remain true to her ominous words in one of Wharton's most memorable opening paragraphs ('His wife had said: "If you don't give her up I'll throw myself from the roof." He had not given her up, and his wife had thrown herself from the roof'[29]); Elsie Ashby of 'Pomegranate Seed' even comes back from the dead to claim her remarried husband and insist on him accompanying her to the grave. In 'Roman Fever', Alida Slade—'awfully brilliant; but not as brilliant as she thinks'—throws what she believes is a winning verbal blow only for the 'old-fashioned' '[m]useum specimen' Grace Ansley to retort with an understated counterblow that in the final sentence of the story sends the scaffolding of respectability crashing: Alida Slade's husband was also the father of Grace Ansley's much-envied child.[30] Sideswipes notwithstanding, Wharton at this stage did not need *A Backward Glance* openly to take on her critics (and her two 1934 pieces for the *Saturday Review of Literature*, 'Tendencies in Modern Fiction' and 'Permanent Values in Fiction' took care of that). While she was not simplistically writing herself into these stories, she was certainly foregrounding a deceptively complex array of women, often middle-aged or elderly, eminently respectable women who are not as they seem. In the presence of such protagonists the reader is forced to look beneath a surface veneer to discover a more complex, often darker, and on occasion even disturbingly sinister presence. The narrative design insists that the reader makes this imaginative leap to arrive at the crux of the story—betrayal, deception, the secret life—and an underestimation of these women often proves costly.

Nevertheless, *A Backward Glance* offered much that appeared at first sight to cement the stately, grande dame image. Indeed, the immediate visuals set the tone. The volume's frontispiece advertised 'THE AUTHOR' to the 1930s reading public with a formal studio portrait of Wharton in choker pearls, a fur drape around her dress, hands concealed by a fur muff, suggesting a woman belonging to another age. In its opening pages, *A Backward Glance* warns that its subject has had to make the best of 'unsensational material' (viii), while the narrative largely looks outwards, and appears to retain a 'seemly' reserve. The written portraits are often of others—Egerton Winthrop, Paul Bourget, Howard Sturgis, among them—with idealised images of Walter Berry, a chapter devoted to Henry James, one Lewis deems 'the most attractive and persuasive sketch of Henry James ever recorded' (522), but Wilson calls 'slightly catty and curiously superficial' (213), while Teddy merits only passing mentions, and former lover Morton Fullerton—as expected—no reference at all. In Lee's definition, the volume appears 'an impressively evasive exercise in good manners and self-screening' (715).

Reviews in turn often foreshadowed the 'benign', 'serene' responses that would accompany *The Buccaneers*. The *Times* reviewer found 'Mrs. Wharton look[ing] back tranquilly over an unsensational but a rich and ample life'. 'She has written one of her most delightful books in this volume of memoirs, evoking a vanished world and investing it with body and warmth and a peculiar leisured and gracious charm,' continued the review before concluding, 'The book breathes serenity and is one of the pleasantest reminiscences that have appeared for a very long time.'[31] The *Saturday Review of Literature* judged *A Backward Glance* to be 'by and large the recollections of a singularly happy life'; Edward Sackville-West in the *Spectator* deemed them 'admirably written and exquisitely well-mannered', while the *Yale Review* ran with the headline 'A Happy Chronicle'. Many reviewers found a reserve that was 'charming', 'delightful', or 'gracious', capturing a privileged, almost bygone age: 'Granules from an Hour-Glass' as the *Saturday Review* phrased it.[32] E. M. Forster, reviewing for the *New Statesman and Nation*, suggested 'the dominant impression is comfort', detecting 'autobiographical monotony' amidst 'constant prosperity', while, in private, Virginia Woolf praised Wharton's placing of colour in sentences, but concluded disdainfully: 'There's the shell of a distinguished mind.'[33] Christopher Morley speculated divisively in his review: 'I can scarcely imagine the youngest generation, hotfoot upon its own desperation, taking time to read Mrs. Wharton's very wise and moving book; yet it might start some interesting thoughts if they did.'[34]

In its opening pages, *A Backward Glance* alerts the reader to difference; like *Italian Backgrounds* before it, this journey will take a less conventional path. The author draws attention in 'A First Word' to contemporary praise for a type of autobiography that '"spared no one", set down in detail every defect, and absurdity in others, and every resentment in the writer. That was the kind of autobiography worth reading!' (*BG* viii). Wharton sets up the contrast: 'Judged by that standard mine, I fear, will find few readers' (*BG* viii). Yet her opening words also implicitly extended a flattering invitation to readers of *A Backward Glance* to consider themselves part of a discerning set who might see 'beyond'. As Blake Nevius observes, 'There is a marked emphasis throughout *A Backward Glance* on the private jokes, private observances, and common interests which, in the successive groups of which Edith Wharton was the center, heightened the sense of "belonging"' (88). It is a club the reader is invited to join. The preface also illuminates once again the author's appeal to a full, connected, cultured life, exactly as we have seen in much of her travel and critical writing. In fact preparations are made before the reader even reaches that 'first word'. *A Backward Glance* is prefaced by literary quotations in English, French, and German from Wharton's beloved Whitman, Goethe, and Romantic giant François-René de Châteaubriand's *Mémoires d'Outre Tombe*, a huge, multi-volume project written over several decades ('beyond the tomb', a threshold from which a number of Wharton's poems were seen to start in Chap. 2). Offering no translations, the author was once again serving notice to her largely US readership of intellect, joined-up-ness, the cultural life, and, in this case, a different kind of autobiography. And again, it was an intricate balance—a writer rigorously pursuing maximum financial returns and sales through a volume advertising itself to an elite. Wharton's authority was stamped on the inside page of the first edition: a long list with forty-two titles to her name. This author was harnessing all the old images to her advantage—signalling authority, wisdom, experience, success.

Lee proposes that *A Backward Glance* is 'to a great extent, a grand old lady's decorous list of distinguished acquaintances, fondly remembered' (715). It is also a volume that invites readers to look again. When Auchincloss did so, he notably found a very different prospect:

> There was a time when I thought it was a slightly slick, cold memoir written for money in Mrs. Wharton's later years, but I now realize that every sentence is really rather packed; and the fact that it is written with a discretion not found in the autobiographies of people like Diana Barrymore does not mean that there is not an enormous amount in it for those who are willing to supply a bit of imagination.[35]

Once again Wharton offers a much bolder text than appearances suggest. Even the referencing is telling. At various stages of its genesis, the author referenced the volume as 'autobiography', 'memoirs', 'memories', and 'reminiscences' (see Stratton 93). Shifts in terminology and their results have troubled some scholars, Goodman noting the author's 'faltering conception of the emerging book as a collection of "memories," "memoirs," "reminiscences," "retrospect," and "autobiography"'.[36] In 'A First Word', Wharton labels *A Backward Glance* 'autobiography'. Goodman observes that Wharton changed the original title from 'Reminiscences' ('Justice to *A Backward Glance*' 96), while Stratton notes that the writer later opted unenthusiastically for a title of 'Retrospect', before 'inspiration struck' with 'A Backward Glance' (93–94). A fact always overlooked, thanks to their rarity decades after publication, is that dust jackets for the volume's first edition on both front and back covers carried the title: '*A Backward Glance/Reminiscences* by Edith Wharton' while the inside jacket blurb referenced the work as both 'memoirs' and 'reminiscences'. In both the terminology employed in Wharton's correspondence during the volume's genesis, and in its advertising, *A Backward Glance* did not quite fit a neat definition, allowing for a flexibility that the author embraced. As we saw in Chap. 6, *The Writing of Fiction* was shown to warn against excessive prescription: 'General rules in art are useful chiefly as a lamp in a mine, or a hand-rail down a black stairway; they are necessary for the sake of the guidance they give, but it is a mistake, once they are formulated, to be too much in awe of them' (*WF* 42). In its openness and flexibility, *A Backward Glance* joins *The Writing of Fiction* in pushing beyond prescriptive boundaries, indicating once again not confusion, but a successful, confident writer taking her own path.

In a letter responding to private praise of *A Backward Glance*, Wharton suggested the process had involved a remarkable level of exposure, missed by the critics: 'I felt a good deal like Lady Godiva during her memorable ride until I had seen the first reviews, and gathered the critics found fault with my excessive reserve.'[37] What Wharton boldly illuminates in *A Backward Glance* is that the 'Lady Godiva' moments of an autobiography, or indeed of a life, are not the big, conventional physical life event markers (marriage, children, career triumphs, etc.) or sensational revelations (nights of passion in a Charing Cross hotel room). They are instead the 'adventures with books', the life of the imagination, connections, the intellect. Wharton's kind of autobiography and its very different hierarchies of importance stood in striking opposition to the decades of tabloid-like 'life coverage' that followed her. It was a thesis in part reminiscent of her early notebook poem, 'The Duchess of Palliano', in which the unhappily married, but faithful titular figure offers the man she really loves what she considers a richer proposition than an illicit affair: 'Will you not rather / Possess the soul he never sought to reach, / And smile to think how little has been his?' (Lilly). Goodman leads the way in recognising methods by which this 'seemingly unforthcoming autobiography' discloses more than is commonly supposed ('Justice to *A Backward Glance*' 95). As Goodman beautifully phrases it, 'What readers generally fail to recognize ... is that Wharton welcomes them into the most private spheres of her being: intelligence and imagination' (100). Indeed, under the benevolent gaze of the grande dame portrait of another age, readers were being offered a radical, subversive take both on what constituted an autobiography and the signpost events of a life. This now seventy-two-year-old author was taking her own advice from *Italian Backgrounds*: almost entirely undetected, *A Backward Glance* would 'deconventionalize' and make it new.

Even what appear the most conventional autobiographical components of *A Backward Glance* come with a warning, as Wharton directs the reader's attention to the form's inherent constructions, artificialities, and falsehoods. It is a strategy that can be traced through the transition from the earlier, unpublished 'Life and I' to *A Backward Glance*. The opening accounts of the published memoir are related not in the first person, but in the third person. They present separate entities. This is the third person story of 'the little girl'—Wharton on the one hand presenting herself as a spectator of her own life, offering a detached third person point of view, but also drawing attention to an artificiality, and presenting 'the little girl' as a character. Labelling chapter one 'The Background', Wharton gives the story a conventional, story-book opening: 'It was on a bright day...' (*BG* 1). She references 'episode' in the opening paragraph, appropriate to fiction; she determines the birth of the little girl's identity; she offers a literary epigraph (Goethe—who else?) to frame her story. An episode that is related in the first person in 'Life and I'—'My first conscious recollection is of being kissed in Fifth Avenue by my cousin Dan Fearing' ('LI' 185)—is repeated in chapter one of *A Backward Glance*, but narrated with the distance and camouflage, of fictional third person:

> ...the little girl peered with interest at the little boy through the white woollen mist over her face. The little boy, who was very round and rosy, looked

back with equal interest; and suddenly he put out a chubby hand, lifted the little girl's veil, and boldly planted a kiss on her cheek. It was the first time— and the girl found it very pleasant. (*BG* 3)

From the beginning therefore, *A Backward Glance* instigates a warning that the reader is entering a narrative realm of artefact and construct, Wharton refusing to pretend autobiographical components are factual, accurate, and 'real'.

In his January 1931 dismissal of the short story collection *Certain People* for the *New Republic*, John Chamberlain concluded: Wharton 'is not at all concerned with world views, or total human views; but she has her prejudices, and these cause an orientation toward a dead life. More often than not she seems to be practising a dexterous but perfunctory technique upon anything that comes to hand out of the past.'[38] By the time of *A Backward Glance*, Conn suggests Wharton's 'attitude towards the old world of convention had...*ossified* into a nostalgic conservatism' (138, my emphasis). The 1934 volume, however, cleverly speaks both to an American readership seeking reassurance and answers about nationhood and identity during the Depression era, and to a wider audience, particularly European, for whom the First World War remained that unforgotten shadow, noted above. As seen in the travel writings of Chap. 4, Wharton again specifically aligns herself and defines herself as *American*. *A Backward Glance* features images of her great-grandparents and grandparents as she traces her family's Stevens, Rhinelander, and Jones lineage, charting the ancestry that helps to anchor and define her. The reader even learns early in the volume of two paintings in the Capitol's Rotunda, depicting her great-grandfather 'in the sober uniform of a general of artillery, leaning against a canon in the foreground of one picture, in the other galloping across the battlefield' (*BG* 8), her family *literally* a part of the nation's history.

What draws the alignment differently from some of the travel writing, however, is that Americans in *A Backward Glance* are explicitly marked and defined as owing much of their identity to Europe. Wharton, for example, references her 'Huguenot great-great-grandfather, who came from the French Palatinate to participate in the founding of New Rochelle' (*BG* 6) and her 'lovely great-grandmother Rhinelander (Mary Robart) ... of French descent' (*BG* 15). Rather than a conventional, unadventurous plod past the signposts of personal biography, *A Backward Glance* offers a national document for its US readership and a cultural map of immigration—at a time when Americans were looking for revalidation during an ongoing, bruising Depression. While spectacularly failing to address the presence of Native Americans and with one reference to the legacy of slavery as part of her discussion of 'the Americans of the original States' (*BG* 7),[39] Wharton returns to her strategy of holding America up to Europe and finding America wanting, as seen in the travel writing—while still identifying as American.

Looking back, the 1934 volume defines 'the most striking difference' between Americans of Wharton's youth and those of the present day as a severing of European connections.[40] The litany of modern inventions—'telephones, motors, electric light, central heating...X-rays, cinemas, radium, aeroplanes and wireless telegraphy' (*BG* 6) give way in significance for Wharton to 'the really vital change' 'between then and now', namely—as the author perceives it—that in her youth 'the Americans of the original States, who in moments of crisis still shaped the national point of view, were the heirs of an old tradition of European culture which the country has now totally rejected' (*BG* 7). Wharton, by contrast, was confirmed in *A Backward Glance* as an American with that 'old tradition of European culture' in her veins. The author's line was both ambitious and potentially controversial, all in the guise of a 'charming', 'gracious', and 'serene' memoir, presenting herself not just as an American, but as an American for the age: cultured, part of an elite club, connected to Europe, but with a distinctive US lineage. Wharton, again, was embedded into an American narrative. In many ways it was a striking extension of her thesis of 'The Great American Novel' (1927), discussed in Chap. 6, in which Wharton argued against the reductive expectation that 'really to deserve the epithet "American"', the 'novelist's scene must be laid in the United States, and his story deal exclusively with citizens of those States' ('The Great American Novel' 152), suggesting instead that that the 'greatest American novel' 'will probably turn out to be very different....Its scene may be laid in an American small town or in a European capital' ('The Great American Novel' 158). Wharton sets up a position in her memoir in which a great *American* for the age does not have to be living in America—and the writer who had not set foot in the country of her birth for over a decade was presenting herself for the role. While Henry James, who many years after the event described in *A Backward Glance* became a naturalised British citizen, entirely failed to communicate in the amusing, but also pointed account of his attempt to get directions (*BG* 242–43), Wharton was the cultured American communicator and survivor, making herself heard and understood.

As Olin-Ammentorp, Goodman and others have recognised (see Olin-Ammentorp 213–22; 'Justice to *A Backward Glance*' 109–11), the First World War remains a tangible presence in *A Backward Glance*. It is assigned its own chapter, but also seeps into other sections, among them 'Paris', 'Widening Waters', 'And After'. 'The War' chapter offers the most personal testimony of the volume. Indeed the author insists she will not retread the territory covered in *Fighting France*, except to describe her 'personal situation' (*BG* 339). Wharton does not provide a historical account of battles and a charting of the course of war in *A Backward Glance*. Instead, the reader learns of the daily pragmatic realities: her difficulties in securing money, problems reaching England, the setting up of a workroom, the author's inexperience in relief work, her agony of sitting useless in England, then the obstacles faced in returning to France (while many rich residents were leaving Paris, Wharton returns), dealing with a 'sudden influx' (*BG* 346) of refugees. The author's charity work is described ahead of visits to the front line, and Wharton pays tribute, in many respects still ahead of her time, to those who 'served' in ways other than fighting on the front line. *A Backward Glance* presents the emergence of new hierarchies and social orders, in a number of ways a new meritocracy: some volunteers 'would drift in vaguely' only to 'turn out to be the future corner-stones of the building', while others 'lucid, precise and self-confident, would … fade away after a week' (*BG* 347). Wharton also explicitly acknowledges and values the contributions of women. Elsewhere, *A Backward Glance* can be dismissive of women—most memorably in Wharton's line about 'the ancient curriculum of house-keeping … swept aside by the "monstrous regiment" of the emancipated: young women taught by their elders to despise the kitchen and the linen room, and to substitute the acquiring of University degrees for the more complex art of civilized living' (*BG* 60). In her chapter, 'The War', however, she recognises that many women came into their own during the years of hostilities:

> Many women with whom I was in contact during the war had obviously found their vocation in nursing the wounded, or in other philanthropic activities. The call on their co-operation had developed unexpected aptitudes which, in some cases, turned them forever from a life of discontented idling, and made them into happy people. Some developed a real genius for

organization, and a passion for self-sacrifice that made all selfish pleasures appear insipid. (*BG* 356)

Notably, though, Wharton does not count herself among them, insisting that as someone 'already in the clutches of an inexorable calling' (356), everything she undertook during the war 'in the way of charitable work was forced on [her] by the necessities of the hour' (*BG* 357). Biographers have challenged this, arguing that the war engaged her full powers and energies (see Dwight 192, Benstock 324), but Wharton was re-emphasising her primary role—writer, not relief worker.

Similarly, Wharton's work that appeared in newspapers during the war often took the form of life writing, the author offering personal testimony. Her extensive piece, 'My Work Among the Women Workers of Paris', published in the *New York Times Magazine* on 28 November 1915, was prefaced with Wharton's statement that she was writing 'without apology in the first person singular', 'therefore' heading her opening paragraph 'My Workroom' (reprinted Olin-Ammentorp 245–52; 245). The piece is notably marked throughout by the 'I' and by possessives: '[m]y ouvroir' (245), 'my workwomen' (248), 'my plan', 'my ninety seamstresses', 'my workroom', [m]y refugee charities' (247), 'our appeal', 'our depot', 'our refugee women' (249)—the author trading on her name for donations (the paper labels her 'Noted American Novelist' [245]), but also signalling the degree of personal investment. Whether or not her involvement was 'forced on [her] by the necessities of the hour', it was also personal, the author demonstrating an American efficiency that was seen to trouble Minnie Bourget in her response to her friend's war work, referenced in Chap. 4. Wharton's targeted letters invited readers to contribute to, and thereby participate in, the famous author's life story, via donations. Another example of life writing inspired by the war was 'Christmas Tinsel', published in *The Delineator* in December 1923. With authors asked to recall their 'most memorable' Christmas, Wharton identified Paris in 1916, when a distribution of presents for refugee children resulted in a rampaging free-for-all, a 'raging mob' among people who had 'hung on the bitter edge of hunger, sickness and sorrow' for 'two bewildered years'.[41] The sight if not 'pretty' was 'instructive' ('Christmas Tinsel' 11). Olin-Ammentorp eloquently suggests that '[i]n a large sense, most if not all of Wharton's postwar work can be seen as a meditation on the question of civilization' (220)—the author concluding here that 'once a year, and even on the brink of ruin, human nature needs Christmas tinsel more than coals and blankets' ('Christmas Tinsel' 11).

More conventionally revealing autobiographical material would be found posthumously in the private pages of 'The Life Apart. (L'âme close)', the work that scholars have labelled the 'Love Diary'—though it was never a term used by Wharton, and in the manuscript 'Life and I', focused on the early years. Entries of the journal 'The Life Apart' run from October 1907 to June 1908, covering the period during which Wharton's friendship with Morton Fullerton turned into an affair. The text of the full manuscript, housed at the Lilly Library, University of Indiana, was valuably published and analysed by Kenneth M. Price and Phyllis McBride in the December 1994 issue of *American Literature*.[42] While Wharton often proved determined to cover her tracks when it came to her private correspondence—she was notably anxious that her letters to Fullerton should be returned (they were not)—the journal she preserved, potentially for an audience beyond the grave. Price and McBride have charted the range of critical responses to this text, spanning interpretations of 'a symptom of weakness' to Wharton radically revising the conclusion of 'a conventional seduction plot', one that led 'not to degradation and despair but instead to an embrace of life' (see Price and McBride 668, 685). Lewis, the first biographer to access the material, suggests its 'mode of expression … was at times uncharacteristically adolescent' and 'did not always escape the clichés upon which strong emotion tends to fall back' (224). Even, perhaps especially, in this journey through an emotional calendar, Wharton often casts her journal as fiction. For example, as Price and McBride suggest, there is a strong sense of audience; it is a work that develops 'as much by a logic of narrative as by the odd turns of life' (665), with much left for conjecture, many omissions (including consummation of the relationship), and ellipses. The sense of audience is controlled: when Fullerton reads and writes in the diary, Wharton tore out the page. The transgression is erased. This is a layered, at times mosaic piece—a flower pressed into its pages as one entry, three poems, silences, Wharton once again requiring an active reader to fill in the gaps. And the conventions of fiction caution a reader to be wary of the text's veracity. By its very format and structure, this is a journal that, like *A Backward Glance*, speaks to connections—but in the journal, connections of the intellect, mind, *and* body. Yet ultimately in 'Life Apart', it is not enough. Wharton writes in her final entry, of the couple's time at Senlis, '"One such hour ought to irradiate a whole life."—Eh bien, non-ce n'est pas assez!' (reprinted Price and McBride 67).

Wharton's incomplete 'Life and I', a fifty-two page manuscript housed in the Beinecke Library, would remain unpublished until 1990. With extensive cut and pasting, many of the sheets are comprised of strips of paper glued together (as many as five strips per page), in what appears to be a composite of two handwritten drafts. There is no surviving typescript, and the project may simply have been abandoned before this stage of composition. It is also possible that for this very personal undertaking Wharton adopted a different material process from that typically used for her work. Despite the familiar cut and pasting of her very physical composition process (many manuscript pages in the author's archive have strips of paper pasted on the original, or an original page might have been cut up before being reattached to additional segments to remake a 'whole'), 'Life and I' offers a cleaner text than is usual at her manuscript stage, with relatively few corrections and revisions, which suggests that Wharton may have extended the project's manuscript phase—producing perhaps an additional, more polished manuscript draft—beyond the point at which her writing would normally have been passed to the typist. Wharton may have been reluctant to hand over a sensitive text to a member of her staff. (Anna Bahlmann to whom the manuscript might have been entrusted had died in 1916, another friend lost during the war.) Alternatively, 'Life and I' may have been envisaged as a purely private exercise from the outset and never intended for the typist—the author testing the bounds of any life writing before embarking in later years on the 'official' memoir, *A Backward Glance.*

'Life and I' stands as a testimony to the author's ongoing fascination with the formative years. (In June 1932 she would advise Mary Berenson that the 'Life of Bernard Berenson', never published, could be vastly improved by 'giving more details' about his boyhood, 'his little childhood in Russia' and his Harvard days [*Letters* 553].) In later life Wharton resolutely depicted herself as having been a shy, solitary, intense child. In 'Life and I,' she accentuates the portrayal, even amending her manuscript description from 'very shy' to 'painfully shy self-conscious child' ('LI' 198), enhancing the miseries of a retrospective portrait of an isolated, misunderstood, 'different' child. Wharton becomes a girl beset by anxieties and phobia; this is a troubled child subject to 'a state of chronic fear', 'untold anguish of perplexity', 'haunted by formless horrors', dogged by 'some dark undefinable menace' ('LI' 191). 'I think my parents by this time were beginning to regard me with fear, like some pale predestined child who disappears at night to dance with "the little people"', the author concludes ('LI' 190). As Lee observes, in accounts of her childhood Wharton seems 'a stranger in the house, a changeling child' (6).

Wharton's mother, meanwhile, is 'capricious', 'illogical', 'indolent'. The charge of 'indolence', one of many Wharton levels at her mother in 'Life and I', will be repeated in *A Backward Glance*. The author claims in both memoirs that as a child she was required to submit every novel she wished to read to her mother for prior approval (see 'LI' 194, *BG* 65), but in *A Backward Glance* it is Lucretia Jones' indolence that threatens to curtail her daughter's reading: 'Being an indolent woman....In order to save further trouble she almost always refused to let me read it...' (*BG* 65). Her mother is painted as distant, severe, and uncaring, notably responding to her daughter's appeal to explain the 'whole dark mystery' of marriage with a lethal combination of 'icy disapproval', impatience, sharpness, 'coldness', and even 'disgust' ('LI' 197). She can also appear the fiercest of critics, Wharton suggesting her first novel was met with a withering, one-line put down:

> My first attempt (at the age of eleven) was a novel, which began: '"Oh, how do you do, Mrs. Brown?' said Mrs. Tompkins. 'If only I had known you were going to call I should have tidied up the drawing-room'." Timorously I submitted this to my mother, and never shall I forget the sudden drop of my creative frenzy when she returned it with the icy comment: "Drawing-rooms are always tidy."
>
> This was so crushing to a would-be novelist of manners that it shook me rudely out of my dream of writing fiction, and I took to poetry instead. (*BG* 73)

It is, however, a contradictory charge sheet across the memoirs that prompts suspicion. On the one hand Wharton's mother is charged with the 'icy', 'crushing' dismissal above and on the other accused of displaying 'an odd inarticulate interest in these youthful productions' and of having 'perpetrated the folly of having a "selection" privately printed' ('LI' 199). In 'Life and I', Wharton pushes the charge, claiming she 'was never free from the oppressive sense that [she] had two absolutely inscrutable beings to please'—God and her mother, her mother being 'the most inscrutable of the two' ('LI' 187). A manuscript study of the unfinished memoir confirms the author's word choice as one of expert precision and realignment: 'I ~~will~~ <must> do my mother the justice to say that, though wholly indifferent to literature, she had a wholesome horror of what she called "silly books", & always kept them from me'—the amendment from 'will' to 'must' appearing to lend connotations of a familial obligation, reluctantly paid ('LI' 191). The Edith Jones of 'Life and I' is the misunderstood, self-made loner, insisting that she experienced 'complete mental isolation' ('LI' 190) and 'never exchanged a word with a really intelligent human being until [she] was over twenty...' ('LI' 194).

Wharton might have got away with it. For many years scholarship bought the autobiographical back-story that the author peddled. There was, after all, a dearth of materials relating to the early years to contradict it, and Wharton's self-portraits served to fill that gap. Despite the vast extant correspondence, the Lewises were compelled to conclude in making the selections for their volume that 'Edith Wharton was thirty-eight years old, [and] had been publishing fiction for nine years ... before someone other than her Scribners editors thought her letters worth retaining' (*Letters* 4). Recent discoveries, however, notably the recovery of the writer's correspondence to Anna Bahlmann, have done much to confirm that Wharton's autobiographical recollections did indeed make for a great story. The collection includes 132 letters from Wharton to Bahlmann, many of them focused on the mystery years of her youth and early married life, with the earliest letter written at Pencraig, Newport, on 31 May 1874, when Edith Jones was just twelve. This fascinating, unexpected discovery opened up a series of altered images, realigning scholars' understanding of the family dynamics, the author's youthful voice and ambitions, and resolutely called into question Wharton's retrospective depiction of both people and events.

The witty exuberance of the juvenilia *Fast and Loose* always appeared to run counter to Wharton's claim to have been a 'painfully shy self-conscious child' beset by terrors, and the earliest letters to Bahlmann are charmingly animated, humorous, and high-spirited. Wharton was evidently an energetic, athletic child and young woman, with skating, bicycling, tennis, archery, and sleigh-rides among her leisure pursuits. She is an avid writer and reader, her learning, reading, and writing not isolated endeavours, but undertaken and encouraged in a supportive environment. Neither are novels forbidden—the myth that the genre was denied to the emerging writer firmly put to rest. Books are shared, gifted, discussed. She is used to hearing her work is 'lovely'—although this clearly brought its own frustrations: 'I have been more than rewarded by your frank criticism', writes the fourteen-year-old Jones to Bahlmann, 'which is so much more of compliment to me than the polite, unmeaning, "Oh, it's lovely," which I so often get when I beg for an honest opinion' (*My Dear Governess* 30–31). Later, during the couple's early married life, her mother is often with them or nearby; Wharton is very anxious about her mother's failing health, while letters from Paris in 1891 reveal that mother and daughter spend every afternoon together. Whatever the reasons for their falling out, Wharton's manuscript word-selection and amendments of 'Life and I', targeting Lucretia many years after her death appear to be those of a daughter with issues still unresolved. The self-rebuttals to Wharton's presentation found in belated archival recoveries also serve to remind us of the fallibility of biographical readings that have at times been put forward as keys to understanding her fictional works (*Ethan Frome* as a veiled portrait of Wharton's own miserable marriage; *Summer* as an expression of the passion the writer experienced with Fullerton; *The Reef* as the author's reflection on the fallout from that affair, etc.). Only one work by Wharton carried the title, 'The Writing of Fiction', but there were evidently other texts that practiced its design.

In her sixties, Wharton began recording entries in a notebook, 'Quaderno dello Studente' (student exercise-book), in which earlier fascination with the child gave way to the concerns of the ageing woman. 'Perhaps at last I shall be able to write down some disconnected thoughts, old & new—gather together the floating scraps of experience that have lurked for years in corners of my mind' ('QS' 211), the writer mused. In a series of entries stretching over a decade from May 1924 to 10 December 1934, Wharton would do exactly that, writing in the notebook citations and contemplations on topics including death, solitude, religion, and the pain of bereavement. The pragmatic and the deeply personal are often closely intertwined—a poem written through the grief of losing Walter Berry would later appear in *Scribner's Magazine* (see Chap. 2); a number of citations would be reused for published work. Even here, however, Wharton was setting the agenda, advertising its value to potential biographers with her note, 'If ever I have a biographer…' recorded on the book's inside cover three years after beginning the diary ('QS' 208).

In fact, the fragmentary record would fail to satisfy future biographers, Lewis labelling it 'disappointingly sparse' (xii). ('Satisfied! What a beggarly state! Who would be satisfied with being satisfied?' demands the author in 'Quaderno dello Studente' in her seventy-first year ['QS' 215]). For all its physical slightness, however, this exercise-book proves substantive, the more revealing for not being covered or cushioned in polished, descriptive prose. Wharton on occasions exposes deep losses and vulnerabilities, while still seizing life. In December 1934, while 'never ceas[ing] to miss' her beloved Berry and her 'two dear maids' ('QS' 215)—namely Catherine Gross, who had worked for her for almost fifty years, and Elise Devinck, her maid since 1914—and while enduring illness and fatigue, and increasingly troubled by 'the present roar of the world', Wharton could still affirm in this exercise book that 'to wake in the morning is an adventure...' ('QS' 215). It is a tone that would be replicated at the end of *A Backward Glance* ('The visible world is a daily miracle for those who have eyes and ears; and I still warm my hands thankfully at the old fire' [379]) and in 'Les Salettes' of *Twelve Poems* (see Chap. 2). This may be a writer whose works are often dominated by motifs of constriction, imprisonment, yet in 'Quaderno dello Studente' the imagery is often transformed to that of movement and escape: walking the tight-rope, a ride through a spring wood, feeling one's wings.

In the final entry of 'Quaderno dello Studente', dated 10 December 1934, Wharton recorded that she had '[r]eached page 166 of "The Buccaneers"' and posed the question: 'What is writing a novel like?' Her answer:

1. The beginning: A ride through a spring wood.
2. The middle: The Gobi Desert.
3. The End: A night with a lover. ('QS' 215)

Just over two years later Wharton would allude to, but censor this entry in a letter to Bernard Berenson:

> in looking this morning through an old diary-journal I have a dozen times begun & abandoned, I found this: (Dec. 10. 1934.)
> "What is writing a novel like?
> The beginning: A ride through a spring wood.
> The middle: The Gobi desert.
> The end: Going down the Cresta run."
> The diary adds: "I am now" (p. 166 of "The Buccaneers") "in the middle of the Gobi desert." (*Letters* 602)

In neither version do the lover and accompanying transitory pleasures materialise. Instead, partly recorded while *A Backward Glance* was in progress, 'Quaderno dello Studente' offers a pared-down version of the composite, lasting pleasures that Wharton will suggest constitute a meaningful life in the published memoir: literature, connections, friendships, reflection, a world of the imagination, and of intellect.

Wharton's life writings are varied, surprising, and often more revealing than supposed. *A Backward Glance* in particular invites us to look again. It is a text for which a firm label proves elusive, reinforced by the fact that the original edition was simultaneously deemed 'autobiography', 'reminiscences', and 'memoirs', as Wharton, much as she had in a literal sense in her travel writing, looked back on individual 'travell'd roads'. In his original essay 'Justice to Edith Wharton' published in the *New Republic* in June 1938, Edmund Wilson determined, 'There is almost nothing even worth glancing at in *A Backward Glance* except a portrait of Henry James' (cited in 'Justice to *A Backward Glance*' 93), displaying a mindset that not for the only time in that piece appeared to undermine the writer for whom he was advocating. Even here, however, Wilson would row back on his dismissal, with specific reference to the worth (or lack thereof) of the volume as a whole deleted from the line in the later, often reprinted versions of the essay: 'The backward glance is an exceedingly fleeting one which dwells very little on anything except the figure of Henry James' (Wilson, 'Justice' 29). What has been persistently read as backdrop and discreet evasion in many ways holds the key to *A Backward Glance*. Once again we have a text in which Wharton defines herself as American. And there is no false modesty: in *A Backward Glance* the author is defining herself as nothing less than an American *for the age*, one rooted in the story of America (cue ancestors and ancestral history) but also one steeped in European culture and traditions in another paean to a full, civilised, connected life. Wharton's American is connected in all senses of the world, speaking both to the now and to the rich low murmur of the past, a connectedness that perhaps resonates even more powerfully with the modern-day knowledge that only five years after the publication of *A Backward Glance*, the world would be wrenched apart by another war. Wharton's published autobiographical writing taps into a popular market, but also resists that market by pushing the boundaries of the genre, appealing to an 'elite', challenging readers' perceptions of what really comprises the signpost events of life, the Lady Godiva moments of autobiography. She plays with her image, she alerts the reader to the inherent artificialities of biographical 'fact', with third person story-telling and accentuating narrative techniques. While scholars largely continue to read *A Backward Glance* as any combination of charming, refined, well-mannered, evasive, and out of touch, Wharton, once again, was taking risks. 'Life is always <either> a tight-rope or a feather-bed', she wrote in 'Quaderno dello Studente' in March 1926 from Ste Claire ('QS' 212). In *A Backward Glance* the author imaginatively walks the tightrope, above the parameters of conventional autobiography, on her own high-wire path. Under the gaze of the grande dame of the frontispiece, a work read as discreet and old fashioned, suggests instead new life writings for a new age.

Notes

1. Letter from Wharton to Vernon Lee, 4 December 1932. Vernon Lee Papers, Special Collections, Somerville College, University of Oxford, courtesy of the Principal and Fellows of Somerville College, Oxford.
2. Virginia Woolf, 'The Leaning Tower' [1940], *Collected Essays of Virginia Woolf* (Hogarth, 1966–1967), Vol. 2, 177. Cited by Janet Montefiore, *Men and Women Writers of the 1930s: The Dangerous Flood of History* (Routledge, 1996), 2. Subsequent references to Montefiore's work are included in the text.
3. Malcolm Cowley, 'A Farewell to the 1930's', *New Republic*, 8 November 1939, 42–44; 44.
4. David Lodge, 'Modernism, Antimodernism and Postmodernism', *The New Review*, IV: 38 (May 1977), 39–44; 41.
5. Peter Conn, *The American 1930s: A Literary History* (Cambridge University Press, 2009), 5. Subsequent references to this work are included in the text.
6. Wharton's planned novel *Literature*, subtitled 'Man of Genius', was designed as a portrait of the American artist in 1913. The author began planning the work in August of that year, its plot tracing the development of a young writer, Dick Thaxter. While this ambitious novel was never completed, a substantial manuscript survives—uniquely, four extant drafts—and a detailed plot summary. Wharton could never quite let go of the rich, raw material of *Literature*. In April 1921, it remained on the literary agenda as she expounded its problems of timings and perspective: 'The war dealt that master-piece *Literature* a terrible blow. I still "carry" it about with me, and long to make it the dizzy pinnacle of my work; but *when* did it all happen? And what repercussions did 1914–1920 have on my young man?...Can't get enough perspective yet.' (Letter to William Brownell, 21 April 1921, cited in Nancy R. Leach, 'Edith Wharton's Unpublished Novel', *American Literature*, 25:3 [1953], 334–53; 341.) In the early, developed chapters of *Literature*, Dick Thaxter will respond to language, the sounds of words, the ecstasy of 'making up' as Wharton claimed she did herself as a young woman. For a discussion of the 'autobio-

graphical similarities' between the young Dick Thaxter and Edith Jones, see Leach, 341–43.
7. 'Adventures with Books', Manuscript, Edith Wharton Collection, Yale Collection of American Literature, Beinecke Rare Book and Manuscript Library. Box 19, folder 581.
8. Melanie Dawson, 'Biography', in Rattray (ed.), *Edith Wharton in Context*, 41–51; 43.
9. 'Saunterings', *Town Topics* 17:25, 23 June 1887, 2: www.everydaylife. amdigital.co.uk. Subsequent references to this article are included in the text.
10. 'Harry Stevens's Death', *New York Times (1857–1922)*, 20 July 1885, ProQuest Historical Newspapers: The New York Times with Index, 1.
11. *Town Topics* 20:3, 19 July 1888, 2: www.everydaylife.amdigital.co.uk.
12. *Town Topics* 62:27, 30 December 1909, 6–7: www.everydaylife.amdigital.co.uk.
13. *Town Topics* 62:14, 30 September 1909, 8: www.everydaylife.amdigital.co.uk. Subsequent references to this article are included in the text.
14. *Town Topics* 66:9, 31 August 1911, 9: www.everydaylife.amdigital.co.uk. Subsequent references to this article are included in the text.
15. *Town Topics* 66:10, 7 September 1911, 7: www.everydaylife.amdigital.co.uk.
16. *Town Topics* 67:22, 30 May 1912, 8: www.everydaylife.amdigital.co.uk.
17. *Town Topics* 66:6, 10 August 1911, 5: www.everydaylife.amdigital.co.uk.
18. *Town Topics* 69:23, 5 June 1913, 9: www.everydaylife.amdigital.co.uk.
19. *Town Topics* 70:12, 18 September: 1913, 8. www.everydaylife.amdigital.co.uk.
20. Susan Goodman, 'Portraits of Wharton', in Rattray (ed.), *Edith Wharton in Context*, 61–70; 62.
21. See Noel Sloboda, *The Making of Americans in Paris: The Autobiographies of Edith Wharton and Gertrude Stein* (New York: Peter Lang, 2008), 43.
22. Letter from Wharton to Cadwalader Jones, 10 October 1933, Beinecke; letter from Wharton to Bernard Berenson, 30 October 1933, cited in Benstock 436.
23. Along with her other acknowledgments of previously published 'chapters' and 'paragraphs' in the prefatory material of *A Backward Glance*, Wharton thanked 'Sir John Murray for kindly permitting [her] to incorporate in the book two or three passages from an essay on Henry James, published in "The Quarterly Review" of July 1920' (*BG* ix).
24. Loring Schuler to Rutger Jewett, 15 November 1932. Cited in Mary Chenoweth Stratton, 'The Making of *A Backward Glance,* Edith Wharton's Autobiography', PhD diss., Pennsylvania State University, 1991, 76–77. Subsequent references to this work are included in the text.

25. 'Beginning The Recollections of a Great Literary Career', *Ladies' Home Journal*, 50 (October 1933), 5, 131.
26. See advertisements, 'A Backward Glance', *Ladies' Home Journal*, 50 (November 1933), 90, 92, 93.
27. Robert A. Martin and Linda Wagner-Martin, 'The Salons of Wharton's Fiction', in Katherine Joslin and Alan Price (eds.), *Wretched Exotic: Essays on Edith Wharton in Europe* (New York: Peter Lang, 1993), 97–110; 108.
28. Louis Auchincloss, *Edith Wharton: A Woman in Her Time* (New York: Viking Press, 1971), 189, 175, 171, 169.
29. Edith Wharton, 'The Day of the Funeral', in Maureen Howard (ed.), *Edith Wharton: Collected Stories* 1911–1937 (New York: Library of America, 2001), 587.
30. Edith Wharton, 'Roman Fever', in *Roman Fever and Other Stories* (New York: Charles Scribner's Sons, New York, 1964), 14, 10, 12.
31. 'A Novelist's Memoirs', *The Times*, 18 May 1934, 9, The Times Digital Archive.
32. Amy Loveman, 'The Life and Art of Edith Wharton', *Saturday Review of Literature*, 10 (28 April 1934), 662; Edward Sackville-West, 'War and Peace', *Spectator*, 152 (15 June 1934), 929; Wilbur Cross, 'A Happy Chronicle', *Yale Review*, 23 (June 1934), 817–20; Christopher Morley, 'Granules from an Hour-Glass', *Saturday Review of Literature*, 10 (2 June 1934), 727. All reviews are reprinted in *Edith Wharton: The Contemporary Reviews*, 513–30.
33. E. M. Forster, 'Good Society', *New Statesman and Nation*, 7 (23 June 1934), 950, 952, reprinted in *Edith Wharton: The Contemporary Reviews*, 524–25; 525; Letter from Virginia Woolf to Ethel Smyth, *The Sickle Side of the Moon:The Letters of Virginia Woolf, Vol. 5*: 1932–1935, ed. Nigel Nicolson (London: Hogarth Press, 1979), 305.
34. 'Granules from an Hour-Glass', reprinted in *Edith Wharton: The Contemporary Reviews*, 520–22.
35. 'Edith Wharton and her Letters', *Hofstra Review* (Winter 1967), 1–7: Louis Auchincloss Material, Wharton Papers, Beinecke. I, too, have looked again. A decade ago, in *The Unpublished Writings of Edith Wharton*, I referenced *A Backward Glance* as 'tightlipped', '[d]iscreet and often evasive', 'constructing a largely public persona' (Vol. 1, xxii). While I still hold that the volume is indeed tightlipped in terms of conventional biographical disclosure, I find it a much bolder and more unconventional work a decade on, as explored in this chapter.
36. See Susan Goodman, 'Justice to Edith Wharton's "A Backward Glance"', *Arizona Quarterly: A Journal of American Literature, Culture, and Theory*, 73: 4 (Winter 2017), 93–115; 96. Subsequent references to this work are included in the text.

37. Letter from Wharton to Robert Greg, 11 June 1934. Cited by Shari Benstock, 'Landscape of Desire: Edith Wharton and Europe' in Joslin and Price (eds.), *Wretched Exotic: Essays on Edith Wharton in Europe*, 40, note 3.
38. 'The Short Story Muddles On', *New Republic*, 65 (7 January 1931), 225, reprinted in, *Edith Wharton: The Contemporary Reviews*, 485–86; 486.
39. In the chapter, 'The Background', Wharton comments that a print in her possession including 'a low-studded log-cabin ...described as the aboriginal Jones habitation ... was more probably the slaves' quarter' (*BG* 17–18). Goodman suggests that '[w]hen she calls her great-grandfather Stevens a "very nearly great man"' and 'casually mentions' the print 'the extent and direction of her irony remains debatable' ('Justice to *A Backward Glance*' 101), while Jennie A. Kassanoff opens the first chapter of her study with this recollection, suggesting 'The rapidity with which this picture of Yankee self-reliance dissolves into its uncanny double—a repressed portrait of African enslavement—is as breathtaking as it is blunt' (8). Wharton 'reads' the picture, volunteers the information that acknowledges her American family profiting from slavery in New York State, often forgotten in dominant discussions of slavery, but immediately moves on.
40. In Wharton's later manuscript reminiscence 'A Further Glance', her originally benign opening line 'When, [gap in text] years ago, I wrote the closing lines of my reminiscences, I thought of myself as an old woman laying a handful of rue on the grave of a vanished age' is altered to 'on the grave of an age which had finished in storm & destruction'. The 'storm & destruction' amendment is carried through to the version posthumously published as 'A Little Girl's New York' in *Harper's Magazine* in March 1938. Wharton, 'A Further Glance', Wharton papers, Beneicke, Box 19, folder 600.
41. Edith Wharton, 'Christmas Tinsel', *The Delineator*, December 1923, 11. Subsequent references to this work are included in the text.
42. Kenneth M. Price and Phyllis McBride, '"The Life Apart": Text and Contexts of Edith Wharton's Love Diary', *American Literature*, 66: 4 (Dec., 1994), 663–88. Subsequent references to this work are included in the text.

CHAPTER 8

Afterword

[I]t is rather lonely at times on the Raft of the Survivors[1]

Edith Wharton's 'adventures with books' (*BG* 70) came to an end on 11 August 1937 at the age of seventy-five. From her earliest, rapturous scribblings as a young girl on 'the big brown sheets' of wrapping paper from parcels delivered at the family home (*BG* 73) through a final battle with ill-health, 'fighting one tidal wave of fatigue after another' (*Letters* 604) to continue work on her last novel *The Buccaneers*, writing and books proved themselves loyal and constant companions. 'In spite of everything I stick to my work,' she wrote as late as April 1937 (*Letters* 604). At the award of her Gold Medal for Literature from the National Institute of Arts and Letters in 1924, Wharton (via her sister-in-law as she was ill and unable to attend in person) had expressed herself 'particularly gratified by the formula used in conferring the medal', namely that 'it is given in recognition of my services to Letters.' 'I have tried to serve Letters all my life', she explained.[2] And so she did.

Wharton's final decade proved typically productive and diverse, with outputs including: *Twelve Poems* (1926); the novels *Twilight Sleep* (1927), *The Children* (1928), *Hudson River Bracketed* (1929), *The Gods Arrive* (1932); short stories collected in *Certain People* (1930), *Human Nature* (1933), and *The World Over* (1936); life writings 'Confessions of a Novelist' (1933), incorporated the following year in *A Backward Glance*

(1934); and a selection of critical writings, including 'The Great American Novel' (1927), 'Tendencies in Modern Fiction' (1934), 'Permanent Values in Fiction' (1934), and 'A Reconsideration of Proust' (1934). At the time of her death Wharton had reached chapter twenty-nine of *The Buccaneers*, and had assembled her collection of stories, *Ghosts*, published posthumously in October 1937, comprising work that had appeared from 1902 onwards alongside a new story 'All Souls", while the project *Eternal Passion in English Poetry*, the anthology selected by Wharton and Robert Norton, with the collaboration of Gaillard Lapsley and a preface by Wharton, discussed in Chap. 2, was published by Appleton-Century in October 1939. Even so, the publication record does not illuminate the full range of material on which the author was working in those final years: Wharton may not have been publishing travel writing or producing complete plays at that time, but she was still writing in these genres, as evidenced for example by her work on *Kate Spain* and accounts of her journeys to Spain, examined in Chaps. 3 and 4 respectively.

Inevitably, however, time caught up, even with 'O Vigorosa' as Berenson affectionately termed Wharton (cited Lee 412). From her correspondence and from the copy of her final diary in the Beinecke archive, covering the last months of her life from November 1936, it is clear that ill health continued to be an unwelcome, but persistent presence. The author maintained her writing and social life as best she could, with diary entries recording motor excursions, visitors, lunches with friends, and much 'pottering' in her renowned gardens at Ste. Claire, but the frailties of old age were increasingly making themselves known. Afflictions may have been varied, but the response was spiritedly consistent: influenza, high blood pressure, sudden collapses, colds all recorded and brusquely dismissed as alternately tiresome and 'a bore'.[3]

When the time came, Wharton's obituaries were respectful and laudatory, if often dull and generic. Reports of the writer's death, formal obituaries, and accounts of the funeral added up to a week's extensive coverage in the international press. The *Times* (London) headline labelled her 'A GREAT AMERICAN NOVELIST', which it upgraded to 'one of the greatest novelists America had produced' in the body of the piece.[4] For the *Washington Post*, Wharton was 'the noted American novelist', while the *New York Times* suggested, 'She might, and should have been, greater, but though she will not rank among the giants, her place of honor in the craft she followed so long and so industriously will be well above the salt. Both in the novel and the short story she stands with the best her country has produced, and some of her work should endure.'[5] With what was surely a nod to Margaret Mitchell's world-sweeping bestseller of the previous year, the anonymous *New York Times* writer continued, 'As the social historian of a New York that has long since gone with the wind, she stands, of course, alone' ('Edith Wharton' 16). The *Washington Post* suggested instead that 'Mrs. Wharton was too much the gentlewoman and a romantic to be considered a historian of the times she conveyed. She daintily stepped over the mud puddles of vulgar life and looked down her letters at the middle classes. Her vision was clear but limited.'[6] For the *Boston Transcript*, Mrs Wharton was 'the occupant of a secluded tower',[7] mirroring the *Washington Post*'s assertion that 'Mrs. Wharton had little traffic with the seamy side of life either in her writing or her mode of living' ('Edith Wharton' 8).

Reputational assessments across the week of Wharton's death could alter within the same newspaper: The *Washington Post*'s 'noted American novelist' of 13 August above had by 15 August been both promoted to and geographically replanted as 'one of the world's most distinguished American-*born* novelists' (my emphasis)[8] rather than American—both shifts likely in reaction to the international responses to Wharton's passing. There was certainly significant American media interest in the French honouring of Wharton. American newspapers were impressed that France was impressed, and in many cases appeared to upgrade their coverage accordingly when French literary stars came out in praise. Reporting on her funeral, the *New York Times* headlined the attendance of 'Leading members of the Paris International Society', while highlighting that the 'French press ... has devoted much space to reviewing her life and literary work, which was discussed as though she was as much a French as an American writer.'[9] Linda De Roche observes that 'unlike the anonymous reports and retrospectives printed in U.S. and British newspapers', the majority of French writers signed their tributes: Edmond Jaloux in *Le Jour*, Louis Gillet for *L'Epoque*, John Charpentier for *Mercure de France*, Raymond Recouly in the *Gringoire*, André Chaumeix in *L'Echo de Paris*, and Philomène Lévis-Mirepoix (as Claude Silve) in *Le Figaro*.[10] A number of signatures carried the prestigious tag of the pre-eminent l'Académie Française, again an association that did not go unnoticed in the U.S. press. The *New York Times* reported in its coverage of 15 August, '"She was a remarkable literary artist," writes André Chaumeix of the French Academy in Echo de Paris. "For the last thirty years she had brilliant success in the United States, but since she took up her residence in France she became even more famous in our country than in the United States"' ('Services in France for Edith Wharton').[11] American reports were also attentive to French tributes to Wharton's First World War record, specifically to the attendance of representatives of the French War Veterans' Association at the funeral 'honouring her for her war work for France'.[12] The veterans' presence prompted a sequence of creative musings: 'Soldiers of France stood guard to the end, remembering the service Edith Wharton gave to their welfare in the World War'; 'she would like that tribute of the old warriors to her memory, perhaps more than all others.'[13]

Wharton was providing column inches to the end. She headlined 'Literati Deaths This Week' for *Variety*, while obituaries paraded often formulaic tags: 'Novelist Rival of Henry James', 'le dernier écrivain victorien', 'Chronicler of Inner Circle New York Society, in Which She Had Been Reared.'[14] As referenced at the outset of this study, a number of obituaries noted that she was the author 'of 38 works', but she was unmistakably defined as a novelist, even as writers agreed almost unanimously her reputation was secured first by *Ethan Frome*, followed by *The House of Mirth* and *The Age of Innocence*. Reinforced by its image of a mature, demure-looking Wharton in profile at her desk, the *New York Times* pitch—'Novelist Wrote "Ethan Frome", "The Age of Innocence" and 36 Other Books'—allied the author to that civilisation long gone with the wind: 'she published thirty-eight books, including that great love-story "Ethan Frome". But her reputation rested mostly upon her achievement as the Chronicler of Fifth Avenue, when the brownstone front hid wealth and dignity at its ease upon the antimacassar-covered plush chairs of the Brown Decade' ('Edith Wharton, 75, Is Dead in France').

Thus Wharton, at her death, was both seen and not seen. And in many ways she had predicted it, as early as June 1925 with her musing to Daisy Chanler, 'as my work reaches its close, I feel so sure that it is either nothing, or far more than they know.... And I wonder, a little desolately, which?' (*Letters* 483). As she wrote of art in *The Writing of Fiction*, her own imagination was always 'the elusive bright-winged thing, in that mysterious fourth-dimensional world which is the artist's inmost sanctuary' (*WF* 119). Wharton was never bound by the imaginative straightjacket in which her critics often sought—and still seek—to confine her. She was versatile, adventurous, radical, and subversive—all while enjoying remarkable commercial success. Her versatility across the genres did not represent brief sidesteps, temporary diversions from what has long been read as her primary role as novelist—each was pursued fully and whole-heartedly and spoke to Wharton's very sense of herself as an artist and her connected vision of art and artistry. Extraordinary confidence and self-belief were required to carry this off. And she did it—often in the face of resistance, condescension and considerable sexism. It is in the genres for which she is least well-known that Wharton is often seen at her boldest, most adventurous, and most radical—which in part explains why a full recognition of those characteristics of her work has been obscured. Her oeuvre also emerges from a study that considers her span of genres as more overtly feminist than we have appreciated: authoritative, unfettered, and unapologetic. Wharton would embrace experimentalism—from the modernist dynamics of her travel writing, to the rewriting of the romantic poetic idyll, the subdued economy of a number of her plays, the controversial nature of her topics, the redefining of hierarchies of importance in modern autobiography to her self-definition in her seventies as an American for the age. She was a gifted poet, a controversial playwright whose work was in demand by some of the most successful theatre practitioners of her time, a trailblazing travel writer, an innovative critic who held the genre's double standards to account and set a different range of priorities, a hugely influential design writer, a writer of the poor. Yet Wharton also had the courage to be unfashionable, to suggest that 'a backward glance' could be a bold and progressive act, rather than one steeped in nostalgia and sentiment, upholding the status quo. The visions of *these* Edith Whartons, however, emerging from the span of genres, have long been obscured.

In an undated poem, 'Finis', Wharton's speaker reflects on a future without books:

> When I grow tired of books, what then?
>
> The postman's ring, the doctor's call,
> The damage done by the plumber's men,
> The rise in wages, the mercury's fall,
> Knitting-needles and crochet-hooks,
> An afternoon nap in a nice warm shawl,
> And now and then, as a special treat,
> A funeral passing down the street.
> That's the way the future looks
>
> When I've grown tired of books.[15]

A seemingly benign scenario, a quirky meditation here, once again masks a vision of domestic horror. This scenario is not in fact of a 'future', but, as the title directs and overrides, indeed 'finis'. Such a world, however, would never feature in this writer's own life or career plan. Edith Wharton—novelist, short story and novella writer, author of works on architecture and design, poet, playwright, critic, theorist, autobiographer, and travel writer—would never grow tired of her extraordinary, and extraordinarily diverse, adventures with books.

NOTES

1. Letter from Wharton to W. C. Brownell, 14 December 1924, cited in Bell 222.
2. Typescript, Edith Wharton Collection. Yale Collection of American Literature, Beinecke Rare Book and Manuscript Library, Yale University, box 19, folder 607.
3. See entries of 14 and 15 January 1937, 10 and 11 February 1937, 8 March 1937, 3 April 1937, 6 April 1937 in 'Dernier journal d'E.W.', Wharton Papers, Beinecke, box 63, folder 1776.
4. 'Edith Wharton', *The Times*, Saturday 14 August 1937, 12, The Times Digital Archive.
5. 'Edith Wharton Dies of Stroke At 75 in Her French Chateau', *The Washington Post (1923–1954)*, 13 August 1937, ProQuest Historical Newspapers: The Washington Post, 26; 'Edith Wharton', *New York Times (1923–Current file)*, 13 August 1937, ProQuest Historical Newspapers: The New York Times with Index, 16. Subsequent references to these works are included in the text.
6. 'Edith Wharton', *The Washington Post (1923–1954)*, 13 August 1937, ProQuest Historical Newspapers: The Washington Post, 8. Subsequent references to this work are included in the text.
7. 'Edith Wharton', *Boston Transcript*, 14 August 1937. Newspaper clipping, Beinecke.
8. 'Edith Wharton's Rites Held in Versailles', *The Washington Post (1923–1954)*, 15 August 1937, ProQuest Historical Newspapers: The Washington Post, 2.
9. 'Services in France for Edith Wharton', *New York Times (1923–Current file)*, 15 August 1937, ProQuest Historical Newspapers: The New York Times with Index, 41. Subsequent references to this work are included in the text.

10. See Linda De Roche, 'Obituaries', in Rattray (ed.), *Edith Wharton in Context*, 83–92; 89.
11. See André Chaumeix, 'Mrs Edith Warthon', *L'Echo de Paris*, 14 August 1937. Newspaper clipping, Beinecke. Chaumeix's tribute was deeply appreciative, but also a little vague, leaning heavily on links to Paul Bourget, and, as the title signals, published with the persistent misspelling of the author's name.
12. 'Edith Wharton, 75, is Dead in France: Novelist Wrote "Ethan Frome"...', '...Special Cable to *The New York Times*', *New York Times (1923–Current file)*, 13 August 1937, ProQuest Historical Newspapers: The New York Times with Index, 17.
13. 'Edith Wharton', *Boston Transcript*; 'Edith Wharton', *The Gazette*, 14 August 1937. Newspaper clipping, Beinecke.
14. 'Literati: Literati Deaths This Week', *Variety* (Archive: 1905–2000), 18 August 1937, 127, 10, ProQuest, 74; 'Edith Wharton Dies of Stroke At 75 in Her French Chateau'; M.Y.M., 'La mort d'Edith Wharton le dernier écrivain victorien' (unidentified newspaper clipping, Beinecke); 'Edith Wharton, 75, is Dead in France...'
15. Edith Wharton, 'Finis', Wharton Papers, Beinecke, box 21, folder 674.

SELECT BIBLIOGRAPHY

Ammons, Elizabeth, *Edith Wharton's Argument with America* (Athens GA: University of Georgia Press, 1980).
'The Art of Fiction', *The Saturday Review of Politics, Literature, Science and Art*, 141 (16 January 1926), 65–66.
'At the Theatres', *The Atlanta Constitution*, 10 March 1901, 15. Online.
Auchincloss, Louis, *Edith Wharton: A Woman in Her Time* (New York: Viking Press, 1971).
Bancroft, Catherine, 'Lost Lands: Metaphors of Sexual Awakening in Edith Wharton's Poetry, 1908–1909', in Alfred Bendixen and Annette Zilversmit (eds.), *Edith Wharton: New Critical Essays* (New York: Garland, 1992), 231–43.
Barnes, Eric, *The Man Who Lived Twice: The Biography of Edward Sheldon* (New York: Scribner's, 1956).
Barnes, Julian, 'Introduction', *A Motor-Flight through France* by Edith Wharton (New York: Picador, 1995), 1–14.
Bauer, Dale, *Edith Wharton's Brave New Politics* (University of Wisconsin Press, 1994).
Bell, Millicent, *Edith Wharton and Henry James: The Story of their Friendship* (London: Peter Owen, 1966).
Benert, Annette, *The Architectural Imagination of Edith Wharton* (Madison, NJ: Fairleigh Dickinson UP, 2006).
Bennett, Lyn, 'Presence and Professionalism: The Critical Reception of Edith Wharton', in Gary Totten (ed.), *Memorial Boxes and Guarded Interiors: Edith Wharton and Material Culture* (Tuscaloosa: University of Alabama Press, 2007), 19–43.
Benstock, Shari, 'A Brief Biography', in Carol J. Singley (ed.), *A Historical Guide to Edith Wharton* (New York: Oxford University Press, 2003), 19–48.

———, 'Landscapes of Desire: Edith Wharton and Europe', in Katherine Joslin and Alan Price (eds.), *Wretched Exotic: Essays on Edith Wharton in Europe* (New York: Peter Lang, 1993), 19–42.

———, *No Gifts from Chance: A Biography of Edith Wharton* (London: Hamish Hamilton, 1994).

Bernardi, Debra, '"Sublimest Heaven" and "Corruptest Earth": Sexuality in Margaret Fuller's Italian Writings', in Sirpa Salenius (ed.), *American Authors Reinventing Italy: The Writings of Exceptional Nineteenth-Century Women* (Il Prato, 2009), 21–38.

Boggs, Tom, 'Review: Five Anthologies', in *Poetry*, 57: 3 (December 1940), 221–23.

'Books and Magazines', *Vogue*, 22: 23 (3 Dec 1903): 755, ProQuest The Vogue Archive.

'Books of Poems by Two Writers', *New York Times*, 8 May 1909, ProQuest Historical Newspapers: The New York Times with Index, BR300.

Boyd, Ailsa, 'From the "Looey suite" to the Faubourg: The Ascent of Undine Spragg', *Edith Wharton Review*, 30:1 (Spring 2014), 9–28.

———, '"The Decoration of Houses": The American Homes of Edith Wharton', *The Journal of the Decorative Arts Society 1850–the Present*, 30 (2006), 74–91.

Bratton, Daniel (ed.), *Yrs. Ever Affly: The Correspondence of Edith Wharton and Louis Bromfield* (Michigan State University Press, 2000).

Bromfield, Louis, 'A Tribute to Edith Wharton', reprinted in Daniel Bratton (ed.), *Yrs. Ever Affly: The Correspondence of Edith Wharton and Louis Bromfield* (Michigan State University Press, 2000), 108–22.

Carroll, Loren, 'Edith Wharton in Profile', Paris edition of the *New York Herald Tribune*, November 1936. Newspaper clipping, Edith Wharton Collection, Yale Collection of American Literature, Beinecke Rare Book and Manuscript Library.

Chance, Helena, 'Interior and Garden Design', in Laura Rattray (ed.), *Edith Wharton in Context* (New York: Cambridge University Press, 2012), 199–208.

Chanler, Daisy, *Autumn in the Valley* (Boston, Little, Brown, and Company, 1936).

Chinery, Mary, 'Re-forming Manon: A New History of Edith Wharton's 1901 Play, *Manon Lescaut*', *Edith Wharton Review*, 35:1 (Spring 2019), 47–74.

———, and Laura Rattray, '*The Shadow of a Doubt*: Discovering a New Work by Edith Wharton', *Edith Wharton Review*, 33:1 (2017), 88–112.

'Clyde Fitch Discusses "The House of Mirth"', *New York Times (1857–1922)*, 4 Nov. 1906, ProQuest Historical Newspapers: The New York Times with Index, SM2.

Coles, William A., 'The Genesis of a Classic', in Edith Wharton and Ogden Codman Jr., *The Decoration of Houses* (New York: W. W. Norton & Co, 1998), 256–75.

Colquitt, Clare, Susan Goodman and Candace Waid (eds.), *A Forward Glance: New Essays on Edith Wharton* (Newark: University of Delaware Press, 1999).
Conn, Peter, *The American 1930s: A Literary History* (Cambridge University Press, 2009).
Corbin, John, 'Topics of the Drama', *New York Times (1857–1922)*, 23 Nov. 1902, 10, ProQuest Historical Newspapers: New York Times.
[Cortissoz, Royal], 'The Secrets of Fiction', 'An Artist on an Art', 'The Art of Fiction', *New York Herald Tribune*, 7 December 1924, 19 April 1925, 31 May 1925, ProQuest Historical Newspapers: New York Tribune/Herald Tribune.
Cowley, Malcolm, 'A Farewell to the 1930's', *New Republic*, 8 November 1939, 42–44.
Davidson, Rebecca Warren, 'Opposites Attract: The Garden Art of Charles Platt, Maxfield Parrish, and Edith Wharton', *Edith Wharton and the American Garden* (Lenox, Mass: The Mount Press, 2009), 61–74.
Dawson, Melanie, 'Biography', in Laura Rattray (ed.), *Edith Wharton in Context* (New York: Cambridge University Press, 2012), 41–51.
de Kay, Charles, 'How To Arrange A House', *New York Times (1857–1922)*, 27 March 1898, ProQuest Historical Newspapers: The New York Times with Index, IMS14.
Drizou, Myrto, 'Edith Wharton's Odyssey', in Jennifer Haytock and Laura Rattray (eds.), *The New Edith Wharton Studies* (New York: Cambridge University Press, 2019), 104–23.
Dwight, Eleanor, *Edith Wharton: An Extraordinary Life* (New York: Harry N. Abrams, 1994).
E. C., 'A Riviera Garden: Sainte-Claire Le Château, Hyères', *Country Life* (Archive: 1901–2005), 3 Nov 1928, 64, 1659, Country Life Archive.
Eadgyth [Edith Jones], 'The Constellation's Last Victory', newspaper clipping, Edith Wharton Collection, Yale Collection of American Literature, Beinecke Rare Book and Manuscript Library.
'Fall Announcement for D. Appleton-Century Company', *Publishers' Weekly*, 136: 12 (16 Sep., 1939), 929.
Fife, Hilda M., 'Letters from Edith Wharton to Vernon Lee', *Colby Library Quarterly* (Feb. 1953), 139–44.
Foster, Shirley, 'Making It Her Own: Edith Wharton's Europe', in Katherine Joslin and Alan Price (eds.), *Wretched Exotic: Essays on Edith Wharton in Europe* (New York: Peter Lang, 1993), 129–45.
Fra López, Patricia, *Edith Wharton Back to Compostela* (Universidade de Santiago de Compostela, 2011).
Franzen, Jonathan, 'A Rooting Interest: Edith Wharton and the Problem of Sympathy', *New Yorker*, 5 February 2012, online.
Fryer, Judith, *Felicitous Space: The Imaginative Structures of Edith Wharton and Willa Cather* (Chapel Hill: University of North Carolina Press, 1986).

Gale, Zona, 'An Artist on Her Art', *New York Herald Tribune*, 31 January 1926, ProQuest Historical Newspapers: New York Tribune/Herald Tribune, E5.

———, 'The Novel of Tomorrow', in *The Novel of Tomorrow and The Scope of Fiction* 'by Twelve American Novelists' (Indianapolis: Bobbs Merrill Company Publishers, 1922), 65–74.

Garrison, Stephen, *Edith Wharton: A Descriptive Bibliography* (Pittsburgh: University of Pittsburgh Press, 1990).

Goldman-Price, Irene (ed.), *My Dear Governess: The Letters of Edith Wharton to Anna Bahlmann* (New Haven: Yale University Press, 2012).

Gómez Reus, Teresa, '"Remember Spain!" Edith Wharton and the Book She Never Wrote', *English Studies*, 98:2 (2017), 175–93.

Goodman, Susan, *Edith Wharton's Inner Circle* (Austin: University of Texas Press, 2011).

———, 'Justice to Edith Wharton's "A Backward Glance"', *Arizona Quarterly: A Journal of American Literature, Culture, and Theory*, 73: 4 (Winter 2017), 93–115.

———, 'Portraits of Wharton', in Laura Rattray (ed.), *Edith Wharton in Context* (New York: Cambridge University Press, 2012), 61–70.

'"Harper's Magazine" and St. Margaret of Cortona', *The Sacred Heart Review*, 26:22, 30 November 1901, 9, https://newspapers.bc.edu/?a=d&d=BOSTONSH19011130-01.2.26

Haytock, Jennifer, *Edith Wharton and the Conversations of Literary Modernism* (New York: Palgrave, 2008).

———, 'Modernism', in Laura Rattray (ed.), *Edith Wharton in Context* (New York: Cambridge University Press, 2012), 364–73.

'"THE HOUSE OF MIRTH.": Drama Made from Mrs. Wharton's Novel Is Produced at Detroit', *New York Times (1857–1922)*, 18 Sep. 1906, ProQuest Historical Newspapers: The New York Times, 9.

'Italian Gardens', *The Speaker: the liberal review*, 26 Nov. 1904, British Periodicals 206–7.

Jayne, Thomas, *Classical Principles for Modern Design: Lessons from Edith Wharton and Ogden Codman's The Decoration of Houses* (New York: Monacelli Press, 2018).

Jones, Beatrix, 'The Garden in Relation to the House', *Garden and Forest*, 10: 46 (7 April 1897), 132–33. Online.

Jones, Edith, 'A Failure', *The Atlantic Monthly*, April 1880, https://www.theatlantic.com/magazine/archive/1880/04/a-failure/376166/

———, 'Patience', *The Atlantic Monthly*, April 1880, https://www.theatlantic.com/past/docs/issues/1880apr/patience.htm

———, 'Wants', *The Atlantic Monthly*, May 1880, https://www.theatlantic.com/past/docs/issues/1880may/wants.htm

Jones, Mary Cadwalader, *European Travel for Women: Notes and Suggestions* (New York: Macmillan, 1900).
Joslin, Katherine and Alan Price, 'Introduction', in Katherine Joslin and Alan Price (eds.), *Wretched Exotic: Essays on Edith Wharton in Europe* (New York: Peter Lang, 1993), 1–16.
Kassanoff, Jennie A., 'Edith Wharton (1862–1937)', in Eric L. Haralson (ed.), *Encyclopedia of American Poetry: The Nineteenth Century* (Chicago; London: Fitzroy Dearborn Publishers, 1998), https://literature-proquest.com
——, *Edith Wharton and the Politics of Race* (Cambridge: Cambridge University Press, 2004).
Kelly, Alice, 'Introduction: Wharton in Wartime', in Alice Kelly (ed.), *Edith Wharton Fighting France: From Dunkerque to Belfort* (Edinburgh University Press, 2015), 1–48.
Kunz, Heidi, 'Contemporary Reviews, 1877–1938', in Laura Rattray (ed.), *Edith Wharton in Context* (New York: Cambridge University Press, 2012), 73–82.
Lanser, Susan Sniader, and Evelyn Torton Beck, '[Why] Are There No Great Women Critics? And What Difference Does It Make?', in Julia A. Sherman and Evelyn Torton Beck (eds.), *The Prism of Sex: Essays in the Sociology of Knowledge* (University of Wisconsin Press, 1979), 79–91.
Leach, Nancy R., 'Edith Wharton's Unpublished Novel', *American Literature*, 25:3 (1953), 334–53.
Lee, Hermione, *Edith Wharton* (New York: Alfred A. Knopf, 2007).
Lesage, Claudine, *Edith Wharton in France* (Prospecta Press, 2018).
Lewis, R. W. B., *Edith Wharton: A Biography* (London: Constable, 1975).
Lodge, David, 'Modernism, Antimodernism and Postmodernism', *The New Review*, IV: 38 (May 1977), 39–44.
'The Lounger', *The Critic: An Illustrated Monthly Review of Literature, Art and Life*, 38:3 (Mar. 1901), 195–97.
Lubbock, Percy, *The Craft of Fiction* (London: Jonathan Cape, 1954).
——, *Portrait of Edith Wharton* (New York: Appleton-Century-Crofts, 1947).
Macheski, Cecilia, 'Architecture', in Laura Rattray (ed.), *Edith Wharton in Context* (New York: Cambridge University Press, 2012), 189–98.
Manzulli, Mia, '"Garden Talks": The Correspondence of Edith Wharton and Beatrix Farrand', in Clare Colquitt, Susan Goodman and Candace Waid (eds.), *A Forward Glance: New Essays on Edith Wharton* (Newark: University of Delaware Press, 1999), 35–48.
Martin, Robert A., and Linda Wagner-Martin, 'The Salons of Wharton's Fiction', in Katherine Joslin and Alan Price, (eds.), *Wretched Exotic: Essays on Edith Wharton in Europe* (New York: Peter Lang, 1993), 97–110.
Metcalf, Pauline C., 'Preface', in Metcalf (ed.), *Ogden Codman and the Decoration of Houses* (Boston, MA: Boston Athenaeum, Godine, 1988), ix-xiv.

Montefiore, Janet, *Men and Women Writers of the 1930s: The Dangerous Flood of History* (New York: Routledge, 1996).
Montgomery, Maureen E., *Displaying Women: Spectacles of Leisure in Edith Wharton's New York* (New York: Routledge, 1998).
———, 'Possessing Italy: Wharton and American Tourists', in Meredith L. Goldsmith and Emily J. Orlando (eds.), *Edith Wharton and Cosmopolitanism* (Gainesville, FL: University Press of Florida, 2016), 110–31.
'Mrs Wharton's Views on the Society Drama', *New York Times (1857–1922)*, 28 Oct. 1906, ProQuest Historical Newspapers: The New York Times with Index, SM2.
Nettels, Elsa, 'Edith Wharton's Correspondence with Zona Gale: "An Elder's Warm Admiration and Interest"', *Resources for American Literary Study*, 24:2 (1998), 207–34.
Nevius, Blake, *Edith Wharton* (Berkeley: University of California Press, 1953).
———, '"Pussie" Jones's Verses: A Bibliographical Note on Edith Wharton', *American Literature*, 23: 4 (Jan 1952), 494–97.
'New Books: Recent Verse', *Manchester Guardian*, 16 August 1909, ProQuest Historical Newspapers: The Guardian and The Observer, 5.
'THE NEWS—NEWPORT/EDUCATION THROUGH THE EYES/Mrs. Wharton Addresses the Teachers on Art in the Schoolroom'. Newspaper clipping, Edith Wharton Collection, Yale Collection of American Literature, Beinecke Rare Book and Manuscript Library.
'NOT TRUE SAYS CLYDE FITCH', Clyde Fitch Letter to the Editor, *New York Times (1857–1922)*, 24 Sep., 1906, ProQuest Historical Newspapers: The New York Times.
The Novel of Tomorrow and The Scope of Fiction by Twelve American Novelists (Indianapolis: Bobbs Merrill Company Publishers, 1922).
'A Novelist's Memoirs', *The Times*, 18 May 1934, 9, The Times Digital Archive.
'Novelties in Theatres…Mrs. Wharton as a Playwright', *New York Times (1857–1922)*, 19 Dec. 1902, ProQuest Historical Newspapers: The New York Times with Index, 6.
Olin-Ammentorp, Julie, 'Edith Wharton's War Elegies', *Edith Wharton Review* (Spring 2004), 6–12.
———, *Edith Wharton's Writings from the Great War* (University Press of Florida, 2004).
Olivieri, David, (Edith Jones/Wharton), *Fast and Loose*, in Laura Rattray (ed.), *The Unpublished Writings of Edith Wharton*, Vol. 2 (London: Pickering and Chatto, 2009), 1–61.
Orlando, Emily, 'The "Queer Shadow" of Ogden Codman in Edith Wharton's *Summer*', *Studies in American Naturalism*, 12:2 (2017), 220–43.
Peel, Robin, 'Wharton and Italy', in Laura Rattray (ed.), *Edith Wharton in Context* (New York: Cambridge University Press, 2012), 285–92.

Peyre, Henri, 'Edith Wharton: The Writing of Fiction', *Revue Anglo-Américaine*, 3 (April 1926), 366–68.
Platt, Charles A., *Italian Gardens* (New York: Harper & Brothers, 1894).
'Plays and Players', *Boston Herald*, 2 Feb. 1901, 17, America's Historical Newspapers: Boston Herald.
'POETRY', *The Scotsman*, 17 May 1909, ProQuest Historical Newspapers: The Scotsman, 2.
Price, Alan, *The End of the Age of Innocence: Edith Wharton and the First World War* (London: Robert Hale, 1996).
———, 'Wharton Mobilizes Artists to Aid the War Homeless', in Katherine Joslin and Alan Price (eds.), *Wretched Exotic: Essays on Edith Wharton in Europe* (New York: Peter Lang, 1993), 219–40.
Price, Kenneth M. and Phyllis McBride, '"The Life Apart": Text and Contexts of Edith Wharton's Love Diary', *American Literature*, 66: 4 (Dec. 1994), 663–88.
———, *To Walt Whitman, America* (Chapel Hill and London: University of North Carolina Press, 2004).
Ramsden, George (comp.), *Edith Wharton's Library* (Settrington: Stone Trough, 1999).
Rattray, Laura, 'Edith Wharton's Unprivileged Lives', in Jennifer Haytock and Laura Rattray (eds.), *The New Edith Wharton Studies* (New York: Cambridge University Press, 2019), 165–89.
——— (ed.), *Edith Wharton in Context* (New York: Cambridge University Press, 2012).
——— (ed.), *The Unpublished Writings of Edith Wharton*, 2 vols. (London: Pickering and Chatto, 2009).
'Recent Verse', *Spectator*, 103 (3 July 1909), 20, 169.
Ricard, Virginia, 'Edith Wharton's French Engagement', in Jennifer Haytock and Laura Rattray (eds.), *The New Edith Wharton Studies* (New York: Cambridge University Press, 2019), 124–44.
———, 'Legendary Spell: Edith Wharton's Italy', in Sirpa Salenius (ed.), *American Authors Reinventing Italy: The Writings of Exceptional Nineteenth-Century Women* (Il Prato, 2009), 69–85.
Ruff, Allan R., *An Author and a Gardener: The Gardens and Friendship of Edith Wharton and Lawrence Johnston* (Oxford: Windgather Press, 2014).
Russell, Vivian, *Edith Wharton's Italian Gardens* (London: Frances Lincoln, 1997).
Salenius, Sirpa, 'Introduction: Women in the Garden of Italy', in Salenius (ed.), *American Authors Reinventing Italy: The Writings of Exceptional Nineteenth-Century Women* (Il Prato, 2009), 5–19.
'Saunterings', *Town Topics: The Journal of Society*, 17: 25, 23 June 1887, 2; 47:5, 30 January 1902, 14–15; 69:23, 5 June 1913, 9; 70:12, 18 September 1913, 8; 17:25, 23 June 1887, 2; 20:3, 19 July 1888, 2; 67:22, 30 May 1912, 8; 66:9, 31 August 1911, 9; 62:27, 30 December 1909, 6–7; 62:14, 30 September

1909, 8; 66:10, 7 September 1911, 7. *Everyday Life & Women in America c.1800–1920*, www.everydaylife.amdigital.co.uk

Schriber, Mary Suzanne, 'Edith Wharton and the Dog-Eared Travel Book', in Katherine Joslin and Alan Price (eds.), *Wretched Exotic: Essays on Edith Wharton in Europe* (New York: Peter Lang, 1993), 147–64.

———, 'Edith Wharton and Travel Writing as Self-Discovery', *American Literature*, 59:2 (May 1987), 257–67.

'SCRIBNER'S SPRING BOOKS', *The Publishers' Weekly*, 75:12 (20 March 1909), 1131.

Sencourt, Robert, 'The Poetry of Edith Wharton', *Bookman*, 80 (July 1931), 478–86.

Sloboda, Neil, *The Making of Americans in Paris: The Autobiographies of Edith Wharton and Gertrude Stein* (New York: Peter Lang, 2008).

Smith, Logan Pearsall, *Unforgotten Years* (London: Constable, 1938).

'Snapshots at Social Leaders: Events and Gossip...', *The Washington Post (1877–1922)*, 29 Aug. 1909, ProQuest Historical Newspapers: The Washington Post, E7.

'Society', *Vogue*, 28: 8 (23 Aug. 1906), iii, ProQuest The Vogue Archive.

'Society', *Vogue*, 30: 5 (1 Aug 1907), 124-B, ProQuest The Vogue Archive.

St. Laurent, Maureen E., 'Pathways to a Personal Aesthetic: Edith Wharton's Travels in Italy and France', in Katherine Joslin and Alan Price (eds.), *Wretched Exotic: Essays on Edith Wharton in Europe* (New York: Peter Lang, 1993), 165–79.

'The Stage', *Detroit Free Press*, 10 Feb. 1901, A7, ProQuest Historical Newspapers: Detroit Free Press.

Stratton, Mary Chenoweth, 'The Making of *A Backward Glance*, Edith Wharton's Autobiography', PhD diss., Pennsylvania State University, 1991.

'Theatrical Gossip', *New York Times*, 8 March 1901, ProQuest Historical Newspapers: New York Times.

Totten, Gary, 'Afterword: Edith Wharton and the Promise of Cosmopolitanism', in Meredith L. Goldsmith and Emily J. Orlando (eds.), *Edith Wharton and Cosmopolitanism* (Gainesville, FL: University Press of Florida, 2016), 251–65.

———, 'The Art and Architecture of the Self: Designing the "I"-Witness in Edith Wharton's *The House of Mirth*', *College Literature*, 27: 3 (Fall 2000), 71–87.

———, 'The Dialectic of History and Technology in Edith Wharton's *A Motor-Flight through France*', *Studies in Travel Writing*, 17:2 (2013), 133–44.

Towheed, Shafquat (ed.), *The Correspondence of Edith Wharton and Macmillan, 1901–1930* (Basingstoke: Palgrave Macmillan, 2007).

Tuttleton, James W., 'Edith Wharton: An Essay in Bibliography', *Resources for American Literary Study*, 3:2 (1973), 163–202.

———, Kristin O. Lauer and Margaret P. Murray (eds.), *Edith Wharton: The Contemporary Reviews* (Cambridge University Press, 2009).

Tyler, Lisa, 'Wharton, Hemingway, and the Architecture of Modernism: Gendered Tropes of Architecture and Interior Decoration', in Lisa Tyler (ed.), *Wharton, Hemingway and the Advent of Modernism* (Baton Rouge: Louisiana State University Press, 2019), 151–66.

Vita-Finzi, Penelope, *Edith Wharton and the Art of Fiction* (London: Pinter, 1990).

Walton, Geoffrey, *Edith Wharton: A Critical Interpretation* (Fairleigh Dickinson, 1970).

Wegener, Frederick, 'Edith Wharton and the Difficult Writing of "The Writing of Fiction"', *Modern Language Studies*, 25:2 (Spring 1995), 60–79.

———, 'Edith Wharton on French Colonial Charities for Women: An Unknown Travel Essay', *Tulsa Studies in Women's Literature*, 17:1 (Spring 1998), 11–21.

———, '"Enthusiasm Guided by Acumen: Edith Wharton as a Critical Writer"', in Frederick Wegener (ed.), *Edith Wharton: The Uncollected Critical Writings* (Princeton University Press, 1999), 3–52.

———, 'Form, "Selection," and Ideology in Edith Wharton's Antimodernist Aesthetic', in Clare Colquitt, Susan Goodman and Candace Waid (eds.), *A Forward Glance: New Essays on Edith Wharton* (Newark: University of Delaware Press, 1999), 116–38.

Wharton, Edith, 'Adventures with Books', Edith Wharton Collection, Yale Collection of American Literature, Beinecke Rare Book and Manuscript Library.

———, *The Age of Innocence* (New York: D. Appleton and Company, 1920).

———, 'America at War', trans. Virginia Ricard, *Times Literary Supplement*, 16 February 2018, 3–5, https://www.the-tls.co.uk/articles/public/america-at-war-wharton/

———, *The Arch.*, in Laura Rattray (ed.), *The Unpublished Writings of Edith Wharton*, Vol. 1 (London: Pickering and Chatto, 2009), 93–115.

———, 'The Architecture of Humanism' review, *Times Literary Supplement*, 25 June 1914, reprinted in Frederick Wegener (ed), *Edith Wharton: The Uncollected Critical Writings* (Princeton University Press, 1999), 130–34.

———, *Artemis to Actaeon and Other Verse* (New York: Charles Scribner's Sons, 1909).

———, *A Backward Glance* (New York: D. Appleton-Century Company, 1934).

——— (ed.), *The Book of the Homeless (Le Livre des Sans Foyer)*, (New York: Charles Scribner's Sons, 1916).

———, *The Buccaneers* (New York: D. Appleton-Century Company, 1938).

———, 'Christmas Tinsel', *The Delineator*, December 1923, 11.

———, 'The Criticism of Fiction', *The Times Literary Supplement*, 14 May 1914, 229–30, The Times Literary Supplement Historical Archive.

———, *The Cruise of the Vanadis* (New York: Rizzoli, 2004).

———, *The Custom of the County* (New York: Charles Scribner's Sons, 1913).

——— and Ogden Codman Jr., *The Decoration of Houses* (New York: Charles Scribner's Sons, 1897).

———, 'Dernier journal d'E.W.', Edith Wharton Collection, Yale Collection of American Literature, Beinecke Rare Book and Manuscript Library.

———, Disintegration', in Laura Rattray (ed.), *The Unpublished Writings of Edith Wharton*, Vol. 2 (London: Pickering and Chatto, 2009), 65–118.

———, *Edith Wharton: Collected Stories 1891–1910*, Maureen Howard (ed.) (New York: Library of America, 2001).

———, *Edith Wharton: Collected Stories 1911–1937*, Maureen Howard (ed.) (New York: Library of America, 2001).

———, *Edith Wharton: Selected Poems*, Louis Auchincloss (ed.) (New York: Library of America, 2005).

———, *Ethan Frome* (New York: Charles Scribner's Sons, 1911).

———, *Fighting France: From Dunkerque to Belfort* (New York: Charles Scribner's Sons, 1915).

———, *French Ways and Their Meaning* (New York: D. Appleton & Co., 1919).

———, 'A Further Glance', Edith Wharton Collection, Yale Collection of American Literature, Beinecke Rare Book and Manuscript Library.

———, 'George Eliot', *The Bookman: A Literary Journal*, XV, May 1902, 247–51, https://babel.hathitrust.org/cgi/pt?id=njp.32101077276895&view=1up&seq=255

———, *The Gods Arrive* (London: Virago, 1987).

———, 'The Great American Novel', *Yale Review* (July 1927), 646–56.

———, *The House of Mirth* (New York: Charles Scribner's Sons, 1905).

———, *Hudson River Bracketed* (London: Virago Press, 1986).

———, *In Morocco* (New York: Charles Scribner's Sons, 1920).

———, 'Introduction to *Gardening in Sunny Lands: The Riviera, California, Australia*', reprinted in Frederick Wegener (ed.), *Edith Wharton: The Uncollected Critical Writings* (Princeton University Press, 1999), 246–47.

———, *Italian Backgrounds* (New York: Charles Scribner's Sons, 1905).

———, with pictures by Maxfield Parrish, *Italian Villas and Their Gardens* (New York: The Century Co., 1904).

———, *Kate Spain*, in Laura Rattray (ed.), *The Unpublished Writings of Edith Wharton*, Vol. 1 (London: Pickering and Chatto, 2009), 137–58.

———, Letter to Mary Cadwalader Jones, 10 October 1933, Edith Wharton Collection, Yale Collection of American Literature, Beinecke Rare Book and Manuscript Library.

———, Letter to Sally (Sara) Norton, 3 June 1901, Edith Wharton Collection, Yale Collection of American Literature, Beinecke Rare Book and Manuscript Library.

———, *The Letters of Edith Wharton*, R. W. B Lewis and Nancy Lewis (eds.) (New York: Collier, 1989).

―――, Letters to 'Miss Paget'/Vernon Lee, 31 December [1902], 11 November 1904, 19 February 1929, 4 December 1932, Vernon Lee Papers, Special Collections, Somerville College, University of Oxford.
―――, 'Life and I', in Laura Rattray (ed.), *The Unpublished Writings of Edith Wharton*, Vol. 2 (London: Pickering and Chatto, 2009), 183–204.
―――, 'A Little Girl's New York', *Harper's Magazine*, March 1938, 356–64.
―――, 'Madame Lyautey's Charitable Works in Morocco' (translation: Louise M. Wills), *Tulsa Studies in Women's Literature*, 17:1 (Spring 1998), 29–36.
―――, *The Man of Genius*, in Laura Rattray (ed.), *The Unpublished Writings of Edith Wharton*, Vol. 1 (London: Pickering and Chatto, 2009), 3–66.
―――, 'Maurice Hewlett's *The Fool Errant*', *The Bookman: A Literary Journal*, XXII, September 1905, 64–67, https://babel.hathitrust.org/cgi/pt?id=njp.32101077276960&view=1up&seq=80
―――, 'More Love-Letters of an Englishwoman', *Bookman: A Literary Journal*, XXI, February 1901, 562–63, https://babel.hathitrust.org/cgi/pt?id=njp.32101077276861&view=1up&seq=908
―――, 'More Money Needed/Continuation of the Work of Decorating Public Schoolrooms Desirable', Letter to the Editor of the *Daily News*, undated clipping, Edith Wharton Collection, Yale Collection of American Literature, Beinecke Rare Book and Manuscript Library.
―――, *A Motor-Flight Through France* (New York: Charles Scribner's Sons, 1908).
―――, 'Mr. Paul on the Poetry of Matthew Arnold', *Lamp*, February 1903, reprinted in Frederick Wegener (ed.) *Edith Wharton: The Uncollected Critical Writings* (Princeton University Press, 1999), 94–98.
―――, 'Mr. Sturgis's *Belchamber*', *The Bookman: A Literary Journal*, XXI, 307–10, https://babel.hathitrust.org/cgi/pt?id=njp.32101077276952&view=1up&seq=319
―――, *The Necklace*, in Laura Rattray (ed.), *The Unpublished Writings of Edith Wharton*, Vol. 1 (London: Pickering and Chatto, 2009), 113–33.
―――, Notebook Poems: 'An Autumn Day', 'Ante-Mortem', 'Browning in the Abbey', 'Cynthia', 'The Dead Wife', 'Death', 'A Dialogue', 'The Duchess of Palliano', 'In the Forest', 'The Inferno', 'The Leper's Funeral and Death (In mediaeval England)', 'Life', 'Lucrezia Buonvisi's Lover (Dying at Viareggio)', 'Lucrezia Buonvisi remembers', 'The New & the Old', 'The Northwind', 'A Patient Soul', 'The Rose', 'Song', 'The Sonnet's Boundaries', 'The Southwind', 'Swinburne', 'The Tomb of Ilaria Giunigi', 'A Vision', 'Weltschmerz', Wharton mss., The Lilly Library, Indiana University, Bloomington, Indiana.
―――, 'Permanent Values in Fiction', *Saturday Review of Literature*, X: 38 (7 April 1934), 603–4.
―――, 'Preface' to dramatisation of *Ethan Frome*, Ms., Edith Wharton Collection, Yale Collection of American Literature, Beinecke Rare Book and Manuscript Library.

———, 'Preface', *Eternal Passion in English Poetry*, selected by Edith Wharton and Robert Norton with the collaboration of Gaillard Lapsley (New York: D. Appleton-Century Company, 1939), reprinted in Frederick Wegener (ed.), *Edith Wharton: The Uncollected Critical Writings* (Princeton University Press, 1999), 253–55.

———, 'Quaderno dello Studente', in Laura Rattray (ed.), *The Unpublished Writings of Edith Wharton*, Vol. 2 (London: Pickering and Chatto, 2009), 205–15.

———, *The Reef* (New York: D. Appleton and Company, 1912).

———, *Roman Fever and Other Stories* (New York: Charles Scribner's Sons, New York, 1964).

———, *The Shadow of a Doubt*, in Laura Rattray and Mary Chinery, '*The Shadow of a Doubt:* A Play in Three Acts by Edith Wharton', *Edith Wharton Review*, 33:1 (2017), 113–257

———, 'The Sonnet', *Century Magazine*, 43 (Nov. 1891), 113.

———, 'The Sonnets of Eugene Lee-Hamilton', *The Bookman: A Literary Journal*, XXVI, November 1907, 251–53, https://babel.hathitrust.org/cgi/pt?id=njp.32101077277000&view=1up&seq=267

———, 'Talk to American Soldiers', Typescript, Edith Wharton Collection, Yale Collection of American Literature, Beinecke Rare Book and Manuscript Library.

———, 'Tendencies in Modern Fiction', *Saturday Review of Literature*, X: 28 (27 January 1934), 433–34.

———, 'The Theatres', New York *Commercial Advertiser*, 7 May 1902, reprinted in Wegener (ed.), *Edith Wharton: The Uncollected Critical Writings*, 78–80.

———, Wharton, 'The Three Francescas', *The North American Review*, 175: 548 (July 1902), 17–30, https://www.jstor.org/stable/25119269

———, 'To the Editor of the Daily News', *Newport Daily News*, 8 January 1896, reprinted in Frederick Wegener (ed.), *Edith Wharton: The Uncollected Critical Writings* (Princeton University Press, 1999), 54–57.

———, 'Translator's Note to *The Joy of Living*', reprinted in Frederick Wegener (ed.), *Edith Wharton: The Uncollected Critical Writings*, 235.

———, 'Untitled' [Play], in Laura Rattray (ed.), *The Unpublished Writings of Edith Wharton*, Vol. 1 (London: Pickering and Chatto, 2009), 67–89.

———, 'William C. Brownell', *Scribner's Magazine*, 84 (November 1928), 596–602.

———, *The Writing of Fiction* (London: Charles Scribner's Sons, 1925).

———, 'You and You', reprinted in Julie Olin-Ammentorp, *Edith Wharton's Writings from the Great War* (University Press of Florida, 2004), 241–42.

'WHARTON AND FITCH CLASH.: Authoress Objects to His Dramatization of "House of Mirth"' Special to The New York Times', *New York Times (1857–1922)*, 23 Sep., 1906, ProQuest Historical Newspapers: The New York Times, 9.

Wiggins, Celeste Michele, 'Edith Wharton and the Theatre' (PhD dissertation, Case Western Reserve University, 1996).
Wilson, Edmund, 'Justice to Edith Wharton' (1941), reprinted in Irving Howe (ed.), *Edith Wharton: A Collection of Critical Essays* (Englewood Cliff, N. J.: Prentice-Hall, 1962), 19–31.
Wilson, Richard Guy, 'Edith and Ogden: Writing, Decoration, and Architecture', in Pauline C. Metcalf (ed.), *Ogden Codman and the Decoration of Houses* (Boston, MA: Boston Athenaeum, Godine, 1988), 133–84.
——, *Edith Wharton at Home: Life at The Mount* (New York: Monacelli Press, 2012).
Wolff, Cynthia Griffin, *A Feast of Words: The Triumph of Edith Wharton*, rev. ed (Reading, MA: Addison-Wesley, 1995).
Wright, Sarah Bird, *Edith Wharton's Travel Writing: The Making of a Connoisseur* (Basingstoke: Macmillan, 1997).
—— (ed.), *Edith Wharton Abroad: Selected Travel Writings, 1888–1920* (London: Robert Hale, 1995).

Index[1]

A
Akins, Zoe, 79
  The Old Maid, 79
Alexander, George, 60
America, 6, 8, 9, 12, 14, 36, 43, 72, 88, 103, 104, 107–111, 115, 124, 125, 127, 164–166, 185, 194–195, 203, 211–212
American Academy of Arts and Letters, 147
American Civil War, 88
American Hostels for Refugees, 43
American Humane Association, 67
Ammons, Elizabeth, 37, 51n31
Anderson, Sherwood, 149
Appleton/Appleton-Century, 45, 148, 171, 172, 186
Archives, 9, 20, 27, 72–73, 77, 114, 172, 173, 198, 210
Arnold, Matthew, 26, 38
  'Resignation,' 26
Art, 92, 95–97, 133
Atlanta Constitution, 65
Atlantic Monthly, 20, 25, 26, 35, 37, 41, 105, 184
Auchincloss, Louis, 23, 50n11, 98, 187, 190

B
Baedeker, Karl, 90
Bahlmann, Anna, 7, 10, 20, 21, 25, 60, 95, 98, 104, 152, 198, 200
Balzac, Honoré de, 158, 160, 162
Bancroft, Catherine, 37
Barnes, Julian, 103
Barnes, Margaret Ayer, 79, 87
  The Age of Innocence, 79, 87
Barrymore, Diana, 190
Baudelaire, Charles, 26
Bauer, Dale, 151
'Beatrice Palmato' (prose fragment), 37
Beck, Evelyn Torton, 155

---

[1] Note: Page numbers followed by 'n' refer to notes.

© The Author(s) 2020
L. Rattray, *Edith Wharton and Genre*,
https://doi.org/10.1057/978-1-349-59557-0

Beinecke Rare Book and Manuscript Library, 57, 58, 68, 77, 97, 112, 139, 210
Bell, Millicent, 22, 150
Benert, Annette, 124
Bennett, Arnold, 171
Benson, A. C., 169
Benstock, Shari, 22, 147, 196
Berenson, Bernard, 95, 149, 160, 210
Berenson, Mary, 7, 88, 97, 198
Berlin, 78
Bernardi, Debra, 94
Berry, Walter, 5, 46, 59–61, 64, 112, 113, 126, 127, 140, 168, 183, 189, 201, 202
Bible, 28, 40
Blake, Mary, 94
Blashfield, Edwin H., 124, 125, 128, 129
Book Buyer, 124
Bookman, 6, 47, 126, 150, 154
Book-of-the-Month, 148, 180
Boston Herald, 61
Boston Transcript, 211
Bourget, Minnie, 108, 109, 196
Bourget, Paul, 19, 90, 108, 125, 189, 215n11
  Sensations d'Italie, 90
Boyd, Ailsa, 124, 137
Boynton, Percy H., 15
  'American Authors of Today,' 15
Bratton, Daniel, 140
Broadway theatre, 3, 79
Bromfield, Louis, 138
Brown, Jane, 136
Brownell, William Crary, 20, 35, 91, 136, 156, 157
Browning, Elizabeth Barrett, 46, 184
Browning, Robert, 6, 23, 26, 28, 29, 39, 41, 46, 152
  'Any Wife to Any Husband,' 23
Burns, Robert, 46

C
Cambridge University, 171, 172
Campbell, Mrs. Patrick, 68, 71, 73, 181
Cannes, 88
Carpenter, F. R., 6
Carroll, Loren, 82
Cather, Willa, 149, 155, 161
  'The Novel Démeublé,' 155, 164, 177n25
  The Professor's House, 161
Catholic Church, 3, 40, 58, 89
Century Magazine, 20, 35, 42, 130, 133
Chamberlain, John, 193
Chance, Helena, 126, 130, 136
Chanler, Margaret (Daisy), 97, 138, 149, 184, 212
  Autumn in the Valley, 118n28, 138–139
Charpentier, John, 211
Châteaubriand, François-René (vicomte de)
  Mémoires d'Outre Tombe, 190
Chaucer, Geoffrey, 29
Chaumeix, André, 211
Children of Flanders Rescue Committee, 43
Chinery, Mary, 58, 84n7, 84n14, 85n23, 85n28
Clark, Kenneth, 171
Codman, Ogden Jr., 12, 35, 73, 122–125, 127–129, 137, 140
Coleridge, Samuel Taylor, 29
Coles, William A., 124, 125, 129
Conn, Peter, 179–180, 193
Cook, Charles, 103
Cortissoz, Royal, 149, 163, 164
Country Life, 139
Cowley, Malcolm, 179
Crane, Hart
  White Buildings, 44

INDEX 233

Crichton, James, 58
Critic, 64, 134, 135
Cummings, e. e.
  is 5, 44
Cutting, Sybil, 168

D

Dante Alighieri, 26, 34
  La Vita Nuova, 26
Davidson, Rebecca Warren, 135
Davis, Fay, 71, 72
Davis, Owen and
  Donald, 79, 81
Dawson, Melanie, 181
De Kay, Charles, 129
De Roche, Linda, 211
De Wolfe, Elsie, 63–65
  The House in Good Taste, 124
Delineator, 196
Denison, E., 131
Devinck, Elise, 202
Dial, 37
Dickinson, Emily, 30, 47
Diderot, Denis, 160
Dodd, Anna, 94
Donne, John, 26, 46
  'A Valediction: Forbidding
    Mourning,' 26
Dorhout, Nynke, 178n36
Dorr, Julia, 94
Dreiser, Theodore
  An American Tragedy, 161
  Dawn, 180
  'The Scope of Fiction,'
    164, 165
Drizou, Myrto, 117n26, 120n56
Du Breuil de Saint Germain,
  Jean, 43, 112
Dwight, Eleanor, 117n19,
  124, 130–131,
  133, 196

E

Eadgyth (pseudonym), 24, 25
Eastlake, Charles L.
  Hints on Household Taste, 128
Edith Wharton Review, 58
Eliot, George, 147, 152
  Daniel Deronda, 152
  Middlemarch, 153
Eliot, T. S., 14, 46–49, 149, 152
Emerson, Ralph Waldo, 47
Europe, 6, 8, 9, 12, 23, 47, 64,
  87, 88, 94, 96, 112, 114,
  123, 140, 179, 193,
  194, 203
Euthanasia, 3, 40, 57, 67, 68, 83

F

Farrand, Beatrix (née Jones),
  7, 135–138
Fielding, Henry, 160
Fife, Hilda F., 49n2
Fiske, Minnie Maddern, 62, 65
Fitch, Clyde, 9, 57, 71, 73, 181
Fitzgerald, F. Scott, 148
  The Great Gatsby, 102, 161
Fitz-James, Rosa de, 112
Florence, 90
Forster, E. M., 189
Foster, Shirley, 107
Fra López, Patricia, 113
France, 5, 8, 13, 26, 41, 72, 74,
  88, 89, 94, 101, 103–108,
  124, 125, 140, 157,
  195, 211–212
Fraser, Malcolm, 131
Frohman, Charles, 3, 55, 57, 60, 63,
  65, 71, 73, 74, 181
Fryer, Judith, 124
Fullerton, Morton, 14, 20, 37,
  38, 137, 159, 189,
  197, 201

G

Gale, Zona, 149, 163–165
Garrison, Stephen, 44, 53n47
Germany, 78, 88
Gibson, Wilfrid Wilson
 'Lament,' 44
Gide, André, 107
Gilder, Richard Watson, 130, 134
Gillet, Louis, 211
Goethe, Johann Wolfgang von, 21, 26, 98, 99, 152, 155, 160, 164, 190
 Faust, 98
 Wilhelm Meisters Lehrjahre, 21
Goldman, Emma
 Living My Life, 180
Goldman-Price, Irene, 21, 50n18
Gómez Reus, Teresa, 112, 114
Gonnelli, Giovanni, 95
González, Marta, 113
Goodman, Susan, 168, 169, 184, 191, 192, 195
Grand Tour, 90
Grant, Robert
 Unleavened Bread, 158
Great Depression, 79, 179, 185, 193, 194
Greece, 94, 97–99, 101
Greek mythology, 28, 48
Greene, Graham, 15, 18n28
Gringoire, 211
Gross, Catherine, 202

H

Hale, Susan, 94
Hall, Adelaide, 94
Hammett Jr, C. E., 22
Harding, Emma, 83
Hardy, Thomas, 26, 62, 164
Harper's Magazine, 2, 13, 20, 35, 39, 40, 59, 135, 181
Havenhand, Lucinda, 126
Hawthorne, Nathaniel, 164, 165

Haytock, Jennifer, 11, 159, 173, 178n42
Heiser, Victor
 An American Doctor's Odyssey, 180
Hemingway, Ernest, 161
Henley, William Ernest, 46
Hergesheimer, Joseph, 149
Hewlett, Maurice, 36, 37
 Artemision Idylls and Songs, 36, 153
 The Fool Errant, 153, 154
Homer
 The Odyssey, 99
Hoppin, Francis V. L., 137
Housman, Laurence
 An Englishwoman's Love-Letters, 121
Howells, William Dean, 15, 25, 72, 167
Hughes, Langston
 The Big Sea, 180
 The Weary Blues, 44

I

Irish famines, 25
Italy, 19, 32, 58, 88–93, 95–97, 116n5, 130–133, 153, 182

J

Jaloux, Edmond, 211
James, Henry, 5, 6, 22, 34, 39, 125–126, 149, 150, 157, 164, 165, 167–169, 184, 189, 194, 203, 212
 Guy Domville, 34
 A Little Tour in France, 103
Jayne, Thomas, 124
Jewett, Rutger, 180, 184, 186
Johnston, Lawrence, 139
Jones, Edith (young Edith Wharton), 5, 13, 20–23, 88, 105, 112, 152, 153, 181, 182, 184, 200–201

Jones, George Frederic (EW's father), 26, 88, 90
Jones, Henry ('Harry') (EW's brother), 25, 103
Jones, Lucretia (EW's mother), 22, 88–89, 199, 201
Jones, Mary Cadwalader, 7, 12, 78, 80, 87, 94
  European Travel for Women: Notes and Suggestions, 93–94, 96
Joslin, Katherine, 107
Joyce, James, 149
  Ulysses, 149, 163

K
Kafka, Franz, 161
Kassanoff, Jennie, 22, 52n40
Keats, John, 29
Kelly, Alice, 105
King Albert's Book, 41
Kingsley, Charles, 46
Kipling, Rudyard, 164
Kunz, Heidi, 150

L
La Fayette, Madame de (Marie-Madeleine Pioche de La Vergne), 160
Ladies' Home Journal, 14, 106, 133, 184, 185
Lamp, 150
Lanser, Susan Sniader, 155
Lapsley, Gaillard, 20, 46, 79, 139, 157, 168, 171–173, 210
Lardner, Ring, 149
Lauer, Kristin Olson, 17n16
Lawrence, D. H., 157
Lawrence, Harry, 97
L'Echo de Paris, 211
Lee, Hermione, 22, 25, 26, 35, 37, 38, 79, 90, 91, 95, 102, 108, 128, 131, 133, 148, 149, 153, 155, 169, 171, 187, 189, 190, 210
Lee, Vernon (Violet Paget), 7, 19, 90, 120n56, 123, 130–132, 135, 155
  Euphorion: Being Studies of the Antique and the Mediaeval in the Renaissance, 19
  Studies of the Eighteenth Century in Italy, 19, 90
Lee-Hamilton, Eugene, 19, 20
  Sonnets of the Wingless Hours, 19
Lenox, 5, 72, 74, 89, 130, 137, 182
L'Epoque, 211
Lesage, Claudine, 89, 97, 100, 108, 117n27
Lewis, R. W. B., 34, 37, 60–62, 68, 139, 183, 187, 189, 197, 201
Lewis, Sinclair, 148, 149, 158, 169
Lilly Library, 10, 27, 29, 30, 39, 112, 197
Locke, Alain
  (ed.) *The New Negro: An Interpretation*, 161
Lodge, David, 179
London, 23, 60, 61, 64, 68, 148
London Evening Standard, 171
Longfellow, Henry Wadsworth, 14, 25, 47, 152
Loos, Anita
  Gentlemen Prefer Blondes, 161
Lowell, Amy, 47
  East Wind, 44
Lubbock, Percy, 7, 36, 151, 157, 166–170, 172
  The Craft of Fiction, 7, 36, 166–170
  Elizabeth Barrett Browning in Her Letters, 169
  Portrait of Edith Wharton, 138, 172
  The Region Cloud, 169
Lusitania, 41
Lyautey, General Hubert, 110, 111
Lyautey, Inès, 111

M

Macheski, Cecilia, 124, 125
Macmillan, 99, 148
Manchester Guardian, 36, 39
Manzulli, Mia, 135, 136, 138, 140
Marbury, Elisabeth, 57, 60
Marinetti, F. T., 102
Marlowe, Julia, 61
Marshall, Scott, 137
Martin, Robert A., 187
Maupassant, Guy de, 78
McBride, Phyllis, 197
McKim, Charles, 127
Medici Society, 97
Melville, Herman, 165
Mercure de France, 211
Meredith, George, 26
  'Lucifer in Starlight,' 26
Metcalf, Pauline C, 124
Meynell, Alice, 46
Milner, H. E., 135
Milton, John, 26, 155
Mitchell, Margaret, 211
Monroe, Harriet
  A Poet's Life, 180
Montefiore, Janet, 179
Montgomery, Maureen E., 96–97, 124
Morley, Christopher, 189
Morris, William, 26
  'The Defence of Guenevere,' 26
Motor car, 92, 102, 103, 110
Mount, The, 5, 13, 74, 122, 130, 132, 137, 182, 185
Murray, John, 90, 205n23
Murray, Margaret P., 17n18

N

Nabokov, Vladimir
  Lolita, 187
Nash, Paul, 106

Nation, 97, 102, 111, 134, 152
National Institute of Arts and Letters, 147, 172, 209
Nature, 23, 28–29, 44
Nevius, Blake, 22, 50n13, 150, 190
Newport, 12, 22, 49n8, 122, 127, 129, 181, 182, 200
Newport Daily News, 12, 127, 129
New Republic, 107, 155, 164, 165, 177n25
New Statesman, 168
New York, 58, 61, 68, 71, 72, 88, 122, 148, 159, 171, 211
New Yorker, 161
New York Herald Tribune, 163
New York Times, 6, 7, 36, 37, 39, 42, 57, 65, 68, 71–73, 83, 182, 210–212
New York World, 2, 20, 25
Norris, Frank
  McTeague, 158
North American Review, 25, 35, 36, 150, 153
Norton, Charles Eliot, 90
Norton, Robert, 20, 46, 97, 168, 171, 210
Norton, Sara (Sally), 7, 90, 104, 131

O

Olin-Ammentorp, Julie, 43, 44, 105, 106, 195, 196
Orlando, Emily, 124, 140
Osprey, 97, 118n28

P

Pankhurst, Emmeline, 41
Paris, 61, 74, 88, 125, 159, 183, 211
Parker, Dorothy
  Enough Rope, 44
Parrish, Maxfield, 12, 130, 131, 134

Paul, Herbert W., 38
Pavillon Colombe, 12, 88, 137, 138, 140
Payne, William, 37
Peel, Robin, 95
Peixotto, E. C., 91
Persephone, 28, 77
Peyre, Henri, 168
Phelps, William Lyon, 15
Phillips, David Graham
  Susan Lenox: Her Fall and Rise, 158
Pioneer/s, 103, 105, 115
Platt, Charles A., 135
  Italian Gardens, 135
Poe, Edgar Allan, 30, 164, 165
Prévost, Abbé Antoine, 9, 60, 160
  Manon Lescaut, 9, 60, 61, 160
Price, Alan, 42, 105, 107
Price, Kenneth M., 39, 197
Priestley, J. B., 167, 168
Proust, Marcel, 160, 162, 164, 210
Publishers' Weekly, 36, 46
Pulitzer Prize, 1, 59, 79, 147, 148, 163

R
Ramsden, George, 119n44, 178n36
Randall, Bryony, 178n38
Recouly, Raymond, 211
Ricard, Virginia, 90, 108, 109, 129
Rice, Allen Thorndike, 25
Richardson, Dorothy, 155
Richardson, Samuel, 160
Roosevelt, Theodore, 43
Rossetti, Christina, 26
Rossetti, Dante Gabriel, 26, 46
Royal Institute of British Architects, 135
Ruff, Alan R., 139
Ruskin, John, 90
Russell, Vivian, 135

S
Sackville-West, Edward, 189
Sacred Heart Review, 40
St James Theatre, 60
St Laurent, Maureen E., 96
Salenius, Sirpa, 89, 90
Santayana, George
  The Life of Reason, 108
Sassoon, Siegfried
  Satirical Poems, 44
Saturday Evening Post, 105
Saturday Review of Literature, 157, 158, 188, 189
Saturday Review of Politics, Literature, Science and Art, 166
Schriber, Mary Suzanne, 111, 118n32
Schuler, Loring, 184
Scotsman, 37
Scott, Geoffrey, 15, 136
  The Architecture of Humanism, 15, 136
Scott, Walter, 46, 153, 160
Scribner, Charles, 105, 163
Scribner's (Charles Scribner's Sons), 35, 36, 68, 101, 102, 150
Scribner's Magazine, 41–43, 46, 57, 90, 104, 106, 123, 134, 154, 156, 175n5, 201
Sencourt, Robert, 46–49
Shakespeare, William, 21, 26, 46
  Julius Caesar, 21
Sheldon, Edward (Ned), 79, 80, 87
Shelley, Percy Bysshe, 26, 29, 99
Silve, Claude (Philomène de Lévis-Mirepoix), 7, 160, 211
Simmons, Ronald, 43
Skidmore, Eliza, 94
Slavery, 194, 207n39
Smith, John Hugh, 36, 79, 97, 168
Smith, Logan Pearsall, 97
  Unforgotten Years, 118n28
Smollett, Tobias, 160

Spain, 11, 94, 112–115, 210
Speaker: the liberal review, 130
Spectator, 15, 36, 37, 91, 97, 189
Spencer, Herbert, 167
Ste. Claire, 45, 53n48, 137–139, 204, 210
Steffens, Lincoln
  The Autobiography of Lincoln Steffens, 180
Stein, Gertrude
  Autobiography of Alice B. Toklas, 180, 184
  The Making of Americans, 161
Stendhal (Marie-Henri Beyle), 160, 162
Stephen, Leslie, 154
Stevens, Harry, 5, 181, 182
Stevens, Mrs. Paran, 181
Stevenson, Robert Louis, 167
Stowe, Harriet Beecher
  Sunny Memories of Foreign Lands, 94
Stratton, Mary Chenoweth, 185, 186, 191
Sturgis, Howard, 154, 168, 189
Sudermann, Hermann
  Es Lebe das Leben, 9, 57, 68, 73
  Heimat, 68
Swinburne, Algernon Charles, 46

T
Teasdale, Sara, 47
Tempest, Marie, 61
Tennyson, Alfred, Lord, 26, 27, 39, 40, 46, 155
Times (London), 7, 189, 210
Times Literary Supplement, 44, 93, 111, 162, 166, 167, 171
Totten, Gary, 102, 103, 110, 111, 124
Towheed, Shafquat, 116n8, 148
Town Topics, 5, 14, 181–183
Traherne, Thomas, 4
  'The Vision,' 3, 4, 151, 163

Travel guides, 8, 90–92, 94, 96, 110, 111, 114
Tunisia, 95
Tuttleton, James W., 47
Tyler, Elsinia, 50n10
Tyler, Lisa, 124, 126
Tyler, Royall, 118n27

V
Van Alen, James, 94, 99
Van Doren, Irita, 111
Vanadis (yacht), 94, 97
Vanderbilt, Cornelius, 122
Vanderhoof, C. A, 131
Variety, 212
Venice, 90, 94
Vita-Finzi, Penelope, 150, 159
Vogue, 130, 137

W
Wagner-Martin, Linda, 187
Waln, Nora
  The House of Exile, 180
Walton, Geoffrey, 150
Washington Post, 15, 137, 210, 211
Wegener, Frederick, 45, 53n48, 111, 151, 152, 155, 156, 159, 176n21
Wenzell, A. B., 73
West, Rebecca, 155, 171
Westminster Abbey, 29
Wharton, Edith and
  ageism, 7, 14, 186, 188
  as American, 8–9, 12, 14, 104, 107–111, 114, 193–195, 203, 211–212
  authority, 2, 8, 28, 39, 95, 100, 109, 111, 114, 151, 170, 174, 190
  'beyondness,' 4, 24, 28, 29, 115

biographical readings, 12, 20, 37, 68, 97–98, 100, 115, 118n32, 173, 201
collaboration, 11–13, 20, 71–74, 123, 126, 134, 136
commercial success, 10, 44, 65, 114, 148
controversy, 2, 3, 5, 11, 40, 65, 68, 82
correspondence, 21, 59–60, 63–65, 78–80, 88, 91, 123, 152, 153, 156, 164, 171, 172, 182, 186, 191, 197, 200
creative process, 20–21, 59, 63–64, 76, 78, 150, 186, 198, 202
critical reception, 6–7, 10, 13, 14, 22, 35–38, 45–49, 58, 114, 124–126, 134, 150, 155–159, 161, 164–170, 189
divorce, 76, 89, 181, 183
elitism, 12, 24, 47, 103, 128–129, 164, 166, 174, 185, 190
engagement, 5, 181, 182
experimentalism, 9, 38, 59, 82, 93, 212–213
female friends, 7
feminism, 7, 8, 13, 34–35, 48, 126, 133, 152, 155, 171, 213
image, 2, 5, 13–15, 148, 149, 151, 157, 165, 173, 183, 185, 187, 188, 193, 203, 212–213
individualism, 4, 8, 12, 38, 91, 95, 100, 115, 159, 174, 188, 213
libraries, 4, 5, 26, 99, 108, 169, 181
longevity, 14, 15, 48, 187, 210
marriage, 89, 98, 201
modernism, 9, 11, 13, 92–93, 100, 105–106, 114, 157–163, 174

obituaries, 1, 7, 210–212
passion, 20, 23, 28, 37–38, 201
public scrutiny, 5, 57, 71–73, 137, 181, 183
racism, 95, 194
rebellion, 2, 5, 6, 91, 174, 192, 203, 213
rules, 4, 24, 38, 158, 165, 174, 191
scandal/gossip, 5, 11, 14, 33, 40, 71–75, 181, 183
sexism, 5–7, 36, 126, 133–135, 167, 169, 170, 181–183
social injustice, 10, 33–34, 56, 66, 69–72, 81
subversion, 2, 11, 82, 151, 191–192, 212
transgression, 2, 5, 10, 32–33, 40, 140–141, 169, 171, 197
World War I, 9–10, 41–44, 101, 104–109, 112, 147, 179, 180, 185, 193, 195–196, 203, 212
Wharton, Edith (works)
    Anthologies, *The Book of the Homeless (Le Livre des Sans Foyer)*, 41, 43; *Eternal Passion in English Poetry*, 20, 23, 45, 171, 210
    Architecture and Design, 6, 8, 12, 13, 121–141; *The Decoration of Houses*, 8, 12, 35, 59, 73, 122, 136, 137, 185; 'Gardening in France,' 12, 136, 139–140; *Italian Villas and Their Gardens*, 6, 8, 36, 89, 91, 126, 130–136, 185; 'Mrs. Wharton Addresses the Teachers on Art in the Schoolroom,' 121, 122; 'Spring in a French Riviera Garden,' 140

Wharton, Edith (works) (*cont.*)
  Critical Writings and Literary Theory, 4, 7, 8, 13, 36, 109, 127, 147–174; 'The Criticism of Fiction,' 13, 162; *Fast and Loose* reviews, 13, 152; 'George Eliot,' 147, 150, 154, 155; 'The Great American Novel,' 13, 158, 165, 194, 210; 'Introduction,' *Gardening in Sunny Lands: The Riviera, California, Australia*, 136, 139; Maurice Hewlett's *The Fool Errant*,' 117n23, 153, 154; 'Mr. Paul on the Poetry of Matthew Arnold,' 39, 150, 153; 'Mr. Sturgis's *Belchamber*,' 154; 'Permanent Values in Fiction,' 13, 157, 188, 210; 'Preface,' *The Book of the Homeless*, 105; 'Preface,' *Eternal Passion in English Poetry*, 45, 210; 'Preface' to dramatization of *Ethan Frome*, 79; 'A Reconsideration of Proust,' 210; 'Review,' *The Architecture of Humanism: A Study in the History of Taste*, 136; 'The Sonnets of Eugene Lee-Hamilton,' 19; 'Tendencies in Modern Fiction,' 13, 158, 188, 210; 'The Theatres,' 62, 65, 73, 150; 'The Three Francescas,' 150; 'Translator's Note to *The Joy of Living*,' 68; 'The Vice of Reading,' 4, 150; 'William C. Brownell,' 156; *The Writing of Fiction*, 2, 4, 6–8, 13, 36, 114, 127, 150, 151, 153, 157–171, 173, 174, 186, 187, 191, 212
  Life Writings, 1, 3, 5, 13, 23; 'Adventures with Books,' 13, 181; *A Backward Glance*, 9, 13, 14, 19, 20, 59, 61, 68, 72, 88–90, 97, 98, 105, 106, 112–114, 122–124, 130, 131, 133, 134, 138, 149, 150, 180, 181, 183–196, 198, 199, 202, 203, 209; 'Christmas Tinsel,' 196; 'Confessions of a Novelist,' 184, 209; 'A Further Glance,' 13, 59, 172; 'Life and I,' 13, 22, 26, 27, 180, 192, 198–200; 'The Life Apart (L'âme close),' 13, 197; 'A Little Girl's New York,' 13; 'My Work Among the Women Workers of Paris,' 196; 'Quaderno dello Studente,' 3, 14, 45, 46, 113, 138, 180, 201, 202, 204
  Novels and Novellas, 1, 7, 9, 48, 55–56, 67, 89, 114; *The Age of Innocence*, 55, 56, 79, 87–88, 114, 147, 148, 180, 212; *The Buccaneers*, 1, 82, 114, 172, 187, 189, 202, 209, 210; *The Children*, 148, 149, 187, 209; *The Custom of the Country*, 55–56, 76–78, 87–88, 107, 122, 160, 167; *Disintegration* (unfinished), 4, 69, 93, 116n14; *Ethan Frome*, 79, 87, 173, 185, 201, 212; *Fast and Loose*, 13, 21, 49n8, 56, 116n5, 152, 153, 200; *The Fruit of the Tree*, 3, 58, 68, 77, 83, 140; *The Glimpses of the Moon*, 148; *The Gods Arrive*, 141, 162, 163, 187, 209; *The House of Mirth*, 4, 9, 23, 36, 55, 56, 58, 60, 66–67, 71, 73, 107, 121, 136, 137, 150, 154, 182, 212; *Hudson River Bracketed*, 148, 162, 163, 209; *Literature*, 61, 163, 180, 204n6; *Madame de Treymes*, 36, 107; *The Marne*, 107; *The Mother's Recompense*, 148, 149, 161; *The Old Maid*, 79; *Old New York*, 6, 180; *The Reef*, 56, 107, 201; *Sanctuary*,

35; *Summer*, 4, 23, 25, 107, 140, 185, 201; *The Touchstone*, 35, 77, 185; *Twilight Sleep*, 114, 209; *The Valley of Decision*, 35, 69, 89, 91, 97, 123, 130, 153, 185
Plays, 2–4, 10, 11, 39, 55–83, 141, 181, 210; *The Arch*, 11, 58, 74–77, 80, 83, 141; 'The Children's Hour,' 58, 77; 'Crichton of Cluny,' 58; *The House of Mirth* (adaptation with Clyde Fitch), 9, 71–73; *The Joy of Living* (translation), 57, 68; *Kate Spain*, 11, 58, 74, 79–82, 210; *The Man of Genius*, 11, 57, 58, 60–63, 66, 69, 83; *Manon Lescaut* (adaptation), 57, 61; *The Necklace*, 11, 58, 76–78; *The Shadow of a Doubt*, 3, 11, 39, 40, 57, 58, 60, 63–68, 77, 83, 124; *The Tightrope*, 57, 59–61, 83; untitled play, 11, 58, 68–72
Poetry, 1–3, 6, 7, 10, 19–49, 101, 114, 139, 152, 201; 'Ante-Mortem,' 8, 29, 39–40; 'Areopagus,' 25; *Artemis to Actaeon and Other Verse*, 3, 6, 10, 20, 35–39, 41, 47; 'An Autumn Day,' 28; 'Battle Sleep,' 42; 'Belgium,' 41; 'Browning in the Abbey,' 27–29; 'Chartres,' 35; 'The Comrade,' 41; 'The Constellation's Last Victory,' 25–26; 'Cynthia,' 33; 'Daisies,' 22; 'The Dead Wife,' 29; 'Death,' 30; 'A Dialogue,' 30–32; 'The Duchess of Palliano,' 31–32, 192; 'Elegy,' 43; 'Euryalus,' 27; 'A Failure,' 25; 'Finis,' 213; 'The First Year,' 44–45; 'Garden Valedictory,' 46, 140; 'The Great Blue Tent,' 42; 'Happiness,' 35; 'Heaven,' 24; 'The Inferno,' 34; 'In the Forest,' 28; 'June and December,' 21; 'The Last Giustiniani,' 8, 34–35, 40–41, 89; 'The Last Token,' 23, 39, 89; 'Les Salettes,' 45, 202; 'Life,' 27, 28, 35, 37–38; 'Lucrezia Buonvisi remembers,' 7, 32–33, 39; 'Lucrezia Buonvisi's Lover (Dying at Viareggio),' 32–33, 39; 'Margaret of Cortona,' 2, 3, 24–26, 35, 89; 'May Marian,' 4, 23, 24; 'Mistral in the Maquis,' 45; 'Moonrise over Tyringham,' 35; 'Mortal Lease,' 37, 38; 'The New & the Old,' 34; 'Nightingales in Provence,' 44–45; 'The Northwind,' 28; 'Ogrin the Hermit,' 37, 41; '"On Active Service,"' 42, 43; 'Only a Child,' 2, 24–26; 'Opportunities,' 22; 'The Parting Day,' 25; 'Patience,' 25; 'Phantoms,' 21; 'Pomegranate Seed,' 41; 'The Rose,' 33–34; 'Some Woman to Some Man,' 22, 23, 39; 'Song,' 27, 28, 31; 'The Sonnet's Boundaries,' 28–29, 38, 51n21; 'The Southwind,' 28; 'Spring Song,' 23; 'Summer Afternoon,' 41; 'Swinburne,' 28; 'Terminus,' 20, 37–39, 51n31; 'The Tomb of Ilaria Guinigi,' 27, 29–30, 35, 89; 'A Torchbearer,' 35; 'The Tryst,' 41–43; *Twelve Poems*, 10, 42, 44, 202, 209; *Verses*, 10, 20–24, 29, 39, 50n10; 'Vesalius in Zante,' 35, 40–41; 'A Vision,' 29; 'Wants,' 25; 'Weltschmerz,' 33–34; 'With the Tide,' 42–44; 'You and You,' 42–44

Short Stories, 1, 48, 187, 188, 209, 214; 'After Holbein,' 187; 'All Souls,' 210; 'Autres Temps,' 88; *Certain People*, 193, 209; 'Confession,' 77, 79–82, 188; 'The Confessional,' 89; '"Copy": A Dialogue,' 57, 77; *Crucial Instances*, 185; 'The Day of the Funeral,' 188; *The Descent of Man and Other Stories*, 36; 'Diagnosis,' 188; 'The Duchess at Prayer,' 89, 134; 'The Fulness of Life,' 24; *Ghosts*, 210; *The Greater Inclination*, 35, 57, 59, 125, 185; *The Hermit and the Wild Woman and Other Stories*, 36; 'Her Son,' 188; 'The House of the Dead Hand,' 89; *Human Nature*, 15, 209; 'The Letter,' 89; 'The Muse's Tragedy,' 89; 'Pomegranate Seed,' 187, 188; 'Roman Fever,' 187, 188; 'Souls Belated,' 88, 89; 'The Twilight of the God,' 57; 'A Venetian Night's Entertainment,' 89; *The World Over*, 80, 82, 209; 'Xingu,' 63

Travel Writings, 5, 8–12, 72, 87–115, 193, 203, 210; 'Back to Compostela,' 112, 113; *The Cruise of the Vanadis*, 11, 94, 97–101; *Fighting France: From Dunkerque to Belfort*, 9, 11, 41, 101, 195; *French Ways and Their Meaning*, 8, 11, 89, 101, 102, 109–111; *In Morocco*, 11, 12, 101, 110–112; *Italian Backgrounds*, 6, 9, 11, 36, 89–93, 95, 96, 102, 103, 106, 115, 161, 185; 'Italy Again,' 92; 'Last Spanish Journey with W. Spain 1925,' 112–114; *A Motor-Flight Through France*, 11, 36, 102–105, 110; 'A Motor-Flight through Spain,' 112; '"Osprey" Notes and Accounts (Yacht),' 113; 'Talk to American Soldiers,' 89, 106, 157

Wharton, Edward (Teddy), 5, 88, 89, 103, 130, 182, 183, 189
Whitman, Walt, 26, 38–39, 47, 190
  Leaves of Grass, 38–39
Wiggins, Celeste Michele, 76
Wilde, Oscar, 60
  The Importance of Being Earnest, 60
Williams, John, 186
Wilson, Edmund, 14, 47, 121, 189, 203
  'Justice to Edith Wharton,' 47, 122, 203
Wilson, Richard Guy, 123, 126, 130, 137, 140
Winthrop, Egerton, 123, 189
Wolff, Cynthia Griffin, 61, 66
Women's suffrage, 6, 93, 98
Women travellers, 8, 12, 93–94, 103, 114
Woolf, Virginia, 148, 149, 154, 155, 157, 161, 164, 165, 170, 171, 179, 189
  Flush, 184
  Mrs. Dalloway, 148, 161
  A Room of One's Own, 170, 171
Wordsworth, William, 26, 27
World's Columbian Exposition, 125, 126
Wright, Frank Lloyd
  An Autobiography, 180
Wright, Sarah Bird, 94, 98, 100, 102, 107, 114

Y
Yale Review, 158, 189
Yale University, 147, 171
Yeats, William Butler, 46

Z
Zola, Émile, 167

CPSIA information can be obtained
at www.ICGtesting.com
Printed in the USA
LVHW090830111020
668492LV00010B/353